Stage Ghosts and Haunted Theatres

Nick Bromley

Nick Bromley

Foreword by Richard O' Brien

Published by LNP Books

Stage Ghosts and Haunted Theatres copyright Nick Bromley 2021
All rights reserved. No part of this book may be reproduced in any form
without permission from the publisher except for the quotation of brief
passages in reviews.

A catalogue record for this book is available from the British Library.

ISBN 978-0-9572683-1-9
First published 2021

Set in 11/15 Sabon with DINEngschrift headings
Typesetting & design by Liz French, lizfrenchcreative@gmail.com
Cover illustration & additional artwork by Simon Seddon, Instagram: s.p.seddon

Photo of Richard O'Brien by Shaun Webb

Printed and bound in Great Britain by Biddles,
King's Lynn Norfolk PE32 1SF

Published in the United Kingdom by LNP Books,
35 Westville Road, London W12 9BB.

To John and Andrew
and all the ghosts
who've weekly walked.

Foreword by Richard O'Brien

Writing this foreword to Nick Bromley's eclectic collection of other-worldly theatrical phenomena, is both a cheerful delight and a challenge. Delightful because of my own connections with so many of the faces and places that are featured here and challenging because I am a committed Darwinist who would happily beat a drum for both Voltaire and Richard Dawkins. In my opinion it is now fatuous to deny that we are an evolved species. If indeed there was any doubt in the first place, DNA has finally revealed the simple, peer-reviewed truth that we all came out of Africa and interbred with other hominids as we made our way around the globe. I have 2.006 per cent of Neanderthal markers tucked away somewhere in my genetic jigsaw puzzle. So, here's the rub, if there is no God, no heaven and no hell, how can I believe in ghosts?

Nick takes us on a breezy ride around the British Isles and Ireland and introduces us to a history of their theatres and of people both living and departed. It is, therefore, an educative and entertaining journey that will, I assure you, elicit a smile and the occasional spooky, goose bumps moment. (Joe Orton's message did the latter for me.)

I like to view myself as a pragmatic rationalist who holds little truck with the paranormal and things that go bump in the night - but then, how do I explain the ball of green, gaseous light that hovered over the pillow on the other side of the bed, flew into my head, juddered down to my toes and up again and then expelled itself and disappeared through the wall on the other side of the room? Or, the bathroom light switch which twitched and snaked with a ferocity of its 'own' accord? Well, dear fellow 'Horatios', there are, indeed, more things in heaven and earth than are dreamt of in our philosophies.

If you are a lover of H.P. Lovecraft and M.R. James you will, automatically, enjoy these spectral tales. If you are not then may this work of great affection lead you to discover those two authors of other worldliness.

A toast: To absent friends and fiends.   *Richard O'Brien*   2019

Contents

Prologue

Interval

An Entre-Acte

Act II - ON TOUR

A Grand Finale

Maud Allan as Salome
(see page 70)

PROLOGUE

D o you believe in ghosts? I would hope so but I suspect that you are just as likely to have purchased this book out of curiosity and are beginning to read it with an underlying degree of uncertainty. After all, you are unsure what it may contain and cautious whether to take it seriously.

If many people wish to believe in ghosts, few have first-hand experience to justify and confirm their hope. They are prey to doubt, worried perhaps that their genuine interest in the supernatural will attract the sneers of those who, having no truck whatsoever for an afterlife of any creed or persuasion, view ghosts as fictions of vivid imagination, even manifestations of hysteria.

Do not despair. Take heart. Those sceptics have never managed to prove incontestably that ghosts are mere figments of illusion and, if the spirit realm does not exist, why is there so much credible documentary evidence in support of them? Why is this world so integral to our lives and such a part of the lore and culture of our society? Plurality of worship is now seldom found but all monotheist religions are united in their absolute certainty of the afterlife. Their interpretations may vary but a mutual anticipation of a

*Harry Loman, the oldest stage door keeper in the world, with
the author in 1971 (see page 32)*

future existence has dominated world history for thousands of years. Gospel 'facts' are intertwined with legends. Today, even in this supposedly scientific age, we are spoon-fed from childhood with benign and bloodthirsty tales from that other half-forgotten underworld of gods and monsters. Fear and belief of the dark are etched deeply into our subconscious.

My own long-held certainty of ghosts has been reinforced by my chosen career. I have been in theatre for over half a century and have worked in too many haunted locations to have any doubt of the existence of the super-natural. Over the years I have gathered stories, tales and anecdotes regarding my profession's apparitions and I have furthermore encountered some myself. I now wish to pass on this evidence from my collection for present and future generations.

My basic contention is that ALL theatres are haunted, but a total investigation is beyond the scope of this first volume. Indeed, at a physical level, it could well be dangerous to prove. The sheer weight of existing data would need a tome of such massive size, that, if dropped, it would transform frailer readers into instant wraiths themselves. Therefore, this edition covers merely some of the United Kingdom's stage ghosts and haunted theatres, together with a visit to Eire and occasional references to overseas encounters.

The precise number of theatres that have existed or still stand in Great Britain is difficult to calculate but one estimate is of around 4000. Sadly, only a diminishing minority still stand today. Over the centuries, the majority have been demolished through design, accident or indifference and many that remain have become degraded. But, together, whatever their current condition, these locations have borne witness to unknown thousands of performances to untold millions of spectators. Would it be so surprising if fragments of the past remain in these storehouses of emotions and memories? I believe surviving particles of energies emanating from actors and audiences are retained within their walls and fabric and allow us to sense or see fleeting glimpses of past events and lives. There are several portals to yesterday, but what better doorways than playhouses?

Theatre is as old as civilisation, and sometimes half-forgotten gods join ghosts in coming seemingly to life. In August 2009 Simon Russell Beale was playing King Leontes in Sam Mendes' production of *The Winter's Tale*. The company was giving two performances in the open air theatre of Epidaurus. This 4th century BC Greek theatre is an ancient marvel, famous for its perfect acoustics. Together with the Temple of Apollo it was part of the Sanctuary of

Asclepius, the most famous sacred healing site of the classical world. As King Leontes, standing in front of some 12,000 spectators, Simon felt that he was in the very birthplace of theatre.

On both evening performances the air was very warm and incredibly still. In Act 3 of the play, Cleomenes and Dion return from Delphi bearing the sealed letter from the Oracle of Apollo. It pronounces that Hermione is chaste, Polixenes blameless, Camillo loyal and Leontes a jealous tyrant who shall 'live without an heir, if that which is lost be not found'. This divine judgment infuriates the King. On each night as Simon cried out passionately that 'there is no truth at all in the oracle, the sessions shall proceed, this is mere falsehood', a little ball of wind, arriving as if from nowhere, hit him lightly in the chest. A coincidence made stranger by his next declaration, 'Apollo's angry, and the heavens themselves do strike at my injustice'. Perhaps the Great Pan is not dead too, but lingers still on Paxi.

This collection is not of such ancient spirits but of some more modern British apparitions. Some are famous, others anonymous, and I must apologise beforehand to the host of ghosts omitted and to the very many theatres not mentioned in this present book. I have tried to evoke a little of the past of these chosen venues and describe the people who helped create and shape their reputations. Some may have more lines than others but, as the saying goes in our business, there is no such thing as a small part.

May I emphasise that these accounts and anecdotes have been either witnessed or told to me in complete good faith and that I have no reason to doubt the sincerity of all who have helped with their contributions. What they have seen or heard are enduring testimonies to past lives, echoes of both the banal and the extraordinary, the triumphs and the tragedies of the stage and of those whose fates have been affected by theatre, be they actors or spectators.

Perhaps on your next theatre visit these encounters may tempt you to linger just a little longer than you would, or should, at the end of the performance. The house lights will come up of course, but they never quite disperse the shadows, do they? And though the auditorium will soon be silent and empty, are you sure tonight you are completely on your own?

Nick Bromley 2020

Overture to Act 1 – A London Run

This supernatural investigation will begin in London for it is not only the United Kingdom's heart of drama but arguably the theatre capital of the Western world. Gallic statisticians may calculate that Paris has more venues and indeed, that city has over eighty in present use as either theatres, operas or music halls. They range from the stately Comedie Francaise to one-man enterprises such as La Comedie des Boulevards, but the inexorable domination of the English language and the sadly growing decline of others means that our West End has the edge where reputation and global marketing is concerned. London's productions and actors are synonymous for excellence in the field of popular and innovative live theatre. New York's theatre world is its only true rival but modern British dramatists have always been on a par with their Stateside counterparts and that art form which was truly American led - the musical - is now no longer solely dominated by Broadway.

Historically London has also the added cachet of bearing witness to Shakespeare's own original productions. He not only wrote them but also acted in them. He is named in the First Folio of 1623 as one of 'the principall actors in all these playes' and most fittingly for this book, if we believe Nicholas Rowe's biography of 1709, he specifically played the role of the Ghost in *Hamlet*. But in all the centuries since his death, there have never been reports of his spirit going about his nightly business at the Globe Theatre, Bankside.

There is sound reason for this, for the authentic site of the original Globe is some seven hundred feet away from today's reproduction, buried beneath the car park of Anchor Terrace. Other would-be psychic investigators may be tempted to hold future nightly vigils on the authentic site but my frank advice is to keep it short. The location is on Southwark Bridge Road, a busy, deadly diesel-fumed thoroughfare. If you are not knocked over and out by the traffic, your lungs could be and you'll be shuffling off this mortal coil sooner than you can shout that it was all much ado about nothing.

Instead, let us start our journey on a street once so famous for entertainment that it was regarded as being the epitome of London's nineteenth century theatre districts. In other words 'Let's All Go Down the Strand', only nowadays you mustn't expect to 'ave' much of 'a banana' and, drunk or sober, you won't stumble across the shades of Edmund Kean and his Wolf Club in the present Coal Hole Pub. That diminutive actor together with the likes of Jack

Bannister, John Liston, William Oxberry and Lord Byron caroused indeed in a tavern-cum-bawdy house of that name, but, again like the Globe, to mis-quote Lionel Bart, 'fings ain't where they ought to be'.

Kean and Co. may have raised merry hell in the original Coal Hole's location in Fountain Court but that building has long since disappeared together with its successor, Terry's Theatre. Vanished too are the Gaiety, the Globe, the Opera Comique, the Olympic, the Royal Strand and the Tivoli. Their ghosts may have gone with them but other spectres still remain close by and to meet them we shall visit the trio of theatres that survive on the Strand, the Adelphi, the Vaudeville and the Savoy.

ACT I
Scene 1: The Adelphi Theatre

It may not come as a surprise to theatrical psychic criminologists amongst my readers to be told that the Adelphi is haunted, for here, at the rear of the theatre in Maiden Lane occurred, on the evening of Thursday December 16th 1897, one of the most infamous murders in stage history. It was a murder which contained many of the elements of melodrama: a dashing, handsome hero, a beautiful woman, a demented villain and dire, predictive dreams; a case of life imitating art, for in fact a melodrama was billed to play on that very night. The Adelphi is a most complex building and it has had several incarnations. Originally opening as the Sans Pareil in 1806, it acquired the name of the Royal Adelphi in 1853, then dropped its regal pretension and was altered, enlarged and rebuilt throughout that century. It indeed became the Century in 1901 before reverting to being the Adelphi again in 1904. The present façade and auditorium is of the 1930s but the back of the theatre overlooking Maiden Lane dates from the 1850s. It has, to its left, a Dickensian side alley, Bull Inn Court, that runs down past the Nell Gwynne Tavern to the Strand. The stage door was situated at the top of this alley in the 1890s but there was also a private door on Maiden Lane itself which led up to the principal dressing rooms.

William Terriss: a matinee idol before the term was invented

Since 1885 The Adelphi had become famous for its melodramas and the leading man of shows such as *Harbour Lights*, *The Union Jack* and *The Swordsman's Daughter* was the immensely popular William Terriss. 'Breezy Bill', as he was popularly known, had indeed become synonymous with this type of show. He had reached his half-century in 1897 but his athletic physique and outgoing vivacity kept the appearance of late middle age at bay. He had a natural charm and swagger. A matinee idol before the term was invented, Terriss fully lived up to his favourite expressions of *Tempus Fugit* and *Carpe Diem*. His bluff, as Ellen Terry said, was colossal and between interludes as a sheep farmer in the Falkland Isles and a horse breeder in Lexington, Kentucky, he played major parts in several melodramas at Drury Lane and the Strand Theatre before joining Henry Irving's company at the Lyceum in 1880. His association with the man he called 'The Guv'nor' was to last on and off for fifteen years but from 1885 he combined Shakespeare at the Lyceum with tours and melodramas at the Adelphi. He was more than your everyday leading man. He was a star.

Many stars have leading ladies and Terriss was no exception to the rule. His was Jessie Millward, his playing partner in twelve productions. Their relationship ran parallel to his marriage and was fully accepted by his wife and family. He shuttled freely between his house in Bedford Park and Jessie's flat in Princes Street in Mayfair. Jessie always played the heroine in their productions but acted the parts with more spirit than they were sometimes written. They were a well-suited item, a couple seemingly smiled on by fortune.

However, in the autumn of 1897, during rehearsals for the revival of William Gillette's *Secret Service,* Jessie began to have a recurring nightmare. She would dream of hearing Terriss calling out 'Sis! Sis!' She would follow his voice until coming to a locked door; she would crash through it and catch him as he fell. Terriss would reassure her that it was just a fantasy but her anxiety was increased by the presence of a man who had started to haunt the stage door, a short, dark man with a squint. She remembered him as a walk-on in past productions, a man with a habit of posing about the stage. The play however opened without incident and the cast began to settle into their run. But, unbeknown to Jessie, on December 15th, Frederick Lane, Terriss' understudy, told three independent witnesses - who would later confirm this statement in writing - that, in a dream the night before, he had seen their star lying on the backstage stairs with blood oozing from his chest.

On the afternoon of December 16th, Terriss and his lifelong friend John Henry Graves arrived at Jessie's flat. Jessie left them there playing chess as she wanted to get to the theatre early to start preparing for the evening performance. As dusk fell, her Hansom cab arrived in Maiden Lane. She and Terriss both had keys for the private door, but, on catching sight yet again of the man standing on the other side of the street, Jessie hurried into the theatre via the stage door entrance.

The villain lurking in the shadows was one Richard Archer Prince, an occasional actor and sometime supernumerary at the Adelphi and known throughout the lower levels of the theatre world as 'Mad Archer'. If madness ran in Prince's family - one half-brother was born insane and another died in an asylum - Prince also suffered from that common delusion that he had all the makings of a great player. Rejections and failure only increased this conviction and it was coupled with a growing belief that a West End coterie, and in particular William Terriss, was conspiring against him.

In the 1880s, Prince had been employed as a super in such Adelphi melo-dramas as *Harbour Lights* but his subsequent acting career had never taken off. His strange behaviour, unpredictability and distinct lack of talent dogged his attempts to become a regular West End actor. Odd touring engagements were matched by abrupt dismissals and long bouts of unemployment and by 1895, a decade after he had first come to London, he was back where he started - a super at the Adelphi in Terriss's *One of the Best*. George Bernard Shaw reviewed the show as 'one of the worst' and Prince must have lived up to the critique for he was not engaged for the next production. Reduced to pawning his belongings and writing begging letters, his resentment continued to grow.

A letter from Terriss actually helped him to obtain grants from the Actors Benevolent Fund but even this source of charity was eventually denied. On the afternoon of December 16th four rejections tipped Prince over the edge. The secretary of the Fund sent a message that his latest application for cash had been turned down and his agent told him, yet again, that there was no work. Henry Spratt, the Adelphi stage door keeper, informed him that Mr Ter-riss would not give interviews and his sister, a prostitute currently working the circle promenade of the Empire Leicester Square, told him to his face that 'she would rather see me dead in the gutter than give me a farthing'.

Shortly before seven o'clock, John Henry Graves and Terriss arrived outside the private door in Maiden Lane. As Terriss bent down to place his key into the lock, Prince ran across the street and struck him twice in the back with a knife. It happened so quickly that Graves thought that Prince was patting his friend on the back and it was only after Prince struck Terriss again, and this time in the chest, that he realised what was happening. Terriss cried out 'My God, I am stabbed!', and Graves leapt on Prince as other witnesses piled in shouting 'Murder! Police!' As Prince was pulled away by Graves and a police constable, Terriss was dragged into the corridor by a crowd of helpers. Jessie cradled him in her arms before he was carried up to the dressing room. The third blow had entered his heart and though doctors arrived within minutes from Charing Cross Hospital, it was impossible to save him. His last words to her were the very same as she had dreamed, 'Sis, Sis'.

FOUL ASSASSINATION OF WILLIAM TERRISS, THE CELEBRATED ACTOR.
FROM DESCRIPTIONS BY EYE WITNESSES.

The Illustrated Police News of Saturday 25th December 1897

Terriss' death truly shocked the Victorian world. Fifty thousand people lined the route as his coffin was borne from Bedford Park to Brompton Cemetery and ten thousand more crushed around the graveside. Henry Irving gallantly escorted Jessie there, together with Seymour Hicks, the late actor's son-in-law, for the Terriss family were united in grief rather than hypocrisy.

At his trial, Prince was found to be criminally insane and he died in Broadmoor in 1937. He achieved the status of 'bogeyman' in his lifetime, for occasional rumours would sweep the West End that he was out and about, auditioning again and refusing to take 'next' for an answer. His victim has reappeared to give substance to the story that, before dying, he had also declared, 'I will come back'.

On the night of the murder, the actor Seymour Hicks was alone in the dressing room with the corpse when he heard a disembodied voice declaim, 'Are there men living such fools as to think there is no hereafter?' He was convinced that it was his father-in-law and that they would meet again.

The composer Lionel Monckton returned home that night still very shaken by the news to find that his grandfather clock, which had been given to him by Terriss, had stopped exactly at the hour of the murder. Shortly after the event, Terriss, wearing a frock coat and top hat, was seen backstage on several occasions, and the door to Jessie's old dressing room would, on a regular basis, be given two sharp taps as if his phantom was requesting entrance. In 1928 this room was assigned to the musical comedy actress June Hillman. Resting between shows on a sofa, she heard not only the taps but had her arms gripped by an unseen force as a green light appeared in front of her dressing room mirror. Sightings of Terriss continued occasionally until the 1970s but there have been no recent reports.

However Breezy Bill's roaming spirit has also appeared at the unlikely venue of Covent Garden Tube Station. According to a report in the Sunday Dispatch of January 13th 1956 he was seen by several members of the staff on the platform and positively identified from a photograph by a Mr Jack Hayden. As the station was only opened in 1906 it would seem a curious location except for the theory that its entrance was built on the site of a newspaper shop in Long Acre which Terriss was known to frequent. Perhaps his spirit still vainly attempts to buy a copy of *the Stage*, rather than read everybody else's as live actors mostly do these days. Or perhaps the Underground is also used as a ghostly form of transport and our tube trains are even fuller than they appear.

Breezy Bill is not the only ghost that the Adelphi possesses. During the run of *Beyond the Rainbow* in 1978, Paul O'Leary, then deputy chief electrician, took his mother round after a matinee to meet the Italian star of the show, Johnny Dorelli, in the number 1 dressing room which was then located at stage level. Arriving outside its door, they heard voices inside the room and hesitated, wondering whether to wait until these other guests had gone.

Suddenly there was a loud knock on the door which was immediately thrown open by Signor Dorelli. Everyone was mystified, for though all had heard the sound, none present had actually knocked. In 1979 Paul, as duty electrics, was shutting down the auditorium lights after an evening show when he saw a young girl standing alone in the upper circle. He called up to her 'You have to leave now' and, knowing the exits were locked and chained, climbed the stairs to escort her out. This proved impossible for, when he arrived, there was of course no one there.

In 1996, Frank Thompson the choreographer and director was then in the cast of *Sunset Boulevard*. One afternoon he was called for a company rehearsal scheduled to take place in the dress circle bar. He duly arrived at the stage door armed with script and score, signed in and went through the pass door which allows access to the corridor which in its turn leads to the dress circle. Slightly ahead of him and walking in the same direction, he noticed a youngish woman also seemingly on her way to the rehearsal. She was wearing a grey dress and her hair was tied in a low bun but, as she had her back to him, he could not identify her. She did not look as if she was in the cast but he presumed she was someone from the production office. The woman went through the door into the dress circle. Frank followed close behind her and saw her mount the stairs to the back aisle and then go through the auditorium doors into the bar. When he too entered, he was amazed to discover that she was nowhere in sight. Surprised at this sudden disappearance, he asked the other cast members where she had gone to and who she was, but his questions could not be answered. No one else had seen her come into or leave the bar although Frank had at the time taken her reality completely for granted. Her identity remains a mystery.

She was not seen there again during that run but perhaps she was in the audience that later watched an improptu performance by the theatre's manager. During Tommy Baxter's management of the Adelphi, the run of *Chicago* was in progress. The orchestra were not housed in their usual pit, but were positioned in full view onstage. In 1998, after a Thursday evening performance, the ushers and front of house had as usual left the building, the fireman had done his checks and Tommy was alone in his office, at the top of the theatre, finishing off some paperwork. Eventually he locked up for the night and made his way down the stairs towards the stage door which he had to reach by walking through the auditorium.

He had had a long, long day and so, to relax a little before leaving, he wandered onto the empty stage, sat down at the piano and started to play an old Scottish ditty. Beginning to feel that he was not alone in the auditorium, he turned to his left, looked out into the house and saw what he could only describe as multiple apparitions, sitting in the stalls and all staring fixedly at him. He promptly, and I think justifiably, stood up from the piano and without so much as a bow, made his exit off stage, out of the stage door and into the pub. Some applause just isn't worth the waiting for.

Scene 2: The Vaudeville Theatre

A few doors away from the Adelphi is the Vaudeville, looking older than its neighbour but in fact only dating from 1870. Designed again by Phipps, the rebuilt 1891 frontage has a slightly pinched appearance and the theatre is indeed long and narrow, extending ever backwards to its stage door entrance in Maiden Lane.

The Vaudeville was owned for almost a century by the remarkable Gatti dynasty. This family's founder, Carlo Gatti, arrived in London in 1847 from Ticino in Switzerland. Like so many other Swiss Italians, Carlo was a dab hand at catering but began his phenomenal career with a humble fast food stall. Gatti was also an ice merchant. He imported blocks hewn from Norwegian glaciers and during one hot summer must have had a Eureka moment for, by 1857, he was selling ten thousand ice creams per day from his pitch in Hungerford Market.

Graduating from street stalls to restaurants, the Gatti family next began to turn their attention to theatres. They opened Gatti's Under the Arches Music Hall in nearby Villiers Street - later to become the Players Theatre - and then gained control of the Adelphi Theatre in 1878. By 1882 Agostino and Stefano Gatti wanted to replace the gas lighting both there and in their nearby restaurant, the Royal Adelaide Gallery, with electricity, but the Westminster Council of the day refused to lay the connecting cables.

The brothers were not to be thwarted. They bought a vacant site on the Vaudeville side of Bull Inn Court, transformed the more masculine of their waiters into muscular builders, and opened an electric substation grandly titled 'The Charing Cross and Strand Electricity Supply Corporation'. The result was that the all-electric Adelphi glowed, shimmered and twinkled, but the gaslit casts at the Vaudeville began to complain that their words were being drowned out by the throbbing noise of the machinery. When that theatre owner tried to take legal action to enforce closure of the substation the brothers simply solved the problem by making a successful bid to buy the Vaudeville from him.

If the Gattis have yet to be sighted as spectres, other phantoms appear at this playhouse. Their favoured location seems to be in the auditorium. Lisa Crawford who works front of house told me that 'when I first started in 2009, I was told by Adam Ellicott, the assistant manager, that he had been physically pushed by an unseen ghost as he was going up the stairs from the foyer to the dress circle. I asked Paul, our then fireman, whether he knew about it and he said that he believed that this particular ghost went back a long way to before the theatre was built when a townhouse occupied the site with its entrance on Lumley Court. It was here that a seamstress had had her throat cut and had haunted the immediate area ever since'.

My research reveals that Lumley Court was indeed constructed in the early 1700s and was a cul-de-sac until the 19th century when its passage was extended through to Maiden Lane. To this day this narrow alley running beside the theatre retains a Dickensian reek of open sewers and desperate evil. It is by-passed by the wary after dark and utterly avoided at the dead of night.

So, if we maintain that no sensible ghost would want to linger there either, but instead could simply drift through the wall and into the fragrant comfort of the auditorium, then we will pick up Lisa's account again. 'I was told by an usher, Roberta, that during one show, she was sitting on the floor just inside the stalls entrance and fixing her make-up helped by a small light close to ground level to show patrons there were no steps, when she saw a woman go past her. In fact, she didn't see all of her. She floated past because she had no legs'.

The next Vaudeville ghost would appear to be audience related. The box office indeed told me that sometimes they had smelt the scent of herbs, but as box office windows always encounter more than their fair share of exotic customers this does not conclusively mean that you can sniff the afterlife in the foyer. But you may be able to see it. Theatre primarily is all about other peoples' problems, be they comic or serious. These dilemmas are what audiences come to watch, though there are times when the patrons themselves bring their own problems with them. Add in the chill factor of the supernatural, and the then front of house management of the Vaudeville had something definitely more substantial to report to me than mere whiffs of rosemary and thyme.

One evening, when the production of *Swallows and Amazons* was playing in December 2011, Thom Southerland, then acting as deputy manager, was asked by Nimax, the theatre's owners, if he could entertain some VIP guests at the interval. This was a regular task which he had dealt with many times, as had his assistant Emily Mathieson. In this case the guests were to be a boy and a girl accompanied by two ladies. Because of the size and nature of the incoming house they realised it could be difficult to identify and pick out their guests in the foyer before the show but they knew that their charges would be sitting in the stalls in row B, seats 4 to7. Thom had therefore organised a reserved area in the dress circle bar and had pre-ordered, as requested, ice creams and drinks.

As the houselights came up for the interval Thom walked down the side aisle with Emily to collect their guests. 'We were very surprised because in total there were three children. There was a boy and a girl sitting between the two ladies, but also another child, a little girl with blonde hair, sitting on the lap of the lady in B7'.

Being conscientious hosts, Thom told me that they had both panicked slightly as they knew they had not set up enough ice creams for three children. As the guests stood up and the girl got off the lady's lap, Thom therefore told Emily to 'sort out the ice creams when you get up there'. Due to the sheer crush of patrons, the guests were unable to stay together and the little blonde girl went ahead upstairs alone. Still separated by the crowd they began to arrive individually at the bar. Thom recalled saying to the first lady, 'We have two ice creams on the bar. Let me get another one and what flavour would you like?' But the lady replied, 'Two's enough. I only have two children'. He now needed to get downstairs to manage the interval from the foyer and so said to Emily, 'When the lady and the other girl arrive, sort them out'. She somewhat failed in this task. Ten minutes later, as the bar bells signalling Act Two started to ring, Emily found Thom and simply told him in a shocked voice that 'there is no other child'. This had been emphatically confirmed to her upstairs by the other lady but both Tom and Emily had seen 'this girl on the lady's lap'.

I do not doubt that they had witnessed a ghost and furthermore a ghost, no matter how young, contravening a basic theatre rule. After all, no auditorium seat for reasons of both health and safety and profit, can be occupied by more than one person at a time.

Scene 3: The Savoy Theatre

The Savoy, now seemingly part and parcel of the famous hotel, actually predates it by eight years for it originally opened in 1881. It was designed by Charles John Phipps for Richard D'Oyly Carte so that the impresario could produce his Gilbert and Sullivan operas in his very own theatre and it was the subsequent huge profits from the likes of *Patience, Iolanthe* and *The Mikado* that enabled D'Oyly Carte to take the next logical step and erect a hotel fit enough to wine, dine and bed not only his audiences but a perennial beaux monde. Enter the theatre's auditorium today and you may believe that you are admiring the stunning Basil Ionides' Art Deco décor which was installed in the 1929 refit, but you will be mistaken for this part of the theatre is an immaculate 1993 reconstruction. This is because, while closed for refurbishment, the Savoy fell victim, like so many others before it, to that ancient enemy of theatre, fire.

The auditorium was completely gutted on the night of February 13th 1990 though the general consensus next morning was that Vulcan had got his priorities absolutely wrong because the iron curtain, having been correctly lowered at the end of the day's work, did the job it was installed for and the antiquated backstage areas were preserved. As the fire still smouldered, Sir Hugh Wontner, then chairman of the Savoy, vowed to his general manager Julian Courtenay, that the theatre would be immediately restored. Sir Hugh may have died just before the reopening but he still maintains a nightly presence in the auditorium. Gaze up at the upper circle ceiling and you will see the striking sky mural painted by Helen Barnes. Look very closely and you will find Sir Hugh's face, wreathed in clouds, peering down at the stage.

As both theatre and hotel have played host to a multitude of stars it would be tempting to relate that some have been unable to resist the desire to reappear on stage. After all, the late Elaine Stritch actually lived in the Savoy for years and the even later Fred and Adele Astaire made it as far as the roof where they were photographed dancing together in the 1920s. But there are no dead 'name' encounters, only the experience of a live head of a backstage department.

In 2008, Lisa Brindley was wardrobe mistress on *Legal Fictions* at the Savoy, an evening of two John Mortimer one-act plays, *The Dock Brief* and *Edwin*. In time-honoured theatrical tradition, the Savoy wardrobe is situated on the backstage top floor and the nearest lavatory was an inconvenience, for it was a five-minute walk away. Lisa discovered however that a nearby pass door allowing access to the front of house, was left unlocked. Deciding to explore, she found to her delight that there was a Ladies in a corridor close by the upper circle possessing that rarity in theatres, the luxury of no less than five working cubicles. The first time she used its facilities she admitted to me that she had 'found it a bit creepy'.

Undeterred, the next afternoon she slipped through the pass door for a return engagement. She had just entered the toilet when she had the sensation

W.S. Gilbert

'that something horrible was glaring at me and then that something ran at me with a whish of petticoats to chase me out the door. I turned and ran'. That evening she told her story to two of the show's understudies. Both claimed to be clairvoyants and the bolder of the duo set off to investigate the location. He returned to advise her emphatically not to ever attempt another visit under any circumstance. 'There are evil spirits there and you have upset them,' he declared. 'You have entered what was originally the site of their house and they are very angry that you're peeing in their front room. Don't go in and do it again'. Lisa, understandably, took his advice.

It would be tempting to suggest that the ghosts of W.S. Gilbert and Sir Arthur Sullivan haunt the theatre for it was the venue of their greatest triumphs but, despite Gilbert's presence troubling some occupants of his London house in Harrington Gardens in the 1970s, I have drawn a blank at the Savoy. However their compositions do link them, if only tenuously, with the ghost of one Frederick Frederici, who was a star bass baritone with the D'Oyly Carte Company.

Frederici played such leads as the Mikado and Dick Deadeye on tours both in the UK and the USA. He even originated the part of the Pirate King in *The Pirates of Penzance* in Paignton in 1879 though he only ever appeared twice at the Savoy in two matinee performances of *Ruddigore* in February 1887. But perhaps, by playing the ghostly Sir Roderick Murgatroyd there, he may have tempted the Fates to take a premature interest in his mortality.

Later that year he sailed for tours in America and Australia and on March 3rd 1888 was appearing as Mephistopheles in Gounod's *Faust* at the Princess Theatre in Melbourne. At the end of the final act he sang his last note and duly descended with Faust into the smoke and fire of Hell by courtesy of a counterweighted stage trap. *En route* he suffered a heart attack and was pronounced dead by the time he had been carried into the Green Room, despite some of the cast being quite convinced that he was with them on stage for the curtain calls.

Sir Arthur Sullivan

Frederici has since been seen on many occasions in the Princess's dress circle, and was seemingly captured on camera in the 1970s. He may not haunt the Savoy but there is another link with the Gilbert and Sullivan operettas which is recalled by old staff members.

Before the fire, the location for the Savoy's follow spots - those hand-guided lamps that magically keep stars in sharper focus and brighter light than other cast members - was at the rear of the upper circle. No matter at what angle one spot was left the night before, each morning it was to be found back in its precise pre-show position, focused exactly on the conductor's stand in the pit. 'Standing by and ready for you, Sir Arthur'.

Scene 4: The Victoria Palace and the Apollo Victoria

Since the middle of the 19th century, true Londoners have been in a minority where the composition of theatre-goers is concerned. Audiences are now international thanks to air travel but from the 1860s railways played a vital part in delivering out of town audiences to the West End. Customers were drawn from all over the country and so many from the South-East leapt out of carriages at Victoria Station that past entrepreneurs accordingly built several places of entertainment close to that concourse.

Massive redevelopment over the years has meant that cinemas such as the Metropole, the Cameo and Biograph have been swept away, but these two splendid theatres, together with their ghosts, are still intact, beacons of hope for an ever never world in what some regard as a wasteland of mundane architectural misconstruction.

At first glance you would presume that the Victoria Palace would be the really haunted partner of the duo. Standing on the site of the Royal Standard Music Hall, the location of Chaplin's London debut, the V.P. was built in 1911 to a Frank Matcham design which alone should carry a certain cachet for any self-respecting spirit. Furthermore, to add to its splendour, it also sports a rather over-gilded statue of the prima ballerina Anna Pavlova. She is in arabesque posture and balances precariously on top of the dome above the front of house entrance. This lofty on-site tribute to an artiste is unmatched by any other London theatre statue. If Sir Bruce Forsyth's bust, weighed down slightly by its chin, only ascended as far as the London Palladium's Cinderella Bar, it is a further theatrical slight that Sir Laurence Olivier has to make do with an undersized statue on the lowly ground level of the riverside promenade outside the National Theatre.

Anna's gleaming golden effigy was commissioned in her honour by Alfred Butt, her producer and the first owner of the theatre. But once erected, the superstitious Pavlova, fearful of courting bad luck, adamantly refused even to glance in its direction. The statue was removed in 1939 at the start of World War II to avoid possible destruction from any terpischorean loathing Luftwaffe pilot, and then promptly lost. What ballet lovers admire today is therefore only a 1960 replica but perhaps, somewhere, the original sculpture is still gathering dust, leaning on the barre of some forgotten private dance studio.

The theatre's own antique veneer of dust has now completely vanished thanks to Sir Cameron Mackintosh. Not that this illustrious producer has, as far as I know, been personally busy with a Dyson, but because, under his new ownership and inspired guidance, the Victoria Palace has been magnificently restored to its full glory while its facilities, on both sides of the curtain, have been brought into the twenty-first century. Full houses watch *Hamilton* nightly but I cannot report with any certainty that the spirits of the Crazy Gang who ruled there for fifteen years are amongst them and up for the rap. Before *Billy Elliot* finished its run in 2016 there were indeed stories of a poltergeist who would lock and unlock the old wig room, throw the wigs around and trash the curlers. Could its identity perhaps have been the Gang's 'Monsewer' Eddie Gray? I have my doubts. That adroit and funny juggler would surely have kept the wigs in constant mid-air and never allowed one to hit the floor. I would suggest rather that when planning applications were granted to redevelop Victoria, the whole ghostly Gang called it a night and decamped to St Pancras.

In contrast, the Apollo Victoria does not disappoint when it comes to the supernatural. Designed by Ernest Wamsley Lewis and William Edward Trent, it opened in 1930 as the New Victoria during London's final major surge of theatre building in the last century. It was basically planned as a 2,500 seat cinema but with the allowance of a wide, shallow stage so that variety shows and bands could be slotted in between the double features. Its site, accessible from both Vauxhall Bridge Road and Wilton Road, allowed for two main entrances and it has a splendid nautical Art Nouveau interior décor, designed by Trent's cousin, Newbury Trent, incorporating a mermaid, scallops and waves. This theme may possibly have been inspired by an underground stream running beneath the site that has been identified as part of the 'lost' river Tyburn. A sump pump is always in operation sub stage and like its counterparts in adjoining buildings keeps the ever-flowing waters at bay. Unlike the vast majority of other theatres, the Apollo Victoria is also strangely devoid of vermin. Their absence, according to one theory, is because the theatre stands on a ley line. The hidden energies transmitted from it, I am told, make it completely rodent free, unlike the nearby Palace of Westminster which is so overrun by mice that the dirty rats spend some £1500 of tax payers' money per week trying to keep them at bay.

I first made the theatre's acquaintance in 1984 when Andrew Lloyd Webber's *Starlight Express* opened. Trevor Nunn's direction, Arlene Phillip's choreography and John Napier's multi-level design, brought to completion by that king of contemporary production managers, Richard Bullimore, ensured that audiences would be continually amazed and entertained and the look of the interior be changed for some eighteen years.

We were far too busy in the early days chasing roller skaters to bother to run after ghosts but there was no denying that the building itself had a strange mixture of atmospheres. Some locations were welcoming but other areas were quite forbidding. The lift was particularly intimidating. It was as old as the building and susceptible to stopping, whether grossly overcrowded or completely empty. Walter, the ancient night security officer, and myself were stuck in it for two hours one night after a show and I still recall that feeling of impending doom. I put it down at the time to the void beneath our feet and Walter's incessant Player's cigarettes but later on got into conversation with our aptly-named wig master, Hugo Byron Wiggins. Hugo related that he too had felt a distinct presence in the lift and this had prompted him to speak about it to a clairvoyant friend who came to visit him in the theatre. After an immediate investigation, she told him that a caretaker had been stabbed and had died in the base of the lift shaft. She then informed him that the caretaker had 'returned to haunt backstage and in particular the lift, hated noise and young people and could be destructive'. Understandably from then on, wishing to leave *Starlight* upright and on my own two feet, I took the stairs.

Walter and Hugo are now working celestial venues but Paul Barrett, the present stage door keeper, has been at the theatre since the *Starlight Express* days. He doubled then as night security too for it was impossible to bring the fire curtain in at the end of a performance owing to the nature of the set and a presence was needed for both safety and insurance.

In August 1999 Paul was working a graveyard shift. At around 4am he began one of his periodic rounds of the building. Switching on the cleaners' light he walked through the pass door into the auditorium. There, sitting in row Q of the stalls in seat number 23, was a man staring at the stage. He was aged about fifty, balding, stout and wearing a wing-collared, frilly-fronted dress shirt with a cummerbund above his trousers. Paul thought he was a 'sleeper', a tramp who had somehow slipped in during the previous show's outgoing to get off the streets and kip safe.

'I called out several times, "hello, hello", but he just kept staring at the stage. "Hello", again I shouted, "you're not supposed to be here." At that the man stood up, turned and walked up the central aisle away from me. He seemed to almost float as he went over the track at the back and out through the curtains towards the steps to the foyer. I ran after him through the curtains but he had gone. There was nothing there but the air there was freezing cold. And that night it had been in the high 20's.'

Keith Schooling, another stage door keeper, also doubled on night security with Paul. Early one morning while doing his periodic round of the building, he heard a crash in the stalls. In *Starlight Express* the cast would tear around the stage and auditorium at great speed during the train races. There were therefore safety nets on the side of the front stalls. Raised for those sitting in the inner paddock, they would be lowered just before shows to help stop skaters landing into the audience's laps. Keith, assuming one of the nets had fallen down from its upright position, went to investigate.

He saw a bald-headed man in his fifties sitting in the centre of the stalls, again in Q 23. Rattled at the sight of this intruder, Keith shouted out to him that he had no right to be in the building. The man stood up and began to walk away before suddenly vanishing. Keith kept this experience to himself until Paul happened to recount his own story of 'Mr Q23'. Neither of them saw him again but, to this day, that particular seat is always found to be pulled down in the mornings in contrast to those on either side of it.

Starlight Express was incredibly popular and standing tickets were sold for the back of the stalls so that the public could stand by the safety rails of the train track to watch the skaters racing by. Because of the amount of high-speed action and the constant risk of accidental collisions, the patrons were closely monitored at all times and, once the show had started, only allowed access to cross the tracks to their seats at specific moments.

With these circumstances in mind, an incident happened on 17th November 1987 to one of the front of house staff and I immediately asked whether she could describe in detail what had happened. Accordingly, Helen Gaume wrote that, 'during a performance while I was ushering, I escorted a latecomer to his seat in the stalls. While we were waiting for a suitable break in the performance I became vaguely aware of a man standing next to me watching the stage alongside us. But whenever I turned my head to see him more clearly he would disappear. After I had seated the latecomer I hastened back to the rear stalls feeling faintly uneasy, recalling a story I had heard from a friend. Apparently whenever a show is forced to stop, a ghost is supposed to appear before the incident, to the side of the stalls. Knowing that this particular friend of mine could be a little fanciful I had simply shrugged this aside, but during this particular performance I suddenly started worrying that she might have obtained this information from a more reliable source. Needless to say, I was stunned when this particular show was forced to stop because debris had fallen onto the track that rings the paddock. The part of the theatre I had been standing in at the time was the exit by the men's toilets in the stalls and it had been that part of the stage that we had all been facing.'

These gentlemen's toilets are situated on the left-hand side of the auditorium and it is from here in the early mornings that staff have often heard the sound of children laughing and singing. There is a macabre explanation for this, for I have been told that during the Blitz in the Second World War, the Civil Defence earmarked certain buildings to be used as temporary emergency morgues and that the stalls area of the then New Victoria was designated to be one of them. Westminster was certainly heavily bombed. The immediate vicinity around Victoria Station alone was hit fifteen times during raids in 1940 and 1941 and later, during the V1 attacks in 1944, the borough's toll of death and destruction was added to by some thirty rockets. If the story of the morgue is an actual fact, it could indeed be a valid reason for the manifestations.

That the theatre still harbours troubled spirits is beyond doubt. In 2014, Norma, one of the present cleaners, was hoovering at half past eight one morning. She was under the stage where there is a purpose-built quick change tent for the cast of Wicked: a basic structure with shelves for boxes of make-up and wig pins. As usual its curtained entrance had been closed shut at the end of the previous night's show. Opening the curtain, Norma stepped inside and immediately felt that there was someone there behind her. Turning around she saw that there was nothing there but that the curtain had been drawn closed again. She reopened it, started to hoover and again found that it had been closed. By now, more than a little rattled, she pulled it open once more and bent down to switch off her hoover. As she stood up she was bombarded by a shower of boxes from the shelves, picked up and violently thrown at her by an invisible hand.

If Norma's experience was unsettling, it pales in comparison with what happened in 2011 to George from Ecuador, the then senior cleaner. One morning at about nine o'clock, George entered the auditorium and went to the front of the stalls. His first job was to check the state of the 'cattle runs', the nickname for the side aisles on either side of the blocks of seats. Looking up, he saw a tall, thin man standing close to the ladies' toilets at the top of the left-hand run. The man, lifting his arm and pointing at George, ran towards and literally through him. The shock of this extraordinary impact threw George to the floor and his screams alerted other members of the staff who found him huddled on the floor of the aisle. Another cleaner and an electrician managed to carry him to the street where George, now as white as a sheet, started vomiting with shock. He was off 'sick' for a week and would never again work alone in the auditorium. *Wicked* may continue to entertain the innocent at the Apollo Victoria but is it possible that something else far less benign, something really wicked, may call this theatre 'home'?

Scene 5: The Criterion Theatre

Time to jump on a bus (or a cab if you've bought the hardback edition) and head to Piccadilly Circus which some visitors believe to be the centre of the capital. Leicester Square may now draw larger crowds but few properly explore its garden and so the majority of tourists miss that quote on the scroll held in the left hand of Shakespeare's statue 'There is no darkness but ignorance'.

Piccadilly Circus by contrast is ablaze with neon light and has Eros to kindle love, Boots the Chemist to help prevent or cure the ill effects of love and the Criterion to indulge our *l'amour propre,* namely theatre ghosts. Indeed the playhouse itself has a slightly detached air these days, another world apart from the teeming hordes that hourly pass it by and seemingly ignore its elegant Second Empire style entrance until, that is, at show time.

Designed by Thomas Verity, the Criterion was originally planned to be a concert hall in the lower part of the Victorian re development of the old White Bear coaching inn. However during its construction, it was decided to turn it into a playhouse and it eventually opened in 1874 as London's first under ground theatre.

The twin problems of ventilation and gas lighting soon became apparent. Asphyxiated audiences are orderly audiences but not guaranteed to clap, let alone return. Pipes to pump in fresh air were therefore installed. Electric lighting followed in 1884, while another improved ventilation system was put in. The theatre safely survived both the Blitz and determined philistine attempts to redevelop the whole site in the 1970s. Today, it's a Grade 2 listed building and correctly so, for the Criterion's original front of house staircases, bars and auditorium have survived intact and together add up to a remarkably fine example of a Victorian theatre design. The whole structure has been retained, the original decoration sympathetically restored, and I would defy anyone visiting today to feel claustrophobic.

I can vouch that before modernisation, backstage was certainly not for the faint hearted. It was indeed catastrophic when I first entered the stage door one early morning in 1971 for the start of *Butley.* The Victorian drains had had enough for that week and had backed up overnight. A lake of stinking sewage lapped and gurgled below in the central corridor and a very old gentleman sitting in a tiny cupboard at the top of the stairs, was telling someone loudly on the telephone that he couldn't "give a shit." He wasn't being bolshie.

He was being literal for it turned out that the toilets had overflowed in sympathy and had also flooded again.

Harry Loman (left) was then ninety-one years old and was - though the Guinness Book of Records refused my submission on a pedantic technical point - the oldest working stage door keeper in the world. Harry had been in the business all his life, starting as one of a clog dancing duo at the age of twelve. He joined Fred Karno's Army where he had taught Chaplin 'a trick or two' and worked with Stan Laurel in the London troupe. He had then been for twenty-five years the funny half of a double act, Low and Loman, appearing with stars such as George Robey, Marie Lloyd and Charles Whittle and had even topped the bill at the Palladium - albeit the other one in Midsomer Norton.

Retirement was a personal choice in those days and he had taken up his new stage door career at the age of seventy-four. The West End theatres were then fairly full of old people working gamely away, though I do not recall such old-timers through rose-tinted spectacles. They were rude and bloody-minded at times, survivors from a harder world, unsentimental about what seldom were 'the good old days'. Harry, beneath the chirpy Kennington charm, could be as tough as they come. Piccadilly Circus' then huge quota of drug addicts, drunks and derelicts were kept firmly at bay and he exercised his authority with impartiality. I once witnessed him throwing Rudolf Nureyev out of the stage door for daring to try to slip in past him, 'the prancin' foreign git'. Even Ingrid Bergman was refused entry until I came to vouch for her. He would sit on sentry duty in his cupboard day and night, in between performing little jigs to keep the circulation going and so enabling him to take a totter down the stairs for a 'wee break'.

The Criterion was originally leased to the actor manager Sir Charles Wyndham from 1875 till 1899. His leading lady for thirty years was Mary Moore, the wife of the dramatist James Albery, and she would eventually become Wyndham's second wife for the last three years of his life. Mary was a very talented comedienne and there is an imposing picture of her, dressed in a white gown, in the theatre's side stalls bar. Work decreed that I would pass her several times each evening en route between the front of house and backstage and one afternoon Miss Moore paid me the compliment of a return visit.

I was underground shuffling paper and had propped the door open to try to encourage the stale air from the corridor to enter into an office that Hitler could have mistaken for his Berlin Bunker. Suddenly something caught the periphery of my vision and I looked up to see the back of someone in white sweeping past the door en route for the main corridor. Thinking it was one of the cast, I shouted out a greeting but to no reply. The cast and crew of

Mary Moore, the Criterion's first leading lady

Butley were a friendly company and so, puzzled by the silence, I went to find out who it had been. Harry and the wardrobe mistress were around the corner gossiping by the stage door. Yes, they had heard me shout out but I was obviously talking to myself as no one had come past them. They were so positive that I began to wonder whether I had seen anything at all. Rather than risk further ridicule I decided to keep the possibility of a psychic experience to myself and had begun to forget about it until one day in the following week.

It was another afternoon and backstage seemed empty when I arrived for work - apart from Harry, of course, in his cupboard, chatting away to one of the front of house ladies. Harry always referred to her as his 'girl-friend' and to back his claim she certainly popped by most days to see him. I said my hellos and then saw that Harry's feet were starting to go into overdrive. It was definitely time for a 'wee break'. Management decreed that the stage door had always to be manned but his girlfriend was quite up for this kind of covering. She took over his seat, Harry descended the stairs to turn left towards the lavatory and I returned to my office. I could vaguely hear her speaking to someone as I unlocked the door but then, suddenly, her words transformed into frenzied screams.

I ran back to the stage door. There stood Harry, halfway up the steps, gazing in puzzlement at his girlfriend who was gasping like a goldfish and pointing at him with a shaking hand. She pleaded for a drink and, after I'd fetched a large brandy from the Captain's Cabin, calmed down enough to tell us what had happened.

As she had waited for Harry to return, a woman in a long white dress had come around the corner from my corridor and had stood at the bottom of the stairs looking silently up at her. She had thought perhaps that she was an understudy and, to be polite, had asked her how she was. The woman didn't reply but continued to stare disdainfully at her and she was just thinking 'what a snob', when Harry reappeared from the direction of the toilet. As he mounted the stairs she saw him literally walk right through the woman in white, completely oblivious to her presence. As he did so the woman just evaporated and vanished.

Harry obviously didn't have much time for dead spirits, for he knew perfectly well that he was a living legend. I am glad to say that in 1977 he was given the Society of West End Theatres Special Award in recognition of achievements in Commercial British Theatre. I am not sure if the Society also knew of Harry's ghost-busting talent but I like to think that Mary Moore, a woman with a reported sense of humour, would have been both pleased and amused.

Scene 6: The Gielgud Theatre

From the Criterion it's but a short walk to the beginning of Shaftesbury Avenue where four theatres standing clustered together are evocative symbols of a sometimes glittering West End. Their collective frontage is indeed something of a West End cliché, for they have featured in countless press photographs whenever a publicist or newspaper has needed an easy shot to represent the success or failure of commercial theatre. I have been fortunate enough over the years to have worked all four but though the Lyric, the Apollo and the Sondheim each have their stories to tell, it is the Gielgud's that I have chosen to explore here.

This theatre opened on December 27th 1906 but, as Sir John was then all but two years old, it was christened the 'Hicks' for it was Seymour Hicks who had commissioned the building and engaged W.G.R Sprague to design it. Hicks was one of the most successful of the Edwardian actor managers. Married to Ellaline Terriss, the daughter of murdered William Terriss, the pair starred together in a succession of musical comedies such as *Bluebell in Fairyland* and *Quality Street*. The huge profits generated from these shows enabled him to build not only the Hicks but also the Aldwych. The *Beauty of Bath* was Hick's first production and was followed by successes such as *Brewster's Millions*. In 1909, Ellaline's illness during the run of *The Dashing Little Duke* obliged Seymour to take over her part, the first recorded incident in a musical of a man playing a woman playing a man and the only known occasion in theatrical history of a husband playing his wife's part in public.

American Impresario Charles Frohman

The theatre's name was changed to the Globe in that same year when the American impresario Charles Frohman took over the management. Frohman was one of the first modern producers. His company dominated the American theatre world and he is credited with inventing the star system on Broadway. This theatrical Titan was unfazed by the outbreak of the Great War. In 1915, at the age of fifty-eight, he booked his passage on the Lusitania to cross the Atlantic to Liverpool to supervise his new season of forthcoming London productions.

The United States was then still a neutral observer of the conflict but the German Embassy had recently publicly warned American citizens of the potential danger of sailing on British liners. This did not disconcert Frohman. When asked by Paul Potter 'Aren't you afraid of U Boats, C.F.?' he replied, 'No. I am only afraid of the IOUs'. The liner set sail on the first of May and was duly torpedoed on the seventh. As the tragedy unfolded, Frohman showed remarkable *sang-froid*. Just before the ship sank, he turned to the actress Rita Jolivet and said 'Why fear death? It is the most beautiful adventure that life gives us'. He was of course paraphrasing a line from one of his greatest successes, J.M. Barrie's Peter Pan: 'To die will be an awfully big adventure'.

It would appear that Mr Frohman's courage was rewarded, for his immediate adventure in the afterlife began on the night he died. That same evening in New York, John Ryland, one of his staff at the Empire Theater on the south-east corner of Broadway and 40th Street, was locking up the fifth floor offices at close of business.

Ryland had gone to the pier only six days before to wish Frohman *bon voyage* and had seen the liner set sail so he was puzzled that not only were the lights on in the impresario's office but that Frohman was also standing by his desk examining some papers and posters that were spread out across its surface. Ryland asked him why he was back and whether there was anything he could do for him. Frohman looked up and shook his head. 'No, you can't help me, John,' he replied. 'Just leave me alone here for a few minutes. Thanks, and goodbye.' Ryland did as he was told, but by now thoroughly perplexed, went to find the House Manager to tell him what had just occurred. The Manager found it incredulous so together they returned to the offices joined by two box office clerks, a press agent and Frohman's office boy Peter Mason. The lights were out, the room empty and the desk uncluttered. Ryland was scoffed at by the others, but he stuck by his story with an unsettling persistence. The next day news came of the Lusitania's sinking.

Ryland continued working at the Empire for another twenty-five years but could never be induced to enter Frohman's room again.

The management of the Globe on Frohman's death passed to Alfred Butt but as well as being a very successful playhouse - Noel Coward's *Fallen Angels* premiered and played there for 157 performances in 1925 - the theatre also gained its premier position on the Avenue because of its close association with the production company that would take its top floor offices in 1937.

This was H.M. Tennent Ltd. and the man who ran 'the firm', Hugh 'Binkie' Beaumont, would become the undisputed czar of the West End for three decades. Binkie's gift for employing talent ensured that he and his small production team seldom made mistakes. From 1936 to 1973 'the firm' produced over four hundred plays, musicals and revues. Binkie had great personal charm and powers of persuasion, an instinctive eye for successful plays and a ruthless business brain that ensured that budgets in all fields were strictly enforced. ·

Playwrights such as Coward, Terence Rattigan, Ivor Novello, Christopher Fry and Emlyn Williams were among his personal friends as well as Sir John Gielgud and many other leading actors of the day. Unless one had lungs for Lhasa and legs of steel, Binkie's offices had to be reached by a lift, small enough to guarantee immediate intimacy if used by more than one passenger at a time. At one point Tennent's had fourteen productions running concurrently in London and this near monopoly meant that Binkie was able to make or break careers. Actors, including future stars such as Richard Burton, Stanley Baker, Peter Barkworth and Virginia McKenna, all discovered by his casting director Daphne Rye, would be placed under permanent contract to perform as cast in plays such as *The Lady's Not for Burning* and *The Deep Blue Sea*.

Binkie's control of his contracted players was extraordinary by today's standards. Ellen Martin who was to marry Stanley Baker, told me how in the early 1950s, she and other actresses would be obliged to visit the offices weekly, take off their coats and shoes and step onto general manager Barney Gordon's scales. If the scales tipped over eight stone they would be fined a crisp pound note per flabby pound of flesh and if that overweight continued, sent to a certain doctor's rooms in Harley Street for a figure changing injection.

Binkie died suddenly in 1973 and his immediate circle have nearly now all gone to join him. I find it curious that there have been no substantiated sightings of him nor for that matter any of the galaxy of stars who played the Globe and, in particular, any glimpses of Sir John. But perhaps the theatre's change of name in 1994 to the Gielgud, when Sam Wanamaker's loving reconstruction of Shakespeare's Globe in Southwark was underway, has something to do with it.

Sir John without doubt deserved such recognition, for his association with the Globe spanned many shows including his seminal production of *The Importance of Being Earnest* which he directed and starred in as Jack Worthing opposite that definitive Lady Bracknell, Dame Edith Evans. So perhaps, having now achieved permanent top billing on Shaftesbury Avenue, his spirit is content to rest in peace, until that is, the next renaming.

*Sir John Gielgud as
Jack Worthing*

However, my last engagement at the theatre made me wonder whether the Gielgud may not be entirely spectral free. One Wednesday evening in November 2013, I was sitting in the stalls watching a technical rehearsal for *Strangers on a Train*. As it was going to be a long journey, I had chosen an aisle seat to stretch out my legs. Just before the interval I felt something brush slowly past my left ankle. I sat up, looked down and around and saw through the semi darkness of the auditorium an indistinct shape scuttling up the aisle towards the stalls bar.

Now, many West End venues have mice. Their 'occasional' appearances may scare patrons even more than ghosts but I must state on behalf of an urgent Society of London Theatres request, that none of these playhouses have rats ('never, never, never'). Pest control officers stalk the West End on a daily basis and should other theatres take a more *laissez faire* attitude towards rodents they are classified as Alternative, Community or Closed.

But whatever had touched my ankle up certainly wasn't a mouse. It was large enough for me to remember my environmental responsibilities, pick up a claw hammer and investigate. Cautiously then, I followed what I thought was its trail up to the corridors and into the foyer. There was nothing visible crouching on the carpet ready to spring up my trouser leg, but, high on a wall, I did indeed find an animal staring boldly down at me. To call it a mere animal is inadequate, for what I was confronted with was a framed photograph of none other than the most famous four-legged theatrical cat of the last century, Beerbohm.

Beerbohm was of course born at Her Majesty's but at an early age was engaged as a mouser at the Gielgud. He was quite correctly put on the official payroll of the theatre and though this charge on the weekly statement was often queried by visiting producers' accountants, it was always to no avail. The master carpenter, the legendary Tony Ramsey, built a home for Beerbohm under the stage in the shape of a miniature theatre with the cat's bedding up-stage centre behind the proscenium arch. But Beerbohm liked to wander and he would always make at least one accidental appearance on stage per show. This was encouraged by most casts. Dame Maggie Smith for one would take him on stage with her and he would gallantly return the compliment. Should a professional feline actor fail to turn up for the show, Beerbohm would take to the part with scant rehearsal and save the day.

Beerbohm - a most famous theatrical cat

He would also choose various actors to share dressing rooms with. Michael Gambon, Peter Bowles, Penelope Keith were all invited in and Beryl Reid so enjoyed his company that each weekend she would take him home with her. Beerbohm could also cause on stage problems but usually after everyone else had gone home.

Sir Michael Codron produced Simon Gray's play *The Rear Column* in February 1978. The play's location was the deepest jungle of the darkest Congo. Eileen Diss, the play's designer, had gone to great lengths to make the set authentic and as a finishing touch dressed it with stuffed exotic birds. The next morning only their feathers remained. Again in 1987, the set of *The House of Bernarda Alba* proved too great a temptation. The stage was covered not just in rocks and sand but also, as the run continued, in many a Beerbohm momento.

On retirement, the old trooper went to share digs with Tony Ramsay. He died peacefully at the age of 20 in March 1995 and was given a front page obituary in *The Stage*. His position was left empty, for Beerbohm was truly irreplaceable and, judging by my experience, he has never really left.

Scene 7: The Lyceum Theatre

If David Garrick is historically associated with the Lane and Beerbohm Tree with Her Majesty's, then the Lyceum is linked inseparably to Henry Irving. The first theatrical knight made it his base for over two decades after he had singlehandedly turned around the fortunes of the theatre and rescued its owner, 'Colonel' Hezekiah Bateman, from bankruptcy. In 1871 he persuaded the American to honour a promise to let him play the Burgomaster Mathias in *The Bells*, an adaption by Leopold Lewis of the novel *Le Juif Polonais* by the prolific French duo of Emile Erckmann and Alexandre Chatrian. The First Night was nothing less than a complete triumph, for the actor's intensity of performance transformed a pedestrian melodrama into a thrilling experience for both critics and audiences alike. After fifteen years of poverty, struggle and apprenticeship, John Henry Brodripp had finally completed his metamorphosis into Henry Irving.

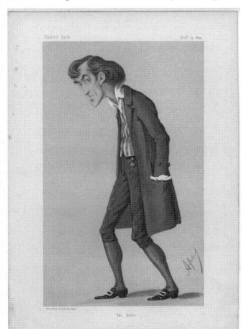

Sir Henry Irving as Mathias in 'The Bells'

Only Mrs Brodripp was unimpressed. She had sat in total silence at the First Night party and remained so on their way home, until Irving announced that this success could mean that they might afford their own horse and carriage. Turning to him, she snarled, 'Are you going on making a fool of yourself like this all your life?' Irving stopped the brougham and walked away into the night. He would never see her again but, in ample compensation, would go on to become the dominant and most famous British actor of the late Victorian stage.

The guaranteed box office appeal of his first extraordinary success meant that *The Bells* stayed in his repertoire throughout his career and he was to play Mathias for the very last time on October 12th 1905, the night before he died in Bradford.

The Lyceum on Wellington Street dates from 1834 and, on visiting it for the first time, it would be natural to suppose that you were gazing on the actual boards that Sir Henry trod. You would be quite wrong. The truth is that the structure of the present building now has no real material connection with the 'Guv'nor' apart from its massive portico columns, for these were swathed in ribbons of black mourning crepe when his death was announced.

What you see instead is the 1996 reconstruction of its 1904 successor, originally planned to be a variety theatre, designed by Bertie Crewe and built in the mistaken hope that it would rival both the London Palladium and the Coliseum. Expectations dashed, it reverted to drama and mostly melodrama. The Lyceum managed to survive the war and continual redevelopment plans, before ending up as what would now be a politically incorrect Mecca Ballroom and venue for Miss World competitions. Now it is thankfully a proper theatre again and has retained continuous ghostly patronage despite its new internal structure. The site has great form for after all, what is now the technical workshop is the site of Bram Stoker's office where, in between balancing the books as Irving's business manager, he penned Dracula on Lyceum-headed note paper.

Kieran McGivern, the master carpenter for the Lyceum before and during *The Lion King*'s arrival, told me that the link with Irving had even been maintained during the days when drama had been banished and the Pasodoble and the Palais Glide held sway. An old cleaner, then employed nightly to polish, wax and buff up the dance floor, had told him in absolute sincerity that he would often hold regular conversations with the 'Guv'nor' about their mutual love of the building, for Irving had a penchant for appearing in the Royal Box punctually at 3.00 am of a morning.

Rob Hayden, technical manager for Apollo Leisure during the rebuild in 1996 was told by one of the box office that when concerts had started to be booked in the 1970s, the decision to hold a séance in the stalls bar ended spectacularly with all the mirrors cracking. There is no evidence the Guv'nor couldn't stomach Led Zeppelin, but maybe he drew the line at The Who.

On one rainy summer's day in 2010, Michelle Allen, company manager of *The Lion King* was standing to watch the start of the evening show from the right-hand side of the Royal Circle. Noticing that a piece of scenery was in the wrong position, she decided to check that it would be cleared in the transition into the second scene. The humidity that day was high, making the air in the auditorium muggy but she was suddenly aware of a sudden fall in temperature to the left of where she was standing. She turned to try to see where this cold air was coming from. As she did so she was tapped smartly on her right shoulder. She swung round but no one was there, at least, no one visible. Wayne Glover, now producer at the Chiswick Playhouse, was working at the Lyceum in 2012 when the royal circle had two bars - the Royal Circle Bar and the Royal Bar. The first was unused by the public as it was planned to turn it into a hospitality room - it is now today's Ambassador Lounge - but it then still had all its fixtures and fittings including bottles and glasses.

'However', relates Wayne, 'it was common knowledge amongst staff that whisky glasses couldn't be stored in there as they would inevitably be broken by an unseen hand. I myself left a whisky glass on the counter after a matinee and indeed, after my break, returned to find it duly smashed.'

An older story that relates to the Lyceum is set in the 1834 building during one of Irving's seasons in the 1880s. A married couple attending an evening performance decided to stay in their box seats during the interval rather than attempt to brave the crush in the corridors and bars.

The house lights were fully up and this allowed them to amuse themselves in the time-honoured manner by examining and damning the dress and appearances of their fellow members of the audience. Just before the start of the second act, the husband noticed that a middle-aged woman in a long silk dress, sitting in the centre of a row towards the front of the stalls, seemed to be clutching a strange looking fur hat on her lap. He examined it through his opera glasses and did an instant double take. To his astonishment, what he had taken to be a hat appeared to be a man's moustachioed and bearded head, whose open eyes were furthermore glaring up at him. His wife had just time to confirm what he had seen and also note the head's long dark hair, before the house lights dimmed and the second act began.

At the start of the next interval, still convinced of what they had seen, they pushed and squeezed their way down to the stalls to get a closer look. The crowd prevented them reaching the woman but they could glimpse her from the far aisle and she appeared by now to have covered the head with a silken scarf. By the end of the performance they were beginning to doubt what they thought they had originally and so clearly seen. To solve the mystery they tried once more to reach her, but when they arrived in the stalls the woman had disappeared into the night. Over time they came to dismiss the whole strange incident as a combined mental aberration. Some years later however, the husband was commissioned to travel to Leeds to evaluate a collection of paintings at the Jacobean manor house of Temple Newsam, then owned by the Ingram family. There he came across a portrait bearing the provenance that it had previously hung at the Lyceum. Turning it over, he found himself gazing once again at the head in the stalls.

You may well, like myself, believe that this is perhaps a little too neat an end to the story. I have yet to find further evidence to support it, so I would like to put forward another hypothesis.

Before Samuel Beazley's 1834 Lyceum, another earlier theatre of the same name opened in 1794 with its entrance where the Lyceum Tavern now stands in the Strand. It was here that Madame Tussaud opened her first wax work exhibition in London.

Madame Tussaud

Marie Tussaud had arrived from Paris in 1802 during that short interlude of peace in the Napoleonic wars after the Treaty of Amiens had been signed between England and France. She brought with her a substantial collection of her best and original moulds. So as not to upset the sensibilities of the many French royalist refugees, she did not display the heads of the executed Marie Antoinette and Louis XV1 but, in order to satisfy British curiosity, laid out instead those of the living Josephine and Napoleon. She placed beside them, as an attraction for the more morbid visitors, a fine selection of the macabre. This included the murdered Marat in his bath and the death masks of such as the Princesse de Lamballe, Madame du Barry, Mirabeau, Hebert, Fouquier-Tinville and Robespierre. The public interest to see them was greatly heightened by the knowledge that she had retrieved and modelled many of their heads immediately after the guillotine had been about its business, and, to stress the point, a fully working model of La Veuve was on display.

May I suggest therefore that what the couple may have seen was not some demented, drama-loving decapitator and her latest victim but the ghost of Madame Tussaud sitting very patiently with the head of one of her extremely life-like creations in her lap, and waiting for the chance to get on stage to reunite it with its body or pop it into the guillotine's wicker basket?

Scene 8: The London Opera House, the Royalty and the Peacock

If you are feeling a little disembodied yourself you may find yourself taking a short cut from the Lyceum to the Aldwych only to find yourself in Kingsway. This is a thoroughly dreary thoroughfare bulldozed in the pursuit of progress through the slums of Holborn in the 1900s. The Kingsway Theatre was blitzed in 1941 but there is one site with a very theatrical past. Look across the road and by Portugal Street you will see the signage of the Peacock Theatre, owned now by the LSE and leased to Sadler's Wells for contemporary dance productions. If you were to wander in of a morning and question the sheer minimalism of movement this is because lectures in global economy are also regularly held here.

The Peacock stands on the site of the Vere Street Theatre where on December 8th 1660 Mrs Margaret Hughes, playing Desdemona, caused a sensation by becoming the first documented English woman to appear in public to a paying audience. A French troupe had indeed tried to in 1629 but *les actrices* had been 'hissed, hooted and pippin-pelted from the stage'. The Peacock is also partly where the London Opera House once stood, an enormous theatre spanning an entire block, designed by Bertie Crewe. This gigantic building was opened in 1911 by the American producer Oscar Hammerstein- the grandfather of one Oscar Hammerstein 11 who achieved immortality through his partnerships with Lorenz Hart and Richard Rodgers.

Mr Hammerstein the First was the only American opera producer and theatre owner whose productions rivalled the Metropolitan of New York. A deal was negotiated whereby the Met paid Oscar $1.2 million on the understanding that he would not present grand opera in the USA for a decade. Cash rich but artistically hamstrung at home, he crossed the Atlantic to take on Covent Garden Opera House and lost. Within two years he returned to America and his theatre was eventually taken over by Oswald Stoll. It had a chequered life as a variety house and cinema, before becoming the Stoll Theatre in 1942. Its location in what was no longer an area dedicated for mass entertainment and its huge capacity of over 2,600 seats meant that it was economically fragile and it eventually succumbed in 1957 to the inevitable fate of that era. It became, of course, an office block. However, even in those cavalier times, artistic council conscience wasn't fully dead and the authorities insisted that a theatre be incorporated in the development, hence the Peacock, or as it was first known - the Royalty. Now this is where things become a bit complicated because, of course, the original Royalty was not at this location but in Dean Street, Soho. Here, in 1840, the actress Fanny Kelly opened her theatre and dramatic academy. Fanny had amassed a fortune in her career and chanced all on this new venture. She had an exquisite 200-seater auditorium constructed which was universally admired, but, backstage, calamity awaited.

An engineer friend, Rowland Macdonald Stephenson, had persuaded her to install under stage his self-designed, but untested, machinery to revolve, fly and change all manner of scenery and so dispense with the cost of a large stage crew to shift the many sets. The first night was scheduled for May 21st. The first disappointment was that Queen Victoria and Prince Albert opted out of the delicate delights of a cultural evening for the more earthy thrills of Astley's Circus. The second was far worse, in fact, it became a disaster.

After the curtain raiser, Fanny had chosen two plays for the evening's entertainment, *The Sergeant's Wife* with *The Midnight Hour* as an afterpiece. During the action and scene changes Mr Stephenson's inventions slowly grinded jerkily into action on cue but with such a cacophony of horse hooves, cranking revolves, rattling chains, clunking cog wheels and shrieking pulleys that the actors' voices were completely drowned out.

Before the opening night, a solitary stage hand had been optimistically hired to oversee this sub-stage engineering marvel but, on finding nothing would move, Stephenson had had to add horse power to set his Emmett like machinery in motion at all. Fanny's humiliation became the talk of the town. Bemused audiences drifted away and the theatre closed at the end of that week and was then half demolished in order to remove both the hapless machinery and the accumulated horse dung.

Fanny would reopen her theatre but bad luck dogged her continually until the time came a decade later when, with her fortune lost, the bailiffs moved in to evict her. She may have left physically but her spirit lingered long. For in 1934, during the run of *Murder in Motley*, the actor Joe Mitchenson, who together with his partner Raymond was to create the Mander and Mitchenson Theatre Collection, saw the lady in Victorian costume sitting in the prompt side box watching a rehearsal.

The Royalty under many different managements carried on, playing host to a stream of historical first London productions - *Trial by Jury* in 1871, *Ghosts* in 1891, *Charley's Aunt* in 1892, Shaw's *Widower's House* and *You Never Can Tell* and Noel Coward's *The Vortex* in 1924 before the whirlwind of the

Blitz fragmented it forever.

Next door to it, at 69 Dean Street, on the top floor of this Georgian house, was the Gargoyle Club of which I have some somewhat hazy memories dating from the 1960s. Stephen Tennant opened it in 1925 at the let's do it age of nineteen. Tennant, whom Evelyn Waugh used as a model for Sebastian Flyte in Brideshead Revisited, created a most popular haven for misbehaviour and attracted the great and bad of Bohemia and Belgravia. The Club's amazing décor of mirrored walls, with Matisse's painting, *L'Atelier Rouge*, hung jauntily on one wall, was probably taken for granted, for most members were up there for fun and not for any of your old-fashioned fauvism. The attraction of an in-house ghost adds to any club's allure but many members and staff over the years genuinely swore that they had seen the spectre of a lady in a high-waisted costume and a large hat decorated with flowers who would materialise before disappearing into the lift shaft. Popular folklore identified her as Nell Gwynne but again I have my doubts. After all, that game girl died in 1687 in Pall Mall and this ghost's description is more fitting of The Gainsborough Lady. However, when the Royalty Theatre's ruins were being levelled in 1953 a skeleton of a woman was found wearing the fragments of an 18th century costume. As that theatre was reputedly haunted by another lady who would grin lewdly and suggestively at patrons before vanishing, could it have been the same ghost, off stage at the Gargoyle, but still trolloping for custom? Whoever it is, she is not the phantom who haunted the Stoll Theatre - née the London Opera House - before its demolition. This was believed to be an opera singer, a discarded mistress of Mr Hammerstein who, like Tosca, had died for love. It is impossible for me to confirm that she would intone '*Avanti a Dio*' as I have found no witnesses to her shade but, if she is no longer willing or able to manifest herself, the Peacock Theatre, below the office block, does have another very curious ghost.

During the 1970s, when it was still named the Royalty Theatre, Paul Raymond moved in with his production of *The Royalty Follies*, featuring lots of lovely girls and very few costumes. One of the featured performers was Miss Nude International whose striptease act had a novel staging. Picture the scene: the lights come up and Miss Nude International climbs nimbly into a huge glass-sided water tank that has been hydraulically raised from beneath the stage. The permanent residents of the tank, two dolphins, Pennie and Pixie, rise rhythmically from the depths, give Miss Nude International a friendly greeting and, to roars of applause and buoyant bubbles, help the lady remove her clothes with some shifty but friendly nips of their teeth.

They don't make acts like that anymore, but, despite all this artistry, *The Royalty Follies* just couldn't pull the audiences in. Now legend has it that the dolphins, left behind when the show folded and forgotten in their darkened tank below the stage, starved to death. This of course is sheer nonsense. Dead they may be now, but on retirement from their busy burlesque careers, they swam out their days at the Woburn Safari Park Dolphinarium. The remains of the tank are still under stage at what is now the Peacock and have helped in the retention of the story, though, as time has passed, Pennie and Pixie have merged together into folklore to become 'Flipper', a rather singular dolphin. Even though no ghost of a mammal is ever seen, there are many people who swear that they have heard its melancholy wails, squeaks and whistles underneath the stage. This is coupled with occasional drops of water found on the floors of the sub-stage corridors, or, could they, by any chance, be tears?

Theatre basements are sunk deep below ground level in London, close to Tube tunnels, drains, rivers and other hidden or best-forgotten passages. Could the 'life' within these be what is really heard or is it indeed the memory of hard times past? I am undecided. My only advice should you wish to investigate such a dank vicinity is - just in case - take a handy tin of pilchards.

It is with some relief for me to now redirect you back to the Aldwych proper and bid farewell to the Peacock. Not the best name for a theatre for it is a bird of misfortune. A peacock feather in the home, so the saying goes, produces old maids and I recall not only the fate of the Pahlavi dynasty who presumed to sit on the Peacock Throne of Iran, but also the cuckolded landlord of the Peacock Pub in Maiden Lane. He and the pub have long gone, but I can still picture the life-like statue of that strutting fowl high up on its pedestal, its opaque eyes seemingly following the nightly vanishings of said landlord's wife, barman and takings. Steeped in superstition, we deemed it far safer to drink at Rules for in those days the waiters were as high as the game by nightfall and if you couldn't afford a cocktail, they'd pour you one anyway. Two olives to every martini if I remember, and, if I don't, a 'pair' correctly describes our next two adjacent theatres.

Penny, Pixie and Miss Nude International -
a hard act to follow

Scene 9: The Novello and the Aldwych Theatres

These twin playhouses are good companions for they were both designed by W.G.R. Sprague and have identical exteriors. They stand like elegant book-ends at each end of the Waldorf Hotel block and though neither have flamboyant ghosts or are infested with hauntings, both are important historical stage memory sites.

The Novello, at its opening in 1905, was christened the Waldorf. It became the Strand in 1909, before the American producer F.C.Whitney took it over in 1911 and renamed it after himself. This hubristic act led to his nemesis in the shape of failed shows such as his *Baron Trenck* and the theatre soon once again became the Strand until it was purchased by Sir Cameron Mackintosh. On its centenary in 2005, he changed its name to honour Ivor Novello, the phenomenally successful actor, playwright and composer of the early-to-mid--Twentieth Century. Until the arrival of Andrew Lloyd Webber, Ivor was regarded as the most successfully consistent musical composer in Britain but he is now largely forgotten by the general public. Some theatre reputations, as opposed to second-hand theatre nostalgia, last only as long as there are enough audiences alive to remember the players, but Ivor deserves better. Here was a man who composed not only 'Keep the Home Fires Burning' during World War I and 'We'll Gather Lilacs' at the end of World War II but also managed to come up with possibly the best line of film dialogue ever written, for when Johnny Weissmuller met Maureen O'Sullivan, he declaimed, 'Me Tarzan. You Jane.'

Ivor lived and died, as it were, above the shop for he had a flat on the top floor of the Strand. Here, on March 6th 1951, hours after performing in his production of *King's Rhapsody* at the Palace Theatre, he suffered a fatal coronary thrombosis. Soon after his funeral, attended by some 7,000 fans, the flat was vacated, the grand piano removed and all traces of its colourful occupant slowly faded away. Or did they?

Ivor was not only talented but a very generous man and a more than enthusiastic host. His parties were legendary and an invitation meant that you had arrived, were desired or, ideally, both. Soon after her first stage success, Margaret Rutherford, as the story goes, was invited by Ivor to one of his soirees and duly entered the lift to carry her up to his flat. She was very nervous for she was a latecomer to the stage and this was to be her first real encounter with what she understood to be its Great and Good. The flat's front door opened and there was Ivor welcoming her in with open arms. Behind him twinkled Douglas Byng, Noel Coward, Siegfried Sassoon, Bobby Andrews and every second chorus boy in the West End. She stood for a moment in amazement, open mouthed in wonder, dumbstruck by the spectacle. 'Why, Ivor!', she enthused with pure sincerity, 'Thank you! Thank you! How wonderful it is, why, I feel I'm in Fairyland!' The players may have all vanished now and the flat has been used until recently only as theatrical offices for such producers as Paul Elliot and Duncan Weldon but it is said, come evening, you can still sometimes faintly hear sounds of laughter and song, no doubt from spirits still fit enough to hoof it up the stairs to the phantom parties.

Like the Novello, the Aldwych Theatre has played host to a huge variety of shows over the years ever since Seymour Hicks and Charles Frohman produced its opening production in 1905, a revival of Hick's *Blue Bell*. Notable landmarks in its history include the series of Aldwych Farces such as *A Cuckoo in the Nest*, *Rookery Nook*, *Plunder* and *Thark* all written by Ben Travers in the 1920s and 1930s, the Royal Shakespeare Company's historic twenty-year occupancy in the 1960s and 1970s together with Peter Daubeny's World Theatre Seasons.

More recently it has housed the offices of the West End's most influential play producer of the last sixty years, Sir Michael Codron. Perhaps his occupancy goads other past impresarios to put in an appearance for, besides the ghost of an unknown woman in the stalls, a fairly common sighting in many auditoriums, an earlier producer has been seen in the auditorium by both audiences and members of the staff.

Annie Hashtari is the Aldwych's house manager and started working in the front of house in 2007. At the end of a performance of *Dirty Dancing* in 2008, a customer approached her and asked whether she knew 'there was a male ghost walking in the stalls near the front of the stage?' Annie, unable to share his vision, listened nonetheless to this 'psychic patron' as he elaborated on what he could see. 'He gave me a description and among other things told me the figure was wearing a black Victorian frock suit, had dark hair parted at the side and also appeared to be looking for someone. I told him I had never heard of a ghost before but he insisted he was there and before leaving said that 'he needs to find her and he hopes to find her soon'. I thought that it was all a bit comical but decided I should tell my manager Ruth about it.

Ruth didn't laugh though. She said it wasn't the first time she had heard such a story. From what the customer had described she said it sounded like Seymour Hicks again and the person he was looking for was no doubt his wife, Ellaline Terriss.'

Sir Seymour Hicks giving his 'Dickie' in 'Blue Bell'

Ruth showed Annie a photograph of Hicks which seemed to correspond with the patron's depiction and it was then that 'other members of the staff began to chime in with their own experiences.'

The stage door keepers, who are the first staff members on duty each morning, still to date repeatedly report on a very strong smell of cigars in the stalls which also seems to permeate the stalls bar. This sensory phenomenon is coupled with the scent of a very floral perfume in what was once a small bar and is now the Nederlander Suite. This room, on the side of the front stalls, was originally a star dressing room with access to the stage, so it would seem appropriate and likely to have been used by both Ellaline and her husband. He may in addition prowl the front of house offices, for a shadowy figure has been witnessed in its kitchen by Sir Michael's own personal assistant, Sandi Pescod. There again perfume sometimes fills the air as does also the aroma of cigars. No one there can explain either odour. I do know Sir Michael enjoys the occasional Villiger - a cigar, he tells me, recommended to him by his great friend Richard Armitage, the son of Noel Gay - though of course, strictly 'off limits'. So perhaps again it is Sir Seymour, impervious to the dictates of Health and Safety, checking the returns and exhaling a phantom Monte Cristo.

Scene 10: The Coliseum

It is time now to backtrack to some more haunted venues. Let us head along the Strand towards Trafalgar Square, for close by, in St Martin's Lane, is another cluster of theatres that merits attention. The Coliseum ranks as good a monument to Britain's late Imperial past as its namesake does for the early Roman Empire but it has the added advantage that it has survived the last hundred years in better shape. It is what some would consider Frank Matcham's masterpiece, designed for Sir Oswald Stoll, who with Edward Moss created national networks of touring and variety theatres at the beginning of the twentieth century.

Stoll's 'London Coliseum' - so none could mistake it for that other one - opened in December 1904. Sir Oswald's aim was to provide family entertainment as opposed to what Marie Lloyd was currently serving up in Hoxton. The belief that well-behaved spectators would be enticed into the first show was aided by the promise that they could watch the Derby from the comfort of their plush theatre seats. Sure enough, the tabs rose to reveal the track and stands, the bookies and punters and six professional jockeys mounted up on proper racehorses. The thoroughbreds were ready and pawing the floor of the central revolve, one of three permanently set into the stage for the then astounding cost of £70,000. At 'Starter's Orders' the revolve started to turn and at the 'Off' began to pick up speed. But the machinery malfunctioned and the revolve began to rotate faster and faster. As it spun ever more frantically, the horses began to lose their footing. Some fell over, others fell off the stage and one horse, together with its rider, sailed majestically over both footlights and orchestra pit to land in the auditorium. Somehow the revolve was stopped but not before the jockey Fred Dent had crashed head first into a stage box and broken his neck. It was small comfort for him to hear that, in the fine tradition of 'the show must go on', the race was repeated the next night but with the added precaution of a safety net.

Early teething problems also guaranteed that King Edward VII's electrically propelled mobile ante chamber, designed to convey the portly monarch and his entourage to the royal box, would blow a fuse and come to a grinding halt as the packed house stood waiting to loyally chant the National Anthem. But such technical hitches were eventually sorted and the Coliseum settled down as the venue for the type of acts Sir Oswald would label as 'class'. Harry

Lauder, Lily Langtry, Yvette Guilbert answered to that description, but bills needed filling so there were such other startling performers as Fraulein Brunhilde, The Tallest Pianist in the World, measuring in at 7ft 11 ins, and Fitz the Boxing Kangaroo.

The most famous ghost of the Coliseum is now a centenarian for he dates from the First World War. Throughout that carnage, soldiers on leave from the Western Front would pack theatres to forget the grim realities of trench warfare for a few short hours and enjoy the happy make-believe world of entertainment. One young cavalry lieutenant became so enchanted with Lydia Lopokova of Diaghilev's Ballets Russes that he spent every single night of his leave watching her dance. He returned to the front only to be killed on his first day back on October 3rd 1918. On that same evening, it is claimed that the dead man was seen occupying a seat in the dress circle. The ghost is reported to have then been sighted on several of the immediate following nights and furthermore recognised by several people who had known the unfortunate lieutenant.

On October 19th, a lady named Emma Martin was watching the show with her father. As the houselights dimmed she claimed she saw a uniformed soldier hurry down the aisle to take up the last vacant seat two rows in front of them. She saw the silhouette of his head as he sat down but then was distracted by what was happening on stage. When she looked at him again he was no longer there, and she had seen no one standing up to walk out. Her father confirmed her story and identified the soldier's badges as being those of a cavalry regiment. After the Armistice, sightings became less frequent and he has not been seen since the 1940s, proof perhaps that there is a sad substance to the saying 'old soldiers never die but merely fade away'.

Scene 11: The Duke of York's Theatre

A little further up St Martin's Lane is the Duke of York's Theatre. It's a charming building designed by Walter Emden for Frank Wyatt and his wife Violet Melnotte and its backstage dressing room block immediately abuts onto the Garrick in Charing Cross Road - another Emden creation.

It opened as the Trafalgar Square Theatre in September 1892 before gaining its current title in 1895. It is a playhouse proper and one that has always attracted plays of the moment. Some indeed for a very short moment, for *Thirteen for Dinner* opened on 17th December 1951 and closed that very night. I like to visualise that evening's creeping feeling of disaster as dinner progresses and the cast surreptitiously pocket the used cutlery as each course dies a dyspeptic death.

The theatre is perhaps most famous for its association with *Peter Pan*. It was here, in 1904, that the first production of J. M. Barrie's play was presented by Charles Frohman, starring Gerald du Maurier as Captain Hook and Nina Boucicault as Peter. Never Never Land has never to this day failed to attract an audience and the original production was remounted annually each Christmas at this theatre until 1914.

The Duke of York's has to my knowledge two separate hauntings. The identity of the first ghost could be either one of two ladies or, for that matter, both. On the stairs as you approach the dress circle bar you will see a picture of Doris Keane. In 1915 this American actress, together with Basil Sydney and Owen Nares, played in *Romance* by Edward Sheldon. Audiences were up for that every night. It played for over 1,000 performances to its adoring public, who, watching Doris as Margherita Cavallini declaiming 'I think I 'ave been mad for jost vone leetle while', disregarded the mangled accent and took her each to be their own, their very own soul mate. Doris would briefly marry Basil and Owen would become one of the matinee idols of the 1920s before coming to a slightly curious end.

In 1943, after the run of *The Petrified Forest* at the Globe Theatre, Nares and Constance Cummings left London to embark on a provincial wartime tour of the play. By the last week of July, the company were deep in Wales performing at army camps and had reached the small town of Brecon. It so happened that an inn on Brecon's High Street, The Shoulder of Mutton, was the house where Sarah Siddons had been raised. On July 31st Nares decided to explore this seldom-visited shrine to the British Melpomene and was directed towards the actual bedroom where Sarah had been born. No sooner had he mounted the stairs and entered the room than he collapsed with a sudden heart attack and died. Though there is no evidence to suggest that his heart attack was triggered by a sudden glimpse of the lady herself, his end could be interpreted as an ultimate artistic homage to the Tragic Muse.

Sarah Siddons' birthplace,
The Shoulder of Mutton Inn,
Brecon

Now it may be his former leading lady Doris Keane who is glimpsed in the foyer of the Duke of York's from time to time, but I believe the other candidate has a stronger claim for, having owned the theatre almost continuously from its opening until her death in 1935, she may still be feeling very proprietorial.

Violet Melnotte was known universally as 'Madame' and by the look of her photographs she would have blended in well at the late Madam JoJos. Her career began in comic operas and she married Frank Wyatt, a star of the D'Oyly Carte Company. She was a tough woman in a tough business. On hearing that a patron had attempted suicide by gassing himself by means of the light in the gentlemen's lavatory, she asked the hospital he had been taken to, to supply her with his name and address. On being told that this was confidential, she angrily enquired, 'who is going to pay for the gas?' Engaged at the age of seventy-nine to her thirty-one-year-old theatre manager, Archibald Patrick Moore, she was enraged not by the outcry at their age difference but by the fact that malicious rumours had put her down as at least 82. The engagement was broken off and Madame died a year later, but not, I believe, of a broken heart. Her real love was the business and it is held that she returns to check it out from time to time.

Apart from being glimpsed during the incomings, she has been seen in the royal box and also in the adjoining royal retiring room, now used for VIP visits. There is a particular story related by a woman named Judy who, as a young girl, came on a theatre visit and was escorted to this room to wait for her family. Left on her own and a trifle peckish, she began to help herself to some crisps from a bowl on the table. As she laid into them, a woman wearing a white evening dress and a sparkling tiara appeared and asked what she was doing. Young Judy replied with the literal truth that she was 'eating crisps'. The woman looked at her, told her that she would allow that and walked

through the door into the royal box. As she exited, Judy's grandmother arrived and caught sight of the lady's back. Judy, knowing the room had a royal connection, imagined that she had met the Queen, but neither our Monarch nor anyone else was found in the box. Judy was able to identify Madame when she was later shown a photograph of Miss Melnotte.

If Violet's face was unmistakable and, to put it mildly, slightly unbearable, the next ghost could be described as unwearable. Its story caused a minor sensation and was investigated at the time by Fred Archer, onetime editor of the Psychic Times.

Violet Menlotte - a tough 'Madame'

In 1949, Thora Hird was appearing in a play entitled *The Queen Came By* at the Embassy Theatre, Swiss Cottage, before its transfer to the Duke of York's. The play was a period piece and, being on a tight budget, the costumes were assembled from what could be found in the Embassy's wardrobe and from local sources. A suitable top was found for Thora on a market stall. It was a velvet Victorian ladies jacket, high collared, tight and short backed and similar to what was known as a monkey jacket or bum freezer.

It was a loose fit when first worn but by the time the show had transferred to the West End it had already been let out to its limits after Thora had complained that it was too tight across her arms, chest and neck. She admitted that she thought it possibly her imagination but the feeling persisted and seemed to get worse with each performance. She was off sick one evening and so Erica Foyle, her understudy, went on wearing the same jacket. She was unaware of Thora's experience, but felt the very same sensation, and, on top of that, saw the ghost of a young woman in the wings wearing the identical jacket. Her story was soon buzzing around the company.

The stage manager Marjorie Page, being bravely conscientious, believed it her duty to try it on. She too felt the constricting pressure of the jacket. Next, the play's director Frederick Piffard decided to have a go. Or rather he persuaded his wife to. She in turn slipped it on and to no apparent ill effect, at least that is until she took it off. Then all saw that around the base of her neck were fresh red weals, as if someone's hands had tried to strangle her.

One can imagine the fear and nervous excitement that now reigned in the Green Room. It was at this point that Fred Archer was called in by Frederick Piffard. Days later, having listened in detail to the experiences of the witnesses, Archer decided to arrange an after-show séance on stage. He invited all involved to watch from the stalls as not one, not two, but three mediums entered from the wings and tried to communicate. None of the mediums had been briefed on what had occurred before they were handed the jacket in turn to aid their psychometry. The first was unable to feel any impression. The second could only feel that it had belonged to a young woman, but the third medium could describe a young girl who had a sense of guilt about something. Somehow or other she had provoked a young man, essentially not evil, into a murderous fury. He saw a pair of hands, 'the rough hands of a workman, tearing at the girl's clothing.' They struggled and then the girl fell backwards and there was 'a splashing as she was forced into a butt of water'.

The medium now saw the man pull the lifeless body out of the butt, carry it up to a room, wrap it in a blanket and then carry it wet and dripping down the stairs again. It was at this point, as the sighting stopped and the medium fell silent, that Marjorie Page charged onto the stage in high excitement to announce that the medium's description of events tallied exactly with the vision she had had when she had been wearing the jacket, explaining that she had thought it so fantastic at the time that she had kept it to herself.

By this time there was a danger of mass hysteria. Fred Archer stopped the session and most people left, but he and a few others stayed behind in Thora Hird's dressing room. Mrs Piffard was persuaded to wear the jacket again. No sooner was it on than she started to breathe heavily and try to wrench it off, crying out that it was getting tighter and tighter. She was so distraught that she did not recognise her husband when he arrived. This time though there were no marks around her neck. Next, a friend of Thora's asked if he could give it a go. He succeeded in getting it on, and then promptly fainted.

It was at this point that Fred Archer decided that emotions were running far too strongly for a subjective analysis. All involved, now aware of the original stories, could quite possibly be susceptible to suggestion. He decided on a fresh approach. Untainted minds were needed.

Everyone from the seance was therefore encouraged to go home, leaving only himself and another journalist at the theatre. With the fireman on duty to guard the stage door, they too left and walked down St Martin's Lane and into a deserted Trafalgar Square. There they found a young couple walking home. Introducing theselves as newspaper men investigating a story, they managed to persuade them to come back with them to the Duke of York's.

Once there, the girl put on the jacket as instructed. She said she felt nothing but the young man had a very different reaction. A strange expression came over his face as he put his right hand on her arm and, as he did so, he told them that something was urging him to squeeze hard. His hands moved involuntarily up towards her neck and the urge became more and more intense, until he suddenly forced himself to let go.

Archer, judging that the young man, rather than the girl, was receptive, next persuaded him put the jacket on. Immediately he began to gasp for breath and cried out 'There is something sinister - like death. It feels as if someone were trying to kill me. But in a just way.' These words had an uncanny echo of what the medium had earlier described. Archer was convinced that the jacket had a psychic influence and was further amazed to discover afterwards that both his random midnight volunteers were interested in Spiritualism.

Needless to say, the jacket was not allowed to make another appearance on stage. It was sold off when the show closed and its fate is debatable, though if one story is true that it was sold to an American collector, could it perhaps hang to this day in the back of a Californian cupboard, waiting patiently for another victim to slip into its embrace?

Scene 12: The Noel Coward Theatre

If we resist temptation and walk smartly past the Salisbury pub, a few more steps up St Martin's Lane will take us to the Noel Coward Theatre. This elegant venue, opened in 1903 and designed by the ubiquitous Mr Sprague was basically an afterthought. Charles Wyndham had bought a parcel of land to build his eponymous theatre in Charing Cross Road. Once it was constructed he sought to sell the unused space behind it, but when negotiations fell through, decided, as one does, that he might as well build another theatre. Unwilling to call it after himself again, he plumped for what it was and named it the New Theatre. After his death, the New was run by his stepson Bronson Albery, one of four West End theatres to come under his control. The New in turn became the Albery in 1973 in honour of his memory until its name changed again in 2006, when Delfont Mackintosh acquired the theatre, to the Noel Coward. 'The Master' was well due eternal top billing and indeed had had his first play produced here, though to be truthful, *I'll Leave It To You* was left pretty much alone by its audiences. A more fitting candidate could have been Gielgud, for it was at the New in the 1930s that he had his great successes with *Richard of Bordeaux* and *Hamlet*, but by 1994 Sir John had already taken up poll position on the canopy at the onetime Globe on Shaftesbury Avenue.

No matter what its name, the venue's greatest success to date is the original production of *Oliver!* But, then again, Lionel's Theatre doesn't sound quite right.

I have not attempted to investigate a rumour that floated around in the early days of my career that there was something 'nasty' lurking in the corridors underneath the stage. After all, back stages are littered with dodgy people, be they dressers or divas. Instead, let me recount a more recent encounter told to me in January 2015.

In November 2014, the actor Kane Verrall, while waiting to start panto, was keeping himself busy at the Coward with some front of house work on *Shakespeare in Love*. One evening, early on in the week, the management decided to close the balcony and move anyone who had booked tickets down to the next level. To comply with safety rules it was Kane's job that night to do a routine check during the show to make sure that no one was up there by either accident or choice. Kane duly did this at the top of the show, and then, after the interval and at the beginning of the final scene, decided to check again. 'I went up, stepped into the auditorium and looked down at the seats. On the left-hand side of the balcony about eight metres away from me, I saw a man with short white hair sitting on the steps bent forward as if watching the show.' Kane took a couple of steps towards him and then knew that something was odd. 'He was there but he wasn't "real", there was something wrong. Until I stepped forward I really believed it was a real person. I froze and began to shiver, turned and left before "he" could turn his face towards me. I went straight down to the manager's office and said there was someone sat in the balcony. Their reply was "You're very pale. You look as if you've seen a ghost". Another usher was immediately detailed to accompany me to check and there was nothing, nobody there. Since then I have tried to find a natural explanation for what I saw, but without success'. No bets taken that Kane witnessed the Bard but even odds it could have been Sir Bronson . . .

If we now zip through St Martin's Court and half a dozen oysters at Sheekey's we will reach another theatrical thoroughfare, for we are in the Charing Cross Road which also plays host to theatres boasting their share of supernatural happenings.

Scene 13: The Garrick Theatre

The Garrick Theatre, named after the most illustrious actor of the 18th century, was built in the 19th century and is believed to be haunted by an actor manager of the 20th. I say believed with a degree of caution as Arthur Bourchier has not, to my knowledge, been positively identified by anyone recently. This is probably because he gave up his lease on the theatre in 1915 and died in South Africa in 1927.

The theatre, designed by Walter Emden, opened in 1889 for another actor manager John Hare, but it was financed by W.S. Gilbert. As usual, the building was to be partly beneath street level but construction was severely delayed when the workmen, digging down, opened up an underground river. Gilbert was in two minds to "go on with the building or let the fishing." But the building won and the theatre opened with Arthur Wing Pinero's *The Profligate*. Hare's management continued through until 1896 and though successful is now chiefly remembered for an uncanny coincidence. To follow up her success in *The Second Mrs Tanquery*, Pinero wrote another play for Mrs Patrick Campbell, *The Notorious Mrs Ebbsmith*. Shortly after the opening a corpse of a woman was found floating in the Thames. She was not only identified as a Mrs Ebbsmith but in her pocket were also two tickets for the play at the Garrick. They were the stubs and so had been used but it would be unfair to blame Mrs Pat's performance on her suicide unless, that is, the portrayal was just too, too accurate.

Arthur Bourchier picked up the reins in 1900. He was an actor who did not believe in small performances. His acting style is best summed up by Gilbert, who, on hearing that he was going to give his Hamlet enthused, "At last we can settle whether Bacon or Shakespeare wrote the plays. Have both the coffins opened and whichever has turned in his grave is the author". Bourchier's office was on the theatre's first floor and Arthur's ghost is said to be encountered on what is called the Phantom Staircase that leads up from there to the roof. Certainly, when I worked there in the summer of 1975, the Garrick then had many of the characteristics of a haunted theatre. The carpeting sucked at one's shoes, the veteran seats bruised one's buttocks and the shabby wallpaper in the stalls would, in wet weather, bulge damply outwards as if searching to dry itself off on one's clothing. The gallery was of course condemned and shut and the abandoned old dress circle bar closed off to the public. This was where Peter Seller's uncle, a onetime Garrick theatre manager, had nightly entertained friends - and so successfully that casts used to complain that he was getting bigger laughs than themselves.

The front of house staff made up for the building's deficiencies for they

Arthur Bourchier - never known to underplay a part

were great characters. They could have been cast for a Mel Brooks movie. We had a hunchback and an ex RSM in the box office and if they hadn't put off the punters from buying a ticket, an 80-year-old Dutch usher, Mrs de Kuyper, would stagger into the Garrick each evening, knock back an enormous neat gin and then, before our eyes, uncoil into the correct upright position to confront them, eyeball to eyeball, and flog them an unwanted programme. The star of the front though was Freddie Booth, a tall, gangly, highly strung man whose arms when agitated would flap like penguins. He wore an old-fashioned commissioner's frock coat topped by a peaked cap a size too small and positioned at a Benny Hill like angle.

Freddie was officially the theatre's link man but as that job had passed away with the gas lighting, he was stationed in the foyer to deal with the public. He was the theatre manager's unofficial right hand man and charming with it. Freddie claimed to have been tapped many times on the shoulder by an invisible hand and to have seen a bottle rise on its own from the bar shelf and crash onto the floor. He would also tell the tale of leaving the manager's office one night to find, standing in front of him, a man in a cloak and hat who vanished. The manager's office was the one once occupied by Mr Bourchier and so he deduced it was him. Freddie has now gone to join Arthur but he has not sent any message to say whether his theory was correct.

Over the years, other strange experiences and paranormal instances have been reported. In 2006, when *You Never Can Tell* was playing, Lin Blakley took over the part of Mrs Clandon from Diane Quick. Lin told me that she had to cross under stage to get from wing to wing and nightly, despite the general backstage warmth, there was a certain spot at the bottom of the spiral staircase that was always as chilled as ice. This sensation is not an uncommon experience backstage and has been reported in various other theatres but I know no locations apart from the Garrick where the house tabs have been seen to go up and down on their own. If that is inexplicable then what about a 1980 performance of *Death Trap*?

Jack Buchanan...still around to give a prompt?

During Ira Levin's murder thriller, the cast suddenly heard their own lines being quietly intoned by a mysterious voice seconds before they were meant to speak them. Putting it down to some maniacal fan in the audience they carried on, but the next night it happened again. Stage management, urged by the DSM, whose prompting skills were now seemingly a bit redundant, put their ear trumpets on and collectively listened. The voice seemed to be coming from the OP side of the stage but there was nobody in that wing. The idea that somebody was playing a practical joke was dismissed and nerves began to get frayed but after a few more intermittent hearings it suddenly stopped and the voice disappeared for good.

It has been suggested to me that Arthur Bourchier supplied the phantom voice, but another likely candidate springs to mind. Let me put a claim in instead for a Scottish actor with remarkable comic timing and a singular sense of fun whose style can still be seen in films such as *The Band Wagon*. Step forward Jack Buchanan, the stage and screen star of the Thirties, Forties and early Fifties. Jack Buchanan also controlled the Garrick from 1947 until his death in 1957.

During my time there, the master carpenter had, in pride of place on his desk, Mr Buchanan's very own glossy top hat. You could look at it and sometimes think you could very faintly hear a voice softly intoning 'Goodnight Vienna'.

Scene 14: Wyndham's Theatre

Set opposite Leicester Square and adjacent to that underground station, Wyndham's Theatre is in an ideal location to attract audiences. It is also one of the most perfect of Sprague's creations. Its front of house décor delights all who view it and casts playing there continuously appreciate its fine acoustics and the intimacy between stage and auditorium. It was built for Sir Charles Wyndham and opened on 16th November 1899 with a revival of the T.W. Robertson comedy *David Garrick*.

Sir Charles Wyndham has never lost his touch

Robertson's play was what is known as a star vehicle. First produced at the Haymarket in 1864 with the comedian Edward Sothern in the title role, Wyndham now took on the mantle of that 'Great Master of his Art' while Mary Moore appeared as the fictitious Ada Ingot. There is a curious picture in the theatre's foyer of the duo embracing in character costume while, behind them, the band of the Coldstream Guards, busbied and blanco'd, tootle merrily away. This is because the Boer War and Patriotism with a capital P were at their heights. Sir Charles could not personally relieve Ladysmith without risking his nightly relationship with Miss Moore but he played the first night as a benefit for the Aldershot Branch of the Soldiers' Wives and Families Association. Hence the band on stage at the curtain call and repeated renditions of 'Rule Britannia'.

Sir Charles had military connections himself for he had actually fought for the Union in the American Civil War. The son of a doctor and for long undecided whether to act or follow his father's profession, Wyndham sailed to 'shake off my love of the stage.' He laid aside his makeup box, picked up his scalpel and with the slightly incongruous help of that great showman P.T. Barnum, joined the army. This was not through a lack of more suitable weaponry but because he was already a fully qualified surgeon. In this capacity, Sir Charles experienced the bloody battles of Fredericksburg, Chancellorsville and Gettysburg before he tired of the carnage. He resigned his commission in 1864 to take up acting again and worked with John Wilkes Booth, Abraham Lincoln's future assassin, before returning to England.

It can be said with conviction that Sir Charles has never left his theatre. He has a strong attachment to the building and would seem to encourage and look after all those who feel the same. This form of support varies in different ways though one is seemingly consistent.

In 2005, Richard Pocock started working front of house at the theatre between acting jobs. He had been up for a national tour of *Present Laughter*. His audition for the role of Gary Essendine 'went exceptionally well and I was very hopeful about getting the part'. The business being what it is, after a week 'I had not heard anything from my agent and so was feeling a touch despondent'. Richard was working the balcony bar and 'at the height of my despondency I was standing in the service area with my back to the optics when I felt three slow taps on the back of my uniform waistcoat by my left hand arm. I immediately dismissed it as a muscle spasm and then, simultaneously realised that it wasn't. The touch was benign. I felt calm and reassured. The next morning I heard that I had got the part and I am convinced it was Sir Charles. Another time around that period, I was sitting in the foyer during a performance with an usher, Henry from New Zealand. We were both reading books with a table between us. Suddenly we both looked at each other and Henry stared at me as if I had tapped him. At that moment he felt his left shoulder be pressed down, and his face blanched. He looked behind at the wall from where the feeling had come from and we were both sure that it had happened. Shortly afterwards he started to work professionally as an actor'.

I can myself support these stories of Sir Charles' tap as I experienced it in the company office in 2015 during the run of *King Charles III*. Not being an actor, I cannot claim a sudden job offer and I await a complete change of fortune for, if I was to say that from then on my petty cash balanced to the penny each week, it would be a blatant example of wishful thinking.

Sir Charles also keeps an interested eye on management. Jennifer Woodburn, then the deputy theatre manager, was convinced during her first week of working, while familiarising herself with the building, that she had 'a really strong feeling that I was being watched and I don't spook very easily but it really did feel like a pair of eyes boring into the back of my head. I felt this especially in the Littlewood Room which is strange when you consider it is the most brightly lit area of the theatre. During that first week I went home and had a very vivid nightmare. I dreamt that I was lying asleep on my side on my pillow and in my dream I opened my eyes and less than an inch away from my face was Sir Charles Wyndham's. It truly frightened me, so much so that I had to tell Emma - the theatre manager - about it the next day. I was describing the dream and I called Sir Charles "Charlie". Em stopped me and told me it's NEVER Charlie, only Sir Charles. I said I'd been calling him Charlie all week! With that she instructed me to introduce myself to Sir Charles via his portrait on our office wall, and assure him of my intention to look after his theatre. Normally I would have thought this silly, but Emma is a very sensible person and not one to suggest ridiculous things, so, due to the feeling that had been following me all week I thought what the hell. When the office door closed I addressed "Sir Charles"as suggested. I can honestly say that from the moment I left the office, that feeling I had of being watched completely disappeared. It wasn't until it had gone that I realised how strong it had been. I've not felt like I've been watched in a sinister way since'.

However, there is more than one ghost at Wyndham's and Paul Minto, the deputy master carpenter, has had first-hand experience. His first sighting was of a woman dressed in a blue ball gown who walked from the stage right of the balcony to its centre before vanishing. Her identity is unknown but there is certainty about the next.

'Fred Denton', Minty told me 'was the live-in fireman during the 1970s. He had his little office-cum-dressing room high above the stage left wing, which was reached then by a now demolished staircase. Fred liked a drop and one night must have had the one too many, for he fell down the stairs and smashed his head in on the stage floor which is where Bill Smith, who was then the master carpenter, found him dead in the morning'.

Minty has heard Fred's heavy footsteps many times stamping up and down the stage right fly floor. One night during *Democracy* he told the cast the story. He was disbelieved until there was a point during the show when all heard the footsteps stamping away. The noise was such that Minty had to go up to the flys and tell the spirit to stop disturbing the performance.

Minty's nonchalant belief in Fred is supported by Rachael Smith-Rawnsley, the stage chargehand. 'In August 2005 I was doing a Saturday matinee of *As You Like It* with Sienna Miller and Dominic West. There used to be a cross over fly bridge and one of my cues was to take a stuffed crow from stage right flys to the stage left flys. This was because the actor Sean Hughes would shoot a gun in the air and, on that cue, I would throw the crow from there down to the stage. Because the bridge was creaky, I had to cross during a song in the show which meant I would wait a long time in the stage left gallery for the song to finish and to do my cue. Crossing the bridge with the crow, I used to use my head torch for safety and to negotiate the steps down on the other side. As I climbed down I saw a man standing, facing me in a navy jacket with very bright blue eyes and with brylcreemed white hair slicked back from his face. He looked in his fifties. I was so shocked that I instinctively turned my torch off and sat down on the steps breathing heavily. When I turned the torch on a few seconds later, he had disappeared. I looked to see how he had exited thinking that he was real and the only way he could have gone would have been down the ladder to the stage left wing which was full of actors and stage management and partially blocked by scenery. The door which went to the outside parapet was shut. I opened it to check and the push bar made a noise which I had not heard. The song was still being sung on stage below. I searched everywhere through the ropes and conduit but no one was there. I gave up and prepared to do my cue, believing that I had seen a ghost. I leaned over the fly rail with the crow in my hand ready to throw, and then received two sharp taps on my left shoulder blade. I said, "I hope you don't mind. My name is Rachael, I work here, you must have seen me around. I hope I am not disturbing you". I knew I was talking to thin air but when I threw the crow I felt a final gentle tap. I left by going back over the bridge to the stage left to do my next cue. An actor was sitting there and asked, "Are you alright Rachael? You look as if you've seen a ghost". When I spoke to Minty about it he said straightaway "You've seen Fred"'.

Scene 15: The Palace Theatre

The Palace occupies a splendid site on Cambridge Circus. It stands alone, a fine, slightly triangular, marbled memorial to its first owner Richard D'Oyly Carte. The producer not only financed its construction from the profits of his Gilbert and Sullivan seasons at the Savoy, but also took a hand in the design of the building. D'Oyly Carte's ambitious aim was to build a theatre dedicated to English Opera.

It was a worthy idea bedevilled by the sheer paucity of such an art form. The Royal English Opera House indeed opened on 31st January 1891 with Sir Arthur Sullivan's *Ivanhoe*. Though some of Sir Walter Scott's novels had been turned into operatic successes by the likes of Bizet, Boieldieu and Donizetti, Sullivan's attempt died in the lists at Ashby de la Zouch. Stumped in his search for another home-grown composer, D'Oyly Carte was obliged to turn to France and present Messager's *La Basoche*, albeit with an English translation by Augustus Harris and Eugene Odin. He was next forced to accept another French invasion in the form of Sarah Bernhardt. The Divine Sarah's acting was always guaranteed to thrill but her singing could turn La Marseillaise into La Bouillabaisse. Frustrated in his quest, D'Oyly Carte threw in the towel. He sold the theatre at a loss to Augustus Harris who, knowing what the public really wanted to see, promptly renamed it as the Palace Theatre of Varieties.

The onset of variety brought an immediate eclectic mix of performers to the Palace. George Robey and Harry Tate made them laugh, Harry Lauder and Cecilia Loftus sang mostly in tune and Little Tich and Anna Pavlova danced, but sadly not together - and all on one evening's bill, for the very first public Royal Command Performance was staged here in 1912. They were supported by three million roses draped around every inch of the auditorium. Overwhelmed perhaps by the floral scent, King George V and Queen Mary gave Variety the royal seal of approval, apart that is from Vesta Tilley, whose trousers, hinting at transvestism, so startled the Queen as she sang *The Piccadilly Johnny with the Little Glass Eye*, that Her Majesty hid her regal minces behind her souvenir programme for the whole of the star's turn.

Vesta's rival and the acknowledged Queen of Variety was Marie Lloyd. She had been banned from appearing in case any of her double entendre songs with their arguably singular meaning would offend royal ears. Marie didn't take it lying down. She staged an alternative show on the same night at the London Pavilion where posters announced 'Every Performance by Marie Lloyd is a command performance - by command of the British public!'

Pavlova, the Prima Ballerina of the Imperial Russian Ballet, first played the Palace in 1910 and her fame has prompted the legend that she haunts the theatre but this, I think, is a story as delicate as the meringue named after her. Perhaps she is the flimsy outline of a dancer seen on stage, or rather half a dancer, as the ghost was reported to be truncated by the stage deck. This is because the floor has been raised since the original stage was laid, but this would not mar a spirited *entrechat*. However, another candidate could well be Maud Allan who as Salome and her *Dance of the Seven Veils* shocked audiences in 1908.

In 1999, Tim Hawes, first trumpet on *Les Miserables,* had his own electrifying experience below the stage. 'I was the last one to leave the band room after a show and was on my way out of the theatre. When I was still under stage and about fifteen foot away from the gents', its big iron door opened and I distinctly saw the back of an elbow and a leg entering the toilet. This triggered a reminder to void the bladder before setting home and I followed in. I was astonished to find that once there, I was there alone'. Simon Garrett was stage manager for both *Jesus Christ Superstar* and *Les Miserables*. He told me that during his time on the latter, he would sometimes check that all cast required for 'Lovely Ladies' were standing by to go on and not still loitering in their dressing rooms or, for that matter, The Coach and Horses. One evening he noticed a tall, angular woman in costume towards the back of the waiting ensemble who seemed vaguely familiar but not instantly recognisable. At that moment the girls were cued on and he moved into the wing to take another look at her. He scanned the stage but drew a blank. Assuming that it was his imagination, he thought no more about it until one afternoon he went up to the balcony during a rehearsal to check out a sightline problem. Job done, he wandered into the balcony bar where a poster caught his eye. It was a Toulouse Lautrec lithograph advertising a show which had played the Palace from January to February 1896, the *Troupe de Mlle. Eglantine*. There, on the right-hand side of the picture next to Eglantine, Cleopatre and Gazelle was the woman he had seen on stage, Jane Avril.

Another incident in this area of the auditorium occurred in 2005 while Michael Ball was playing Count Fosco in *The Woman in White*. It happened when Graham Thompson, covering for the manager, decided one quiet afternoon to do an inspection of the front of house levels. Reaching the top level, he passed through the balcony bar and had begun to open the door at the end of the corridor that leads into the auditorium. When the door was at a forty-five degree angle he saw a reflection of the corridor behind him in the glass panel. But it now was not an empty corridor. Standing there was a gentleman wearing a very long black coat, a black trilby hat and carrying a walking stick in his hand. Graham's immediate thought was to wonder who on earth the man was and how he had got into the corridor, as the theatre was not yet open to the public. He let go of the door, turned around to ask if he needed help and was faced by an empty corridor. The sighting of a presence in the balcony was also reported by Pat Selby, Emile Littler's right-hand man, in the 1960s.

Ivor Novello keeps a spectral eye on the quality of performances

One ghost can be positively named, for Ivor Novello has been firmly identified. Since his last live performance on the Palace stage in *King's Rhapsody* on March 5th 1951, he has made several return appearances. The producer Emile Littler was then owner of the Palace and stated that he saw him watching successive shows from a seat in the back row of the dress circle in the 1950s. Ivor also disrupted a 1980 casting session by moving around the circle to such a degree that the distracted singer stopped in mid song to complain and staff were sent rather uselessly to investigate. I do wonder if Ivor's prowling that afternoon was prompted by some very wrong notes in a wobbly key for he was usually impeccably polite in life.

During a matinee of *The Sound of Music* in 1962, he appears to have changed his location, for, during Act 1, he was seen by the cast in a circle box wearing a rather dashing, red-lined cloak. The box was of course found to be locked and empty at the interval for, no doubt, Ivor had climbed the mountain and didn't want to be seen hanging around for any old lonely goatherd.

The sartorial addition of a cloak has provoked an alternative theory that the watcher could have been Charles Morton, the music hall impresario, who was lured out of retirement to help manage the theatre's transition to variety after D'Oyly Carte's operatic failure. Not only nuns and Nazis may have seen Mr Morton for the 'Father of the Halls' does not appear to be a shy, retiring spirit.

Charles Morton, the 'Father of the Halls' sporting his 'mutton chops'

During the run of *Les Miserables*, the box office was relocated from the front of house foyer to a new position on the Shaftesbury Avenue side of the theatre. During the refurbishment, the builders would often see a man wandering around in top hat and tails, and, not being *au fait* with fashionable French revolutionary wear, assumed him just an actor filling in time before storming the barricades. His distinctive and persistent presence on the wrong side of the curtain was reported to management but the culprit was unidentifiable until photographs were discovered of Mr Morton, similarly attired and bewhiskered, leaning up against the original box office.

Pauline Loraine, the Palace Theatre manager between 2000 and 2008, told me that one evening when the house was coming out from the show, a member of the audience had approached a duty manager in the dress circle to ask whether it was allowed for people to sit on each other's laps. When asked why, she explained that throughout the evening there had been a lady balanced on the lap of a gentleman with mutton chop side whiskers.

Again, on another performance of *Les Miserables*, a patron approached the manager to enquire specifically about the identity of a curious character who, in the middle of a scene, had appeared suddenly on stage left and had walked across the front of the stage from wing to wing. She described the intruder as being a man wearing a long frockcoat, a top hat and, moreover, mutton chop whiskers. Pauline recalls that 'later, when we were refreshing a display by the auditorium bar we found a picture of Charles – and there he was with his mutton chops'.

Scene 16: The Phoenix Theatre

O n the other side of Cambridge Circus is one of London's more modern theatres. I use modern in the relative sense, for the Phoenix opened in 1930 during a year which ushered in four other West End houses. It was built on the site of the Alcazar, a music hall with a difference in that there were three separate stages in the main room. Audiences, instead of being trapped in their seats, were thus able to move from turn to turn before mounting upstairs to where 'Beautiful Artistes' and 'Posing Models' were on view for an extra bob.

The new theatre's first production on August 18th was Noel Coward's *Private Lives* starring the author together with Gertrude Lawrence, Adrianne Allen and Laurence Olivier. Reportedly written in four days, the comedy was a huge success though it only played the Phoenix for three months owing to Coward's dislike of long runs. However this triumph ensured that he had an affection for the theatre and would return to it again in 1936 with Gertie in *Tonight at 8.30*. In 1952 he tried once more with *Quadrille*. This time he was unsuccessful, for he had written the show not for himself but for the American husband and wife team of Alfred Lunt and Lynn Fontanne and, as a review said, 'The play's the thing but not when the Lunts are on stage'.

The Phoenix has experienced mixed fortunes over the years but most recently it has had two great successes. Firstly, *The Canterbury Tales* opened in 1968 just after the Theatres Act had abolished censorship so allowing Nicky Henson to nightly majestically crow 'I Have a Noble Cock'. Its long run of over 2000 performances was overtaken, however, by *Blood Brothers* which played for an astounding 21 years. During its tenure, the part of Mrs Johnstone was played for a considerable time by Stephanie Lawrence. Stephanie had shot to fame after taking over the role of Eva Peron from Marti Webb during *Evita's* run at the Prince Edward. She left to portray her idol Marilyn Monroe in *Marilyn: The Musical* but it folded despite her winning an award for her performance.

I worked with her on her next show *Starlight Express* and recall her complete identification with Marilyn and her bewilderment that that show had failed. Stephanie had a vulnerability similar to her idol, despite a defensive, hard-nosed toughness that alienated some and amused others. All knew she was very talented but for a long time the shows chosen or the parts given never gave her the chance to really shine, until *Blood Brothers* came along.

Mrs Johnstone was the perfect role for her at this junction of her life and it took her to Broadway where she was nominated for a Tony and won a Theatre World Award. Despite this recognition Stephanie's fragile side continued to create problems and this included battles with the bottle which she would sometimes win, draw or lose. Sadly she lost completely in 2000, dying tragically young at the age of fifty.

Twelve years later, during a performance of *Blood Brothers*, the Deputy Stage Manager who was standing in the prompt corner glanced up to see Stephanie on the other side of the set. She was in her Mrs Johnstone costume and was standing just offstage of one of the set's doors as if waiting for her entrance. She appeared so life-like that he accepted her presence before realising that she was dead. Her presence was felt by other members of the staff which surely reinforces Napoleon's theatrical maxim to Mme Georges that some parts are worth a second visit.

Scene 17: The Harold Pinter Theatre

We must backtrack westwards past Leicester Square to this playhouse as it is now named; it opened originally as the Royal Comedy Theatre in 1881. The arrival of a new venue to provide respectable entertainment in this area was welcomed by the Daily Telegraph for 'Panton Street in the Haymarket has for very many years past enjoyed a dubious reputation owing to the nu merous 'night houses' once existing in this vicinity'.

Designed by Thomas Verity, it was one of the last London theatres to have to rely on steel pillars to ensure that weighty customers in the circle would not end up sitting on the laps of those in the stalls. It also soon lost its regal moniker, perhaps because Victorian sentiment deemed it disrespectful to laugh at the Saxe - Coburg - Gotha family.

Nevertheless, as the Comedy, the theatre saw a huge variety of humour, ranging from Andre Charlot and C.B. Cochran revues where the likes of Douglas Byng playing 'Boadicea - Queen of the Obsceni' declaimed, 'O, those ru-id Druids', to Terence Frisby's skilfully-crafted *A Girl in My Soup* and onto the anarchy that was Spike Milligan's *Son of Oblomov*. It has also housed many of the works of David Baron. 'David who?', do I hear some of you ask?

That was the stage name used by Harold Pinter in the 1950s. Pinter's plays have had such influence on British playwriting that, to honour his memory, the theatre took his name in 2011. Harold's shade, though hopefully pleased, does not appear to have returned to haunt the scene of his past triumphs. I can disclose however that there is the distinct possibility that another dead playwright did so when I was working there.

In 2009 I began rehearsals for a new play by Simon Bent entitled *Prick Up Your Ears*. It was a stage interpretation of the doomed relationship between Joe Orton and Kenneth Halliwell, a three-hander with Chris New as Joe, Matt Lucas as Kenneth and Gwen Taylor as their landlady. To add to the angst, Peter Mackintosh's clever design made their bed-sitting room become progressively more and more claustrophobic as the story neared its inevitable tragic ending. Violent death is seldom silent and I well remember Daniel Kramer, our director, at the end of one rehearsal, skilfully creating the sound effects for the skull cracking, brain splattering moment with the aid of a busy claw hammer and a pliant water melon.

Orton and Halliwell's close contemporaries Kenneth Cranham and Thelma Holt together with Joe's sister Leonie came to meet the company at rehearsals and shared their memories and reminiscences. By the time we opened our pre London tour in Richmond we felt as if we knew the couple intimately and were all confident that the show would grip the audience, quite unaware that it would also leave its mark on us.

Was Joe Orton responsible for the series of strange mishaps that dogged **Prick up Your Ears?**

At first, the series of accidents and incidents that happened were put down to natural causes and normal mishaps. It started with little things. In Richmond, the *Pal Joey* record sleeve was found one morning to be ripped open. In Salford, the record player broke and a misjudged hammer blow sent Chris New to be checked up in A&E. In Brighton, Joe's lamp and Ken's lampshade broke, the telephone fell to pieces and the blood sachet in the pillow burst before the cue was reached. Nothing too sinister but it was when we arrived at the Comedy, as it still was named, that the mishaps multiplied and became more bizarre.

The ceiling of the set was designed to descend as the atmosphere darkened so as to visibly add to the feeling of oppression and claustrophobia and this action was achieved by motor-driven chain hoists. During our previews, the ceiling developed a worrying disparity between its actual speed and the readings on the control box, and once, when being set back to its opening height, it ascended at such speed that it struck and lifted the bridge just upstage of the iron. Coupled with this, the set's white wall stuck while sliding out and the collage wall jammed while sliding in. The sense that the show was possibly jinxed was reinforced for me on the afternoon of the opening night. Firstly, the chief electrician, while checking a lamp's position, was blown off his feet by an electric shock and was carted off to hospital. An hour or so later at around 6.15 pm, just before the house was to be opened, a corner of the cornice which ran along the top of the walls of the set fell with a crash to the floor, just missing the production manager Gary Beestone and myself as we stood on stage waiting for the front of house manager to arrive. Jumping back and into action, we held the house and screwed the cornice back into position. Job done, we dropped the curtain, opened the auditorium doors and nervously rechecked all the props and furniture as the first nighters jostled and scrambled to their seats.

It was a relatively trouble-free performance if you discount the front door handle falling off, the communication cans between the electrics board operator and the prompt corner failing, the typewriter mic feeding back and the reel-to-reel tape recorder emitting strange noises. Notwithstanding these malfunctions, by the time we were safely into the last scene we judged that it should be plain sailing until the final curtain.

As the box set made it impossible to watch what was happening on stage from the wings, Gary and I sat in the company office to listen to the end of the show via the tannoy speaker. The very last thing we would hear would be the recorded sound of the hammer blows crunching into Joe's skull. Would the sound effect fail? As the first amplified blow came over the speaker our fists punched upwards in triumph, only to suddenly stop in mid-air. For, in perfect synchronisation with each hammer blow, we witnessed the office wash basin shake violently as something else gurgled in time in the waste pipe below it. At last the hammer stopped its carnage, and instantaneously the basin stilled and the pipe fell silent. Needless to say, we backed, open mouthed, out of the office towards the stage and curtain calls.

Our belief that Joe was up to his little tricks continued to be reinforced throughout our short run. The down stage right prompt corner was so unnaturally cold at times during performances that our DSM Anna Cole had to wear gloves and an overcoat. Drawers jammed, lampshades broke and our ASM Morag Lavery would continually report small props going missing only for them to reappear later in unlikely places. Further proof occurred on the night of October 9th. During a quiet moment in Act 2, while I was standing with Anna in the prompt corner, we both heard a loud knocking from the other side of an old metal door set into the side of the stage wall. I went over and opened it to discover that it led into an empty coal cellar. As I closed the door I looked up to see above me a written sign bearing the legend 'MIND YOUR HEAD'. I didn't take it personally. Perhaps I should have done, for, during the interval change on November 5th, a metal sheet above the central door of the set crashed onto my head leaving me stunned and dazed. A normal state some may say, but my conviction that it was Joe would be reinforced a few years later.

By then, the Comedy Theatre had become the Pinter even if the great man himself had not been renamed Harold Comedy and I was back again for a production of Ayckbourn's *Absent Friends*. My DSM on this show was Kirsty Nixon and towards the end of the run we were both asked to do a revival of Joe's *What the Butler Saw* at the Vaudeville. Our deals were done on a Friday and before the Saturday matinee we sat in the company office discussing the new job. The conversation turning to the late Mr Orton, I recounted my *Prick Up Your Ears* stories to a slightly sceptical Kirsty.

Being both a consummate professional and not having a clue as to what the butler had actually seen, I decided in between shows to find a copy in one of the Charing Cross Road's second hand bookshops. My luck was in, no bookcases fell on my head and for a total of £1.99 I came away with a scraggy old paperback of Joe's complete works. On the front cover there was an illustration and on the back the iconic photo of Joe, legs sprawled akimbo on a sun lounger, wearing some bulging white swimming trunks and a provocative smirk. Not wishing to have the photo staring at me all night long, I put the book front cover up on the desk and went in search of a sandwich.

On my return I found that someone had apparently turned the book over for Joe was there again face up. I flipped him over, but, by the interval of the evening show, his face had reappeared twice more. As the office door was always open I was sure someone was playing games. But all those questioned denied it, and we started Act 2 with the mystery unsolved.

Half way through the act, Kirsty began to have strange, unusual problems with the sound system she was operating and I had to go the corner to help. Sure enough, when I returned to the office, there was Joe back on top again. 'Stop all this mucking about Joe', I shouted and left him to lie upright until curtain down. Our final task after a performance each evening was to write up the nightly show report. As Kirsty and I filled in the information, she confessed that she had turned the book over that first time before the show. Our assistant stage manager Fran Beaumont next admitted that she had too.

'How many times?' I asked. 'Only once', she replied. The report was finished but I paused before saving it to file. 'That still doesn't account for the other two times', I said. 'It's got to be bloody Joe', and hit the keyboard to save the report. The screen went suddenly and totally blank. Something was wrong. I clicked the keyboard again in frustration and a message appeared. We all stared at it in disbelief but there it was before our very eyes.

It simply read: *it wasn't me.*

Scene 18: The Old Vic

It would be quite wrong to ignore the current demand for diversification and so I invite you now to boldly join me in crossing the Thames by courtesy of the Strand Bridge Company to prove that South London too can offer up some theatre ghosts. You will not fall in the river for the bridge exists under another name. The Strand Bridge, conceived in 1809 as a money-making toll crossing was opened in 1817 but renamed as Waterloo Bridge after that famous victory where the Iron Duke, with some little help from the Prussians, managed to decisively better Boney. Luckily French visitors to London seldom take offence at the bridge's name. They are mostly oblivious to their defeat, for in French history the battle is known as that of Mont St. Jean. Realising that the Lambeth marshlands would soon be dryly accessible from central London, three entrepreneurs, Messrs Jones, Dunn and Serres, set about the construction of another temple to the dramatic arts.

The Royal Coburg Theatre opened on May 11th, 1818. It was common knowledge that local theatre enthusiasts enjoyed drama (melo) and drink (fiery) in equal proportions but the management hoped to attract a more refined audience. They announced that they would have 'all the avenues to the theatre well lighted, while the appointed additional patrols on the bridge road - and keeping them in their own pay - will afford ample security to the patrons of the theatre'. Sadly, the Royal Coburg never quite succeeded in establishing a respectable reputation - Edmund Kean, no stranger to disorder, told his audience that 'in my life I have never acted to such a set of ignorant, unmitigated brutes as I have before me'.

In vain attempts to lift its reputation from the gutter, the theatre was renamed both the Royal Victoria and the New Victoria Palace but it was still habitually referred to as a 'Blood Tub'. But in 1880 the theatre was taken over by Miss Emma Cons, a philanthropist and avid social reformer. Its name was changed to The Royal Victoria Hall and Coffee Tavern, for temperance now ruled the day and performers were supplanted in some dressing rooms by the Morley College for Working Men and Women. Her niece Lilian Baylis joined her in 1898 and took over the management in 1912.

By then, the theatre, now known locally as the Old Vic, was dedicated to innovative programmes of concerts and opera. Lilian knew no fear. Between 1914 and 1923 she created theatrical history by attempting and succeeding against great odds in presenting every play in Shakespeare's first Folio. She became a true legend in her lifetime, an extraordinary, idiosyncratic producer, an idealist, whose pioneering companies at the Old Vic and later at Sadler's Wells led to the creation of the National Theatre, the English National Opera and the Royal Ballet. She also became a bit of a legend in her lunchtimes for part of her down to earth lifestyle seems to still linger in the theatre.

Lilian Baylis - a legend in her lifetime...and after

Ned Seago, the stage door manager with 'thirty years at the Old Vic' told me that during her tenure, Lilian would come down into the stage left prompt corner towards the end of a show's matinee, and there, using a handy gas ring, fry up sausages to feed the company and herself between shows. Both audiences' and actors' noses were regularly assailed by the smell which, drifting down towards the centre of the stalls, intertwined with the scent of bloaters and coffee, courtesy of Pearce and Plenty, purveyors of 'good portions for little money' in the foyer. If the bloaters have long kippered off, the aroma of sausages has often been smelt since Lilian's death and are indeed still sometimes around in this present century.

In September 2011, the Irish actor Robert Sheehan was giving his first London performance in *The Playboy of the Western World*. Unaware of the story, he came to the stage door saying that he could smell sausages in his dressing room. He had already been to see his fellow actor James Greene to ask him 'are you frying up in here?' and James - not understanding what he was talking about - had guided him on to Ned. 'Robbie told me "I get this overpowering smell of sausages,"' said Ned, 'and I replied, let me tell you a story'. Further olfactory evidence has been supplied to me by Jonathan Coy. 'There were times when a fry up could clearly be smelt by the ground floor dressing rooms near the stage door. I was last there doing *Noises Off* and the basement canteen that was there in Olivier's time had long gone. So it must have been Lilian's sausages!'

In 1937 Lilian's planned programme of shows included *Macbeth* with

Laurence Olivier in the title role. During the three weeks of rehearsal, 'the Scottish play' duly had its full share of traditional misfortune. Lilian's dog was run over and killed, a collision in a taxi left director Michel St. Denis with his head stitched and swathed in bandages, Motley's elaborate set would not fit on the stage and Olivier temporarily lost his voice through stress and a cold.

With the company's morale at low ebb, Baylis reluctantly agreed to a postponement of the opening and replaced St Denis with Tyrone Guthrie. He set about intensive re-rehearsals with the cast as the carpenters set to circumcising the scenery. It was during a new blocking session that Olivier, who had been sitting in the wings, missed death by both inches and seconds.

Summoned on stage, he stood up and moved from his chair just before a 25 lb stage weight hurtled down from the flies and crushed it to pieces. Next, the announcement that Lilian had been taken ill was badly received by all, and their grief was compounded two days later by the news of her death from a heart attack on November 25th 1937, the day before the dress rehearsal.

Performances are only cancelled if a monarch dies and the First Night duly took place as advertised. Lilian's customary seat in her stage box was empty but she was not completely absent. As curtain up was held by half an hour, by way of protest at the delay her portrait flew off her office wall and crashed to the floor.

Towards the end of 1992 Patti Boulaye was cast as Carmen in *Carmen Jones*. During her rehearsals she asked if she could watch an evening show and I, as company manager, duly arranged a seat through Ned for her in the prompt side box. As she watched the performance she heard a noise behind her and, turning around, saw that the handle to the box door was moving up and down and rattling. Thinking that it was myself she got up and opened the door to discover - no one. The box of course was where Miss Baylis would sit.

Lilian's ghost may also visually appear at the Old Vic. In July 1989 the Katona Joszef Theatre's production of *Three Sisters* was playing at the theatre. At the end of each evening Ned Seago would do a round of the building checking that all was secured and in order before finally going home. He told me, "I had done the third floor backstage and was on the second floor on the prompt side of the building. I opened the door which leads into the corridor that spans the building and saw through the glass window of the opposite door the figure of a woman. There are staircases on both sides so thinking that she was one of the Hungarian actors and that we'd missed each other on the way down, I followed her to let her out of the stage door which of course was locked. As I came through the door on the first landing I saw her literally walk through the bricked-up doorway just to the side of the stage door. I knew immediately she wasn't a live Hungarian and think that it could only have been Miss Baylis doing her rounds."

Producers come and go in British theatre but few individuals have been so pivotal in the creation and shaping of our artistic institutions and modern theatrical heritage. I do believe that, as she made it so world famous, Lilian still walks about her Old Vic quite unchallenged.

Scene 19: The New Wimbledon Theatre

Having braved both the Cut and Lower Marsh I hope you have retained enough guts for one more South London location before our return to the West End. Unlike the nearby England Lawn Tennis and Croquet Club's Centre Court, Wimbledon Theatre aspires to host spectator entertainment not just for a fortnight, but all year round. It's in its blood really, for it has been a touring venue for much of its history.

The theatre was the last addition to John Brennan Mulholland's small suburban circuit joining his Metropole, Camberwell and his King's Theatre, Hammersmith. It was designed by Cecil Masey and Roy Young, who incorporated a Turkish bath in the basement for the exclusive use of the male members of the casts and staff. Whether any ladies penetrated the steam clouds is a mystery but I fear that in that era of masculine domination, they most probably had to make do with the brisker, brackish waters of the River Wandle.

The theatre opened on December 26th 1910 with *Jack and Jill: or the Hill, the Well and the Crown*. Panto titles, if not the actual shows, may have shortened but Wimbledon has never abandoned the chance to stage these seasonal box office winners, always so bang up-to-date with all the current gags and stars and often justifying the claim that the home of London Pantomime is in the Borough of Merton.

Audiences are attracted from far and wide with some even coming from the other side and the ghostly spectators are headed by Mr Mulholland, whose portrait hangs in the dress circle bar, for he himself likes to keep an occasional proprietary eye on his theatre.

One morning in 2004, at around 10.30am, Griff Owen, the then front of house manager, was standing on the side of the front row of the dress circle talking to the assistant house manager Adam Lister when he realised that, despite the access doors to the dress circle being chained up, another man appeared to have got in and was standing in front of seat B27. 'I asked Adam, "Who is that man?" but Adam replied 'Which man?" He said he couldn't see anybody. I was just about to ask the gentleman "Can I help you?" when he turned around and started to walk into the auditorium left box and disappeared. It was only afterwards that I realised that the man I had seen was the same man in the portrait in the dress circle bar.'

Other members of staff during the 1960s and '70s told of seeing a man in elegant evening clothes sitting in the same seat. At around the same time as Griff's experience a staff member came to him in a state of shock to report that he had had an encounter with another anonymous ghost. Before starting his shift for an evening show the young usher had been laboriously climbing the seemingly never-ending stairs to the upper circle. As he put his hand on the bannister to drag himself up, another hand enveloped his own. A most charitable gesture except that there was no arm or body attached to it.

J.B. Mulholland is not only in the circle bar...

The hand may have belonged to someone else other than Mr Mulholland. Between 1955 and 1962 the actor manager Peter Haddon ran a repertory company at Wimbledon, mounting over 300 productions. He died while his own play *Ghost Squad* was being performed. He too has since been seen in the same Dress Circle box and when not visible the aroma of his cigar has been reported coming from that vicinity. The box must be fairly crowded at times for the theatre's own Grey Lady has been spotted there too. Actor Ben Stock came across another late employee. He told me that, 'my experience happened around May 1996 while I was performing in the *Hiss and Boo Music Hall* starring the late great Danny La Rue. I was backstage - upstage right - and was aware of a little man with a flat cap on, over in the upstage left wing. I smiled and thought no more about it. Later on, I asked where he was and was told that other people had experienced a presence - sometimes in human form or in the form of a shadow.'

I am told by Marq English that the shadow has been seen by at least three members of the staff. Marq is the stage door supervisor and as befits a paranormal researcher and the author of *Paranormal Surrey*, he maintains a keen interest in the theatre's spirits. The psychic Sally Morgan, who has often toured to Wimbledon told him that one evening she saw the ghost of a woman in the upper circle wearing a 1950s maroon dress. She also confided that she had felt the presence of an actor from the 1930s on the stage. This performer, like so many others in the business, had needed a second part-time occupation to make ends meet. But his choice of a career in Armed Robbery Between

Scenes apparently misfired. With the law on his heels he had fled back to the theatre and, in a vain attempt to escape, fell from the dress circle to the stage and naturally to his death. It's a story that's open to interpretation but supported possibly by reports of the sound of something heavy but invisible landing occasionally on the stage.

Mike Lyas, the one time general manager, was unconvinced of the supernatural until one evening while working late, a woman wearing Edwardian clothing appeared in front of him, and this lady seems to have been seen again on two occasions by two other people in the stalls. There may also be another ghost that dates from a possible earlier era. In March 2013, Marq received a phone call at the stage door from a lady asking to speak to the manager. He asked, 'what is it regarding?' and the lady replied nervously, 'Oh no, I'm being silly, don't worry. I'm sorry. Thank you for your time'. Marq asked if she was sure he couldn't help her and the lady replied cautiously, 'Well, do you have anything odd happening at your theatre?' Sensing that she had seen something, he grasped the nettle. 'When you say odd, do you mean paranormal odd?' and the lady then explained that the night before she had come to the theatre with her sister who was in a wheel chair. It was a full house and they were in seats H1 and 2 in the stalls. As the houselights went down her sister glanced to her right and saw a man over six feet tall, standing in the side aisle. He was dressed in black with boots, a long coat, a goatee beard and a wide brimmed hat. She described him as looking like 'a puritan'. The man stared at her for some ten seconds and then faded away. Her sister was so shaken by this apparition that she had been unable to even talk about what she had seen until they had got home.

Who was this figure? Levellers and Diggers no doubt lurked about the fields of Merton in the 17th century, indeed the New Model Army's 'Putney Debates' took place unsurprisingly in nearby Putney and John Lambert, one of Oliver Cromwell's generals, lived in Wimbledon, but this Puritan pot pourri proves nothing. The immediate past residents of Stanhope House, the building that formerly stood on the theatre's site, either Dr George Walter Brabyn 'Physician and Surgeon' or Maurice Klein, 'Wine Merchant' would, unless partial to fancy dress, seem too modern so perhaps it may be an earlier occupant of that mansion. However, I will hazard a guess that the spirit was a costumed actor from a past production: perhaps Peter Haddon himself. After all, if it's your show in your theatre, why not nip out front to check up on your fellow cast and count your house?

Scene 20: Her Majesty's Theatre

Back now we must go, across the river to the West End, and down the Hay-market to arrive at Her Majesty's Theatre. Facing the front of house, you may be mystified by the incongruous New Zealand House that threatens its left flank. This is because the theatre was originally but half of a larger building design by J.C. Phipps, the other half being the Carlton Hotel. Contemporary critics may have been sniffy about the architectural merits of the finished site but Cesar Ritz and Auguste Escoffier ensured that the hotel's facilities and grill room were as successful as the adjoining playhouse. But in the Blitz of 1940, the hotel was very badly bombed and what was left of the site was demolished after the war for the present grim tower to be erected.

That the theatre was spared destruction and survives so successfully to this day is both providential and fitting for it is sited on hallowed if previously charred theatrical grounds. That is because Her Majesty's - and the possessive adjective changes with the sex of each succeeding monarch - stands on the site of three previous theatres, two of which went up in smoke in 1789 and 1867.

Sir John Vanbrugh, the dramatist and architect of that most theatrical of palaces, Blenheim, built his Queens's Theatre in 1705. This, becoming the King's Opera House with the ascent of George I, was the setting where some twenty-five of Handel's operas and the composer's first oratorio were performed. Vanbrugh's theatre was a victim of arson by persons unknown and its successor opened in 1793, and was, at the time, the largest theatre in England. It was widely used as a musical and ballet venue, playing host to the British premieres of the operas of Mozart and Rossini and later those of Bellini and Donizetti. Jenny Lind caused riots but not the fire that destroyed this building as it was an overheated stove rather than an overheated fan that started the blaze. The third theatre of 1868 was constructed in the shell of the old. It had some success with opera premieres again, such as *Carmen* and Wagner's *Ring* cycle but became an out of date venue because of the advances in Victorian theatre technology.

It was demolished in 1892 to make way for the present Her Majesty's which opened in 1897. Regarding its exterior and interior design for the first time, many younger readers may very well imagine that *The Phantom of the Opera* has been in residence ever since, for the Second Empire décor seems quite compatible with the musical.

This is not so, but myths do surround a very, very, very long run. Not to be confused with marathons, V.V.V.L.R.s are sometimes defined as shows that are so ancient that the only original parts left are their titles. Luckily, to date, this is not the case with this production which continues to entrance nightly, following in the fine tradition of such shows as *West Side Story, Fiddler on the Roof* and *Balalaika,* for Her Majesty's has been a musical house for much of its existence despite the best intentions of the actor who caused it to be built.

Step forward Sir Herbert Beerbohm Tree, who paid for the construction of 'my beautiful theatre' from profits raised during his ten-year tenancy of the Haymarket and in particular from *Trilby,* an adaptation of George du Maurier's book in which he played the sinister, manipulative hypnotist, Svengali. Tree was an actor manager of quite epic proportions who banished the word 'small' from his vocabulary. He was as Shaw said, 'the despair of authors' and as Mrs Patrick Campbell re-marked, 'the friendliest, most enthusiastic, most hospitable and most infuriating of creatures'. His spontaneous wit was part of his personality. He advised the younger members of his casts to 'keep your vowels and your bowels open' and de-manded from some skittish ladies-in-waiting in *Henry VIII,*'a little more virginity, if you don't mind'. He was by all accounts a superb character

Sir Herbert Beerbohm Tree as Svengali

actor, a master of the makeup box whose transformations would astonish his fellow performers. His enthusiasm for getting into character was such that his portrayal of Lord Illingsworth in Oscar Wilde's *A Woman of No Impor-tance* prompted its author to declare that 'every day Herbert becomes *de plus en plus* oscarisé. It is a wonderful case of nature imitating Art'.

Tree believed that the business of the stage was all about illusion and, in his perpetual quest to achieve an audience's belief in what they were watching, employed the best of everything. His casts, authors and designers were of top quality and he lavished fortunes on sets, costumes and music. He detested long runs and programmed a continual repertoire of new plays and revivals coupled with an annual Shakespeare festival. His passion for the works of the Bard was matched by a fervour for the ladies. He had many mistresses, fathered three daughters by his wife and some seven further illegitimate children including the film director Carol Reed. Lady Tree seems to have been resigned to his behaviour but did draw the line occasionally. On one particular evening Tree had asked the very handsome young actor Esme Percy back to his house to discuss his part over supper. Lady Tree entering the dining room, took one look at Percy and said, 'the port's on the sideboard, Herbert, and remember it's adultery just the same'.

*Tree as Nero: qualis
artifex pereo*

Perhaps this may account for the rumour that his presence has been felt by technicians in and around the backstage crew lavatory.

Sir Herbert's office at Her Majesty's was situated high up on the fourth floor in the dome of the theatre, complete of course with a chaise longue for casting sessions. Here, in its baronial style hall entered via huge studded wooden doors, Tree would host elaborate after-show suppers and parties. This room has had a chequered usage over the years. It was the first location in 1904 for Tree's Academy of Dramatic Art which would become the RADA. It has since been variously misused as a rehearsal room, a storage space and as offices for Stoll Moss. Raymond Lane, a late manager of the theatre, would also subject it to Masonic Lodge meetings. Raymond had a limp as curiously so did all the other members of the Lodge. They would foregather in the nearby Captain's Cabin pub and then, fortified for the ascent, limp in line up the stairs to don their regalia in supposed privacy. However, set in the wall panelling was a hidden door which gave access to the mansard roof. Behind this would sometimes hide Syd, an old theatre dayman. Syd would upset the proceedings by using six inch galvanized nails to scratch the panelling's inside wood in an eerie fashion. He was never discovered, but this human manifestation was not the only presence. The room until recently was a decidedly uncomfortable place to visit alone, if for nothing more than sudden and inexplicable drops in temperature.

The atmosphere was indeed deemed so frightening that staff would refuse to enter it at night.

If Tree can still be found there chilling out, he also has access to all other areas. Laurie Sautereau, flyman and chargehand at the theatre for many years, recalls working late nights during fit ups and set refurbishments and having to cross often from the prompt side fly floor to the other side by the bridge above the stage. He would allow for the fact that the building was cooling down to account for the creaks and cracks of the timbers but could never explain why he would repeatedly hear footsteps on the bridge a beat behind his own but could never, no matter how many times he turned around, see who was stalking him.

When Sir Herbert wishes to be visible he seems to favour an appearance on a Friday, possibly because in his time everyone would be in attendance on that day to receive their wages in cash. In 1977 during a performance of *Cause Celebre* by Terence Rattigan, Glynis Johns and other members of the cast saw his figure standing at the back of the stalls. He has been observed on the royal circle staircase and sometimes in his favourite box in the dress circle level, auditorium right, which is where Lauren Bacall said she saw him in 1972 during the run of *Applause*. Tree has also appeared in both wings and at the back of the set during *The Phantom of the Opera's* occupancy. We must feel some sympathy that he has to endure the music of the night, night after night after night after night. He may be therefore somewhat peeved at the seemingly never-ending success of this present production. Indeed, Sir Herbert was fated to die in 1917 before the close of another musical's annoyingly long run, for the success of *Chu Chin Chow* prevented him from taking his theatre back and recommencing his own productions. He declared that particular show to be mere 'scented hogwash', and without doubt he will certainly still be at Her or His Majesty's when the Phantom should ever finally vanish, waiting eagerly in the wings or in his box to welcome, perhaps, 'oh yes! Indeed, a play, my boy! A play!!'

Scene 21: The Theatre Royal Haymarket

There is no better way of making a first acquaintance with our next haunted theatre than to take an early evening diversion into St James' Square. Stand with your back to the statue of William III and look down King Street towards the Haymarket. There, bathed in the last rays of sunset or lit by lamps as twilight deepens, is the splendid original front portico of Nash's Theatre Royal with the Union Jack fluttering proudly on its flagstaff. You

will not be disappointed, either, by the interior, though first appearances can be deceptive; the auditorium may have an equal whiff of Georgian refinement, but in truth it is an elegant Edwardian fake, created in 1904.

Backstage however, the theatre of today basically remains as it was built in 1821, right next door to the site of the Little Theatre in the Hay which opened in 1720. It was there that in 1747 Samuel Foote set out to challenge the supremacy of the two patented theatres, Drury Lane and Covent Garden. Foote was an astonishing mimic and comedian. He launched his bid with the

Samuel Foote - an astonishing wit, mimic and comedian

satirical *The Diversions of the Morning* and followed its success with *Tea Parties,* and *Auction of Pictures and Tastes,* both of which circumvented the strict laws governing theatrical performances and enabled him to freely mock society's great and good to the delight of those omitted. Mr Foote's mordant wit both frightened and delighted his contemporaries and the desire to get one up on him and have a joke at his expense led to his losing a leg but, by way of amends, gaining a Royal patent for his theatre. Foote forcefully continued his acerbic career, stomping his way on his cork leg from success to success until fate in the form of a footman intervened. The actor was put on trial at Westminster accused of a sexual assault on his lackey John Sangster with intent to buggery. For fear of libel actions, the exact accusation and Sangster's testimony were not published in the newspapers but it was of course the talk of the town. Salacious rumours abounded and Sangster was renamed Roger the Footman in contemporary ballads. The accusation was possibly due to the intrigue of some of his enemies and in particular the bigamous Elizabeth Chudleigh, Duchess of Kingston, whom he had mercilessly satirised. Foote was found innocent by the jury but, as so often happens, mud sticks. Health already ruined and reputation now sullied, he sold his theatre lease to George Colman and died a year later on October 21st 1777 at the Ship Inn, Dover, en route to what was implied to be exile in Calais.

Despite his importance in the history of the theatre I can find only slight evidence of Mr Foote's presence at the new Haymarket, though part of his old house, which backed onto the Little, forms the corridor to the Royal Box. He does not seem to have hopped next door - apart from possibly two curious occasions. These incidents, however, must wait until some of the numerous appearances of a later 19th century actor manager have been described.

John Baldwin Buckstone is synonymous with the Haymarket. He ran the theatre from 1853 until 1878 and produced and acted in well over a hundred plays and entertainments. Buckstone's fare, in contrast to Foote's, was mainly

The celebrated Mr Buckstone - sighted by a host of actors

wholesome, often family orientated and eminently Victorian which of course pleased his most important patron. Indeed, before Albert's death and her flight from public appearances to play a very long private run as the Widow of Windsor, Queen Victoria attended some forty-six performances at the Haymarket.

Victoria puts the present Royal family to shame with her enthusiasm for all forms of theatrical entertainment. She was a constant, avid supporter of London's theatres. Melodramas and operas were devoured and ballets adored. She saw most of Shakespeare's canon, admiring the verse though critical of those that lacked action for, above all, she loved the spectacular. Her favourite forms of drama were comedy and farce and Mr Buckstone, the Queen's favourite comedian, was a past master of those arts. Buckstone was also a prolific writer of some 150 plays, mostly written in the years before he turned to acting and management. The titles of some of his pieces give us a flavour of his work: *Buckstone's Adventure with a Polish Princess*, *Mr Buckstone's Ascent of Mount Parnassus*, *Keeley Worried by Buckstone* - so audiences had no need to worry who would be playing on the night.

He was described as the comedian with a chuckle, a genial, broad comic who could milk a laugh out of the driest drama. Cast as the First Witch in Charles Kean's 1848 production of *Macbeth*, his unique voice caused a show stop with audiences shrieking uncontrollably with mirth. Photographs show a man with a generous mouth and kindly, knowing eyes. He ran a happy theatre for, as a star turn, he did the unusual by employing high quality actors and giving them high quality parts. Edward Sothern for one, became a huge draw in 1861 with his creation of Lord Dundreary in *Our American Cousin* which ran for 496 performances at the Haymarket and was the play whose curtain call Abraham Lincoln tragically missed. Sothern incidentally was a famous practical joker who played his jests with such intensity that many of his friends missed his funeral in the belief that he was fooling them yet again.

It should be mentioned that not all of Buckstone's castings met with Royal approval. The American Charlotte Cushman playing Meg Merrilees in *Guy Mannering* looked, the monarch thought, 'like the most frightful witch in *Macbeth* and was quite hideous to behold.' The unfortunate actress went on to ruin another of the Queen's evenings with her portrayal of Romeo, for 'no one would ever have imagined she was a woman, her figure and voice being so masculine, but her face was very plain.' Her Majesty had unknowingly hit the nail on the head for Miss Cushman favoured what were then known as 'strong female friendships'.

Mr Buckstone wisely avoided the Bard as much as possible and concentrated on new works or revivals of Farquhar and Sheridan but his final year at the Haymarket was dogged by box office failures and ill health and he retired to decay and die in Sydenham in 1879. His ties with the theatre remained though, for, within a year, his spirit had re-crossed the Thames to take up residence again.

There have been several sightings in the last hundred years. In 1926, Drusilla Wills stated that when she was appearing in *Yellow Sands*. 'I was backstage speaking to a friend when an elderly man in an old-fashioned suit passed between us. I remarked about him to my friend and discovered that she hadn't seen him.'

In 1949, Sir Donald Sinden was appearing in Henry James' *The Heiress,* a play set in the 1850s. Descending the stairs from their dressing rooms on the top floor for their entrance, he and Gillian Howell would pass the star dressing room occupied by Sir Ralph Richardson. By the door was a window overlooking Suffolk Street. One evening as they came down they saw Sir Ralph staring out of the window with his back to them. They called out 'Good evening, Ralph', carried on to the stage door level and then came to an abrupt halt. Both realised that Sir Ralph was onstage. The man they had passed was wearing a perfect costume for the piece, except that his clothes were authentically period.

Charlotte Cushman - Queen Victoria was not amused

In 1963 Michael Flanders and Donald Swann were performing *At the Drop of Another Hat* when the ASM in the prompt corner, Olga Bennett, saw a figure of a man in a long black frockcoat standing behind Flanders' wheel chair. Her immediate reaction was to try to bring the curtain in as she thought a deranged stagehand must have wandered on but, as she stared at him, the stranger vanished in front of her eyes. Neither Flanders nor Swann had noticed him but both were convinced of the truth of her story.

In December 2005 Martin Shaw returned to play the Haymarket. 'I was doing *A Man for All Seasons* and in the famous dressing room 10, probably the most beautiful in any theatre in England. I was visited by my partner and a friend of hers; both are psychic in the generally accepted meaning of the word, in that they experience things generally considered to be outside 'normal'. My partner's friend is partially blind and she had been brought by Kaz to see the show. During our quiet conversation they both started and exclaimed simultaneously. "Did you see him?" said Lynne. "I felt him," said Kaz, and they both happily described the person who had entered. Lynne said he was flamboyantly dressed, did a little dance and placed a scarf around my neck. All these details were confirmed by Kaz who 'sees' through feeling. Such things I gather are hard to describe in physical terms. At first I thought it was Oscar Wilde, who had inhabited that room and where I had myself been installed when appearing in *An Ideal Husband* in the very theatre that premiered it. I later learnt that the famous Haymarket ghost was a Mr Buckstone, and the description offered by Kaz and Lynne was exactly as the historical record. Neither had heard of him before, or indeed had known that the Haymarket was haunted'.

Are ghosts capable of acknowledging and even honouring, their new afterlife companions? They are it seems if they are actors, for Mr Buckstone appears to have risen to the occasion in 1998. Dame Judi Dench had come to the theatre to attend Michael Denison's memorial service. As she left the foyer to descend the stairs to the stalls she saw in front of her 'a man in a black frock coat. It was in the middle of the day and he was not at all ghostly'; by the time she got down the stairs he was gone, 'but there was no door he could have gone through'.

Most photographs of Buckstone show him as a beaming Mr Pickwick-type character but these date mainly from after he had become lessee of the theatre and was well into his fifties. In fact he gave his first performance at the Haymarket in 1833 when he was 31 and I believe therefore that the next encounter captured him at this period of his life.

In September 1977 Googie Withers and John McCallum were appearing in Somerset Maugham's play *The Circle*. Their daughter Mandy, then 16 years old, came backstage after a show to meet them. Googie and John had a host of visitors that evening and while they entertained them in their dressing rooms, Mandy decided to explore. ' I went on stage to look around. The stage was faintly lit but the auditorium was in darkness. You could however still see the seating and especially the boxes to the side of the stage. Looking to the box to the right of the stage (the royal box) I saw what I thought was a person sitting in the shadows of the box. He was looking at the stage, not me. He looked to have dark curly shoulder length hair and was well dressed, maybe with a waistcoat. He was middle aged and was just sitting there staring at the stage.' Mandy turned around and exited the stage to rejoin her parents. As they left she told the stage door keeper not to close up, 'as there is still a man in the audience. Apparently that spooked them all a little!'

I first worked the Haymarket in 1966 as an ASM on *The Rivals* and, without question, totally accepted the general consensus that the theatre was haunted. Indeed, the building's appearance and atmosphere fully complemented its reputation for being full of ghosts. It was mostly unmodernised backstage and that included many of the staff. It still had a resident property master who would always wear carpet slippers in the wings and a master carpenter who could be found at his lathe turning out fine mahogany dildos for those in need or in the know. The licensee was Mrs Sylva Stuart Watson who firmly believed in the spirit world and would, it was rumoured, be heard talking to those that lingered in or floated by her office. It was the last London house not to have a show relay or tannoy system. Instead we relied on a call boy who would run furiously up and down the corridors knocking on dressing room doors to remind the actors which show they were in and give them their standbys to come down to the wings. This was effective until Saturdays' second shows when the Guinness would sometimes get the better of the timings. Then voices would rise on stage, lines would be repeated and a splattered staccato of frantic footsteps be heard on the stairs. Sir Ralph was playing Sir Anthony Absolute and Dame Margaret Rutherford, Mrs Malaprop. There was a hierarchic code of behaviour in those days. The brief was that when one met Sir Ralph on the stairs one 'steps aside, murmurs "Sir" and ignores the parrot sometimes on Sir's shoulder'. Sir would duly sail past me, seemingly oblivious to my presence whilst nodding his head in concentration for his next scene. When he eventually spoke to me it was to ask kindly for a pin. For Dame Margaret had mistaken the matinee for the evening performance and had prematurely swallowed her ration of sleeping pills for her journey home. That night, pin poised, Sir Ralph hovered around her in their scenes, ready to plunge it in the moment she nodded off but, despite some eloquent yawning, she pulled through her scenes without need of puncture. She was usually of course magnificent in her role, her chins wobbling in time to her malapropisms like waves of quivering pink blancmange.

During my time on the show, Anthony Chardet, in his time H.M. Tennent's top company manager and Marlene Dietrich's favourite stage director, was having a drink with me in the old Buckstone Club just across the street from the stage door. The subject of Haymarket ghosts came up and he told me that while he was looking after Dame Margaret in the 1962 production of *A School for Scandal*, there was a cast changeover party on stage. At the end of the evening he remembered he had left his overcoat in the wardrobe which is situated on the top backstage floor. Cursing the stairs, he stopped at the entrance to the top corridor to get his breath back and saw the fire door in front of him very slowly open and close, but revealing no one behind it. Tony was not one to believe in ghosts and tried several times to replicate what had happened. But though he opened every window and door to create a draft, the fire door stayed resolutely shut.

I was very envious of this encounter but experienced nothing until I returned some years later as company manager on *Crown Matrimonial*. One evening, rather than go out front, I was standing in the stage right wing where the masking flat allowed a partial view of the stage and so made it possible for me to check that everyone in the cast wasn't misbehaving royally. As I watched, my eye was drawn to the box on the dress circle level where the present lighting desk is now situated. I could distinctly see someone standing in the shadows wearing what appeared to be evening clothes. Our audiences then were, at best, only up to a suit and tie so I thought that it could only be Anthony Peek, the general manager of the theatre, who always wore a dinner jacket on duty. At this time of the evening he was usually drinking a gin and tonic and watching the news on his office television so I was intrigued to know what he was up to. I walked round the back of the set to the prompt corner on stage left, through the pass door and up the stairs towards the box. The door was closed. As it was just before the interval, I waited for the applause at curtain down to open the door and find out what was up. Nothing was up for nothing was there. Mr Peek's office was locked and empty and I discovered that he had gone home at least half an hour before. I questioned the attendants in the foyer and they told me that they had let no one in and seen no one going into the box. Finally I checked the box office returns and they confirmed that the box was unsold. Had I possibly seen Mr Buckstone? If I had opened the door before the interval my suspicions might well have been confirmed.

Buckstone's ghost seems to be often present in what was his old office. This had then a door leading directly onto the stage. It is now blocked up and the room is used as a principal dressing room. A voice has here been heard reciting lines. The other 'star' dressing room upstairs also has a presence, for when Jack Lemmon was using it in 1986 when he appeared in London to play James Tyrone in *A Long Day's Journey into Night* he complained that something had scared him when sitting alone with the windows shut, for the door had opened and slammed by itself three times.

Although it has been reported that Sir Patrick Stewart also encountered Mr Buckstone, I myself believe that he must have met a far more recent ghost. In 2009 *Waiting for Godot* arrived at the Haymarket after an eight week tour. As Patrick told me, 'One night, just as we were getting close to the end of Act 1, Pozzo and Lucky had just gone off and I was looking stage left to where they had gone off and then turned to my right to speak to Ian (McKellen) who was playing Estragon. And as my eyes swept across the edge and the front of the stage there was a man standing on stage, on the stage left, quite close to the box. I looked back and he was still there and my first thought was that "someone has climbed out of the box and if they've done that then they don't wish us well." So, I looked at Ian and Ian came to look worried and looked back at me. I turned again to look at the man, to look for him, and he was not there, he was gone. But I saw him and the moment the curtain came down - Ian and I finished both the acts staring into one another's eyes very close together, saying "shall we go? Yes let's go", and, as the stage direction says they do not move - but as Ian was looking at me, his face was getting more and more anxious - and finally, when we were out of sight of the audience he said to me "What's happened? Something's happened". I told him there was a man on stage with us and he said, "Where? Where?" And I said he was standing down stage left. He was wearing a belted Norfolk jacket. I think he had a shirt – a rather old fashioned check shirt with a tie underneath the jacket and he was wearing cavalry twill trousers and suede boots. That's how clearly I remember seeing him. I was only looking at him for a few seconds but it was so shocking to me that there was someone on stage with us that the image imprinted itself.'

Sadly this seemingly twentieth century apparition remains anonymous but, if I may quote from Harold Hobson's review of the original 1955 *Waiting for Godot* production, the impression this intruder made seems akin to 'Something that will securely lodge in a corner of your mind as long as you live'.

During *The School for Scandal* the stage level dressing room - Mr Buckstone's old office - had been assigned to Margaret Rutherford. She and her husband Stringer Davis lived in Gerrards Cross and would train back and forth during the run. Stringer was by then a fixture in any play she did for it was written into all her contracts that he would be assigned a part. Managements had no problem with this for a small part for Stringer meant a large part of the responsibility for looking after their leading lady was safely in his hands.

They were an inseparable couple and Stringer fussed and tended over her devotedly. During the play's run a railway strike was announced and the management agreed, on the night before the day it was due to happen, to let the two of them sleep over in the dressing room and so ensure that they would have no trouble getting to the theatre. There was ample space for a camp bed for Stringer while Margaret commandeered the large sofa. Sleeping pills were no doubt swallowed but it was an unusual night all round.

For the very next day Margaret announced to Anthony Peek that she had seen a ghost and gave interviews about her experience to both the Psychic News and the BBC. The core of the story is that she saw somebody inside the large cupboard where her costumes were hung. At first a leg appeared, a 'hairy leg' and then the full figure of a man whom some, when she described him in detail, thought to be Mr Buckstone. She also declared that, 'I was really very pleased so I stroked his leg and thanked him for coming.' Stringer saw nothing but confirmed that he heard a door slam and Margaret calling out. A hairy leg is comic. It could certainly have been Buckstone's but comedy is not confined to one era. I wonder therefore if by any chance the limb she felt could have been Mr Foote's remaining lally?

To date, one of the latest visitations of a spirit on stage occurred on the evening of December 19th 2015 a mere few seconds after 10pm. If this sounds both particularly and suspiciously precise, it is due to the fact that it happened at the curtain call immediately after the end of a play and so the exact timing is recorded in the show report.

The second show on Saturday December 19th marked the 100th performance of *Mr Foote's Other Leg* since its very first preview at the Hampstead Theatre and its subsequent transfer to the Haymarket. The late Mr Foote, thanks to Sir Michael Codron, had been fittingly brought home in an artistically acclaimed, celebratory play by Ian Kelly for it was the one-legged comedian and actor who had managed to obtain the theatre's coveted Royal Charter in 1766.

At the end of the show, the lights came up from their fade to black out for Simon Russell Beale to take his first solo bow before beckoning on his fellow actors for the company bow. As Forbes Masson who was playing Mr Hunter waited to go on, he heard the sound of one of the supernumeraries, Canavan Connolly, as usual applauding the actors from his position behind the black surround that masked the wings from the audience's sight. However, as Forbes started to walk on stage, he saw from the corner of his eye that upstage of him and to the left of the dressing room truck there was what appeared to be a pair of white-sleeved outstretched arms and that the hands of these arms were clapping energetically but noiselessly together. Forbes's immediate thought was that somehow Canavan had walked onto the stage but he realised almost simultaneously that he could still hear the hidden supernumerary clapping away in the wing. He turned his head fully upstage to take another look, only to discover that there was now nobody there. At the end of the call he explained what had happened. We investigated and were able to confirm that no one from the crew had strayed on.

Forbes did not see anything other than these disembodied arms and hands and so we could only conjecture here the strange possibility that Mr Foote himself might have returned once more to applaud both the centenary of our production and the justice of his artistic resurrection.

Spiritual interest in our production continued. On the matinee of December 31st 2015 Sophie Bleasdale, our Miss Chudleigh, was also 'waiting to do my bit as "Stage Hand", excited for what the rest of the night had in store for me. As I walked on stage and proceeded to collect various bits of furniture to take them off for a scene change, I noticed in the corner of my eye that there was a figure standing at the front of the stalls, stage right. For a split-second I assumed they must be standing up to let someone past them and out into the aisle. After a few more moments, whilst I was still collecting various bits to take them off, I noticed that this figure - dressed all in white, or at least very pale - was still standing there, just staring at the stage. He/she hadn't moved. It felt odd, and not particularly normal, for someone who was just standing up politely to let someone go for a mid-show loo break! A shiver went up my spine. I left the stage feeling odd and immediately told everyone I could grab my hands on.'

As we all know, things have a way of happening in threes. At the end of the second show on Twelfth Night, January 6th, Joseph Millson was waiting first in line in the stage left wing, to come on for his curtain call and watching Simon Russell Beale take his solo. 'My line of vision meant that I could see directly into the royal box. My eyes, which have 20:15 vision, were drawn to look at the back wall of the box because it looked white. What I saw, and I know it may sound ridiculous, but what I saw looked like a comedy Halloween costume, a white sheet over a person with two large comedy eye holes. I thought for a second that it was someone playing a joke, but, as I continued to stare, it dissolved in front of my eyes.'

If Mr Buckstone is the dominant ghost he is certainly not in sole spiritual occupancy of the Haymarket. Others possibly include David Edward Morris, the leaseholder of 1821, and the novelist and playwright Henry Fielding, the creator of *Tom Jones*. And we must not forget the ladies.

At the back of the royal circle is a wide and elegant promenade. This is separated from the actual auditorium by floor to ceiling wooden walls inset with glass windows and two glass panelled doors. On the opposite wall, by each staircase leading to the foyer are a pair of full length framed mirrors. It is a handy location for staff and creatives to watch the show from and indeed for those discerning theatregoers who prefer to arrive late and view a more muffled performance while the ice tinkles away in their gin and tonics. The only distraction, apart from melting ice, is that when watching at certain angles, the reflection of the window glass shows the mirrors close behind you.

In 1990, Paul Eddington and Angela Thorne were playing to full houses in *London Assurance*. It was a production full of gusto set in 1841, that cross over period between the tail end of the rakish Regency and the respectability of Victoria and Albert. The lighting on stage was at times purposely dim and the promenade was equally dark when the house lights were out. Walter Oscar, who had just joined the staff , was watching a performance from here, when, some twenty-five minutes into the play, he saw, reflected through the glass, two ladies who appeared to have stepped through the mirror directly behind him. He turned around in astonishment to face them as they passed him by and recalls that his hair literally stood on end.

Walter was so shocked that he did not see where they went to, but, minutes later, they returned towards him. This time he could see that, 'their faces were made up theatrically as if ready to go on stage, elegant and detached. They were wearing dark emerald green velvet long dresses with trains.'

He watched them stroll along the carpet seemingly unaware of his presence and then, walking straight into the mirror from which they had appeared, they vanished into oblivion. Walter is convinced that one of the ladies he saw was Sarah Siddons, for her appearance seems to match pictures he has since researched. However the Tragic Muse had retired from the stage well before Nash's Haymarket was built and so, as so often, a mystery remains.

One evening in 1996, on the last night of *The Master Builder*, Frankie Zambra, the company manager, had arranged to meet her friends in the show's stage management team at the end of their Get Out. She arrived at the suggested time and, as the stage door was seemingly unmanned, walked unannounced onto the stage to find them. The set had gone, the dock doors were closed and the stage itself was swept and empty. She was wandering down the stage left wing towards the pass door, when, out of the corner of her eye, she saw a figure standing in the gloom of the auditorium. She stopped and focused on it and could make out 'the form of a butch- looking woman in a long flowing gown. But as I stared at her she just dissolved right in front of me.'

The mysterious Muriel Aked - be sure to acknowledge her

Just then, Frankie's friends arrived from their upstairs dressing room and together they all searched the stalls. Nothing was found but they implicitly believed her story as I do, for she may well have seen Charlotte Cushman or even, perhaps, Muriel Aked.

A mill owner's daughter from Bingley and a skilful character actress, Miss Aked appeared in over 40 films including *The Life and Death of Colonel Blimp* and *The Wicked Lady* but I can only find one credit for her at the Haymarket, namely *Barnet's Folly* in 1935. Mysteriously however, her photograph hangs prominently on one of the walls of the staircase leading up to the dressing rooms. No one knows why, but no one dares to remove it. The belief persists in acknowledging her as one ascends or descends the stairs. This brings good luck, but failure to address the lady can result in being tripped up or pushed down by an angry, invisible hand. So, may I advise all earthly Haymarket visitors on mounting the stairs, to touch the picture frame and to bid Miss Aked a loud and cheerful 'Hello!'

After all, why tempt fate?

INTERVAL

Theatre intervals are just too short unless you're at the Opera and then they're just too long. By the time you've reached the bar, you may have crossed it so no need to ask for whom those bells are ringing. Get straight back to your seat or rather, why leave it at all? Here are some brief encounters to keep you busy until the second act . . .

AT DARLINGTON THEATRE

Darlington Theatre is haunted both by Signor Pepe who founded the theatre in 1907 and by Signor Pepe's best friend. Ian Stephenson, the general and company manager, grew up in Darlington and while still a student spent much of his spare time working at the theatre. Regularly every Sunday in the early 1980s, Ian would go into the theatre office via the stage door and turn around the FOH posters and leaflets for the next week's show. The offices were on the first floor above the box office which was adjacent to the main building. To reach them one had to go through the stage door, and up two flights of stairs to the first-floor corridor of dressing rooms which had an entrance to the annexe.

On this particular Sunday there was no Load In and Ian was on his own from midday for some four hours. 'I had all the keys to the F.O.H areas and while going to put them back I heard the distinct sound of footsteps coming up the staircase on the other side of the door which led to the theatre. No one came up. The stairs were empty. I turned to lock that door and then as I started down the staircase the hairs on my head stood up. I could feel the air literally turn from warm to cold. This sensation stayed with me until, as I turned the key to lock the stage door, I felt this extraordinary release. On Saturday mornings, the stars of the visiting companies would turn up for coffee with the supporters' club and say 'hello'. This would take place in a bar where originally the rear stalls had been. While doing the conversion the builders discovered Signor Pepe's dog buried in the ground. While coffee was being served one day, a little three-year-old boy pointed down to the ground and cried 'Dog! Dog!'"

AT FAIRFIELD HALLS, CROYDON

In 2012, on the 50th anniversary of the Halls, the CEO Simon Thomsett had made arrangements to celebrate the occasion with a Gala Evening in the Concert Hall. The London Mozart Players were to perform some of Wolfgang's best to an audience that included several local MPs, Mayors, Council dignitaries, the Bishop of Croydon and HRH the Prince Edward, Earl of Wessex.

Throughout that day, the staff and volunteers worked tirelessly to make sure that everything would look its best. It had been decided that the Prince's party should not be seated in the Royal Box as it did not have the best sight-lines and Simon had issued instructions that it should be locked up to ensure that no none else would be tempted to break protocol and use it. At the end of the first movement of the opening concerto, Simon looked about to scan the house's reaction, and, to his surprise, saw a man sitting in the royal box. 'I was very angry that my briefing had been blatantly ignored,' he reported, 'and worried that the man could well cause trouble. In the interval, once I was sure the VIPs were being properly looked after, I went to eject the intruder with a member of security. The door was, as had been instructed, indeed locked and, on opening it, we found the box to be empty.'

AT THE QUEEN'S THEATRE, HORNCHURCH

The late New Zealand born actor Terence Bayler was appearing at the old Queen's Theatre, Hornchurch during the Christmas of 1969. He was playing the Demon of the Forest in *Babes in the Wood* - 'an alarming figure in green and brown makeup and costume, with twiggy extensions on my gloves and, of course, green sequins on my eyelids. Thus attired, I had to deliver an invocation calling the evil spirits of the forest to entrap the two innocent babes.' Terence did not want to frighten any young children in the audience and especially his own, for it was to be their first theatre visit. The pantomime's sets and costumes were Victorian in design so Terence thought that 'if I played the Demon as an absurdly hammy and rather drunken Victorian actor, it might amuse the adults and seem to the children to be a silly rather than a really threatening figure. And there was a bonus bit of business – I could sway, both as a tree - and a drunk.' Anthony Carrick the director agreed to this idea and Terence, entering as tradition demanded of villains from stage left, duly played his scene in front of the house curtain while the Babes and their nurse stood by behind it waiting to play their bedtime sketch.

One of the Babes was Ian Trigger, 'a very funny, very short actor' and they would often travel home together on the tube during the six week run. One night the subject turned to ghosts. Terence related that as a child he had heard his Irish grandmother's stories of ghosts in the old country – 'on one occasion she spoke of an area haunted by a turkey on a bicycle -and, on seeing Ian's amusement, I intoned "it was something in the form of a turkey". Ian laughed at this and replied "I'm just a wee Scots agnostic."' The next evening Terence delivered his spooky, swaying invocation and exited. As soon as the bedroom scene finished Ian came off stage 'seeming really disturbed and asked me "how did you do that?" Apparently as I began the incantation, a rocking chair on the bedroom set began to rock violently, and then stopped abruptly when the speech ended.' Ian, thinking it was a joke, had walked around the chair as it moved, expecting but failing to find either string or wire. From then on, Terence shortened the summons, made it much more silly, and the chair rocked not.

AT THE NEW END THEATRE, HAMPSTEAD

The New End theatre lived up to its name by closing in 2011. It had bravely opened in 1974 as a fringe venue, having been converted from its former use as the New End Hospital's mortuary. The hospital itself expired shortly after the theatre opened. It had been originally a Poor House before becoming a hospital for psychiatric patients and treating wounded and shell shocked World War I soldiers. Its latter life was as a centre for endocrinology - the treatment of gland-related diseases. The tunnel under the road linking the mortuary to the hospital had been sensibly blocked up when the theatre opened, but this could not prevent the passage of visitors from the afterlife. The theatre's stage area was where the bodies, including that of Karl Marx, had been laid out and the original raked seating, where hospital staff and other interested parties could observe proceedings, remained. Lights would flicker and strange and inexplicable noises be reported.

The artistic director, Ninon Jerome, was working there in 2009. Late one evening during a technical rehearsal she and her team heard the laughter of children and the sound of footsteps running up and down the stairwell. A search was instigated but all the exterior doors were naturally found to be locked. I myself too remember a strange and forbidding atmosphere in the auditorium but then we were performing *Beyond Therapy* to strange and forbidding audiences of Hampstead psychologists.

AT THE TABARD THEATRE, CHISWICK

The Tabard, above the pub of that same name, would appear to have a most benign and helpful ghost. One morning in 2013, during the run of *The Mikado*, the assistant stage manager, Kristina Kreculji told the general manager Simon Reilly that there had been an inexplicable happening.

She recounted that, at the very end of the previous evening's show, it had been discovered that one of the set's Japanese sliding paper doors had come off its hinges. As it was late, rather than attempting an immediate repair, she and the crew placed the door safely upright, off stage in the stage left wing, so that it could be fixed back the next day. As usual the theatre was locked up for the night, but when Kristina came the next morning to open up and to make good the damage, she discovered that the door had already been fixed back and was now hanging in its correct position. Together, she and Simon then checked through the entire overnight CCTV footage from the security cameras only to draw a complete blank. Nobody human had entered the theatre overnight.

AT THE NEW THEATRE, OXFORD

In 2012, during a tour of *Grease,* Lisa Brindley, the wardrobe mistress and Ashleigh Duckworth, her deputy, arrived for a morning Get In. They had been forewarned about a reputedly haunted top floor dressing room and found it had been assigned to the boys ensemble for it was spacious enough to accommodate them all.

Together, Lisa and Ashleigh entered the room, walked down its short staircase into the dressing area, assembled the wardrobe rails, hung up all the costumes and set out the boys' footwear as quickly as possible, mindful as they were that 'something' might suddenly appear. Their job done, Lisa led the way up the stairs to make a speedy exit. On reaching the safety of the corridor, she shouted back at Ashleigh, 'Thank God, it's not haunted!' With that, the dressing room door, which was wedged firmly open with a rubber door stop, slammed shut in Ashleigh's face, leaving her in dismay in the 'empty' room. They told their story immediately to the DSM, Lorraine Kearin, who, a week later, because of their continual fear, was obliged to accompany them to the room and stay with them while they did their Saturday Get Out.

AT DARTINGTON HALL

Martin Shaw was touring in 1968 with the Bristol Old Vic's production of *War and Peace* and when the company arrived to play at Dartington Hall, the cast were all assigned bedrooms to sleep in. Martin's room, which he was sharing with fellow actor Marshall Jones, was rectangular with the door on one long side, a window on the other and with two single beds each in a corner. 'There were some pretty girls studying there, and I returned late after some socialising. I quietly opened the door to find Marshall awake, his light on and clearly agitated. "Why have you been knocking on the bloody window?", he asked. I pointed out that there was a hefty drop outside the window and knocking on it would be impossible. After a few more grumbles we both turned in. I awoke just before dawn with a sense of absolute terror, every hair standing on end. I lay for a few seconds considering it must have been a nightmare. The feeling remained however and glancing at the window opposite I saw a hooded shape standing silhouetted in the dawn light. Next, the shape moved towards my bed, and instinctively I hit out, and put on the bedside light. This awoke Marshall and he angrily asked me in so many words what the f... was I doing now? "Nothing. Just a dream", I answered, but clearly my face indicated more, for he asked me more seriously what had happened. I told him and then he told me what had happened to him before I'd arrived. He'd been asleep, but was wakened by a hand on his shoulder. He was then lifted from the bed slightly and rearranged. The hand then patted his shoulder. He sat up and put on his light which is when the knocking on the window began. Minutes later I walked in, and he felt unable to communicate what had happened for fear of ridicule. Next morning at breakfast I reconnected with one of the girls from last night. "How did you like sleeping in the Old Infirmary?", she asked. "Old Infirmary?" "Yes, this was a priory." I stayed silent, and then she said. "Did you know it's haunted?" More silence, then: "There's a nun who often goes round nursing people on the top floor."' Martin calls that 'a three-way corroboration' - an unarguable verdict for me.

AT THE GRAND THEATRE, LEEDS

While Victoria Holt was appearing as Charlotte in *Oliver!* at the Grand in November 2012, she looked out front one evening during a scene 'and saw a woman sitting in the auditorium right on what I thought was an usher's seat. She had really long hair which seemed to be wet, was dressed in what appeared to be grey robes and was leaning forwards, clasping her hands as if in prayer. We were there for five weeks and I saw her three times. After the third time, I decided to take a look at the usher's seat. I went into the auditorium and, there wasn't one!'

Charlotte couldn't believe it wasn't there and even banged on the wall where it should have been attached. She asked the ushers what had happened to the seat and they said it didn't exist. 'And on the last night I saw her again on the 'missing' usher's seat, sitting upright this time. . .' Some shows grow on both the living and the dead.

AT THE LEICESTER HAYMARKET

Some Roman cities such as Silchester died with the final departure of the legions but not Leicester, for it has soldiered ever onwards. It has survived an infamous sacking - in this case I refer not to Claudio Ranieri's in 2017 but to the city's in the English Civil War of 1645. If the football club's Premier League success was thought by all except native Rat-eyes - a nick-name referring to the Roman name of the city, *Ratae Corieltauvorum* - to be quite extraordinary, then the discovery of King Richard III's butchered skeleton beneath the concrete of a Social Services carpark could be described as perhaps uncanny. It is fitting then that this particular city's second oldest existing theatre can claim to be haunted and in this case by a spectre younger yet older than the building.

The Leicester Haymarket was only opened by Sir Ralph Richardson in 1973. The theatre was built above and on a site which had previously contained an array of shops and pubs. Having allowed Frank Matcham's huge and splendid Palace Theatre to be demolished in 1959, followed also by the Royal Opera House in 1960, the city council in a fit of civic remorse agreed to redress their actions which had resulted in this cultural wilderness and the Phoenix was opened in 1963. But this theatre's capacity was under 300 and a bigger venue was needed to make shows economically viable. Once built, the Haymarket's early days were steered by its artistic directors Robin Midgley and Michael Bogdanov. Amongst its early successes were several runs of *Joseph and the Amazing Technicolour Dreamcoat* and the 1977 revival of *Oliver!* directed by Midgley and Larry Oaks. This starred the late Roy Hudd as Fagin and was later transferred to London by Cameron Mackintosh.

During a *Joseph* production, one of the backstage staff working late noticed a small boy dressed in an old-fashioned sailor suit playing around one of the costume skips. Assuming him to be one of the Artful Dodger's mob he was told firmly to leave the stage and go home. This he did, for he suddenly vanished. Other staff have recorded their impressions of 'Dennis', named after 'Dennis the Menace' because of his unseen habit of pushing and grabbing at people, skipping about and turning the backstage lights on and off.

During *Oliver!* Robin Midgley was sitting in the stalls when he felt his leg being poked sharply by a finger. Looking down he saw that no one was there, but, on returning home, discovered small bruises on his leg. At other times the child's reflection has been seen in dressing room mirrors by casts and crew but the face always vanishes when challenged. His appearance indicates that he is definitely of another era and it is believed that he must have met his death in a building since demolished to make way for the complex in which the Haymarket sits. Tradition has it that he may have fallen down a well or been crushed by a runaway beer barrel. Two possible, if fanciful, ends, but tales of a ghost's mortal demise should always be dramatic.

AT YORK THEATRE ROYAL

York claims to be the most haunted city in Europe, and this is certainly helped by Harry Martindale's sighting in 1953. For he saw some twenty legless Roman legionnaires marching through the cellar wall of the Treasury House, a building on the site of the old Roman road. Ignore such theories as cannibalism amongst those native tribes outside the gates of Eboracum or severe noble rot in a *miles pede's* wine ration. The reason for this mass loss of lower limbs is simply because the road is some fifteen inches deeper than the present cellar floor. However, when it comes to the Theatre Royal's particular ghost, height is quite irrelevant.

The Grey Lady is thought to be the spirit of a nun from the medieval hospital of St Leonards which previously stood on the site of the present theatre. Not that she manifests herself clearly, for she appears, once the air temperature has significantly dropped, as a grey mist and it is believed that her sighting guarantees a success.

One documented instance is in August 1975 when the company were in rehearsals for Richard Digby Day's production of Dodie Smith's *Dear Octopus*. Evelyn Laye was starring as Dora Randolph and in one scene was required to sit at a piano and sing a verse from the Kerry Dances. As she began to sing, the other cast members were amazed to see a small white cloud of mist traversing the middle of the dress circle. There was no logical explanation, no human or atmospheric activity, for the dress circle was empty and locked. All watched amazed as the mist contracted into a tiny ball and then disappeared. The cast demanded a break to restore nerves and concentration but when rehearsals eventually recommenced, and at the very moment Miss Laye started to sing again, the white cloud of mist reappeared and repeated its performance. Most of the cast, unaware of the legend of the Grey Lady, were convinced that they had witnessed a supernatural sighting. The show of course was a great success and this report lends credence to the belief that this theatre's Grey Lady is a benevolent spirit. Let us credit the appearance and disregard any malevolent thought that this particular nun couldn't bear Miss Laye's top notes.

AT THE GARRICK CLUB

It is a personal disappointment that I have to date failed to find evidence that David Garrick haunts any of our existing theatres. Here's the first actor of the modern age whose reputation and renown, some two hundred and forty years since his death, has endured to this day and yet not even a glimpse of the great man, let alone his famous Hamlet wig, which would rise as if by terror at the sight of his father's ghost, has been spotted on a stage. I would like to lay the blame for his absence on Sheridan who had the old Drury Lane Theatre pulled down in 1791 to make way for his new theatre but nonetheless...

Wait! Problem solved! Author and Garrick Club member Brian Masters has come to my rescue, for he recently gave me the following story:
'About twenty years ago, enchanted by his vivid though painful depictions of the Windsor Castle fire, I commissioned Alexander Creswell to paint two watercolours of the Garrick Club for me. With his expert eye for design and impact, he chose one of the Coffee Room in full splendour, and another of the grand staircase, which is the initial view of every visitor, and the cherished welcome of every member. The results were stunning.

I asked the Secretary whether I might put both pictures on show at the club for a few weeks, in order that other members should enjoy them before I squirrelled them away for my private delight. This was readily agreed, and two easels were set up on the landing outside the bar, in the corner, offering a perfect glance or more prolonged study. They went up on Thursday, I believe. In those days the club was closed from Friday evening to Monday morning; thus nobody was in the building for the long weekend, and everything therein was safe.

On Monday I received an anguished call from the Secretary to inform me that one of the pictures had been found at the foot of the stairs, smashed and somewhat damaged. Alexander immediately called round to inspect, confirming that the frame would need to be replaced, and the picture itself mildly touched up. A van duly arrived to collect it. Within a couple of weeks the repairs had been completed and the pictures returned, ultimately to adorn the walls of my village house in France.

But there was the enduring mystery of how the accident came to pass. It appeared to be impossible. Had the picture fallen off the pegs which supported it securely on the easel, it would have fallen downwards and would be found at the foot of the easel, still on the landing. But that, manifestly, had not happened. It was on the floor below. To get there it had to fall upwards and hurl itself over the banister to its fate. That too could not happen. Human agency seemed to be certain. But there was nobody in the building, and, in any case, who would want to indulge in such frivolous, pointless destruction, and why? The clue came when I heard what the driver of the van had said when he came to collect the picture: 'So that ghost 'as been at it again, 'as 'e?' It was the first I had ever heard of a ghost at the club, and none of the older members could elucidate, either. The picture which had thrown itself over the banister was the one which depicted that very staircase. Normally it is photographed from below, looking up at the first half landing. For his composition, Alexander had elected instead to place himself on the first landing, enabling him to include the front entrance seen from above, and the sweep upwards to the big landing, seen from below. That meant the only place he could stand as he was working was in the corner of the first half-landing, with his back to Garrick's chair. Thus the chair was the only feature missing from the finished picture. David was not at all happy to be banished from a picture of the club which bore his name, and who can blame him. He had long been in control of his own publicity. Even after death . . .?'

AT LINCOLN'S INN FIELDS THEATRE

So, having managed to give Mr Garrick if not an appearance then at least a presence, it seems fitting to end our interval with a tale of a contemporary work that amazed Georgian audiences in one of London's lost theatres.

The Lincoln's Inn Fields Theatre stood on the site now occupied by the Royal College of Surgeons. There, in 1723, John Rich, who would also later have an astounding success with *The Beggar's Opera*, presented on the 20th December a Joseph Addison play, *The Drummer,* and followed it with a new afterpiece entitled *The Necromancer or Harlequin Doctor Faustus* in which Rich played the part of Harlequin himself using the pseudonym of 'Mr Lun'.

For the finale, it was reported that 'the Doctor waves his Wand, and the Scene changes to a wood: a monstrous Dragon appears, and descends about half way down the Stage, and from each Claw drops a Daemon representing divers Grotesque figures *viz.* Harlequin, Punch, Scaramouch and Mezzetin. Four Female Spirits rise in character to each Figure, and join in an Antick Dance; As they are performing, a Clock strikes: The Doctor is seized by Spirits, and thrown into the Dragon's Mouth, which opens and shuts several times, 'till he has swallow'd the Doctor down, belching out Flames of Fire, and roaring in a horrible Manner. The Dragon rises slowly; the four Daemons that dropped from his Claws, take hold of 'em again, and rise with it; The Spirits vanish; and other Daemons rejoice in the following words: 'Now triumph Hell, and Fiends be gay, the Sorc'rer is become our Prey.'

Rich used a veritable armoury of special effects and magic tricks that would put our current pantomimes to shame. He created a frenzy for Harlequin shows and this particular afterpiece packed 'em in whenever it played. The profits from this and *The Beggar's Opera* enabled him to build a new theatre in Covent Garden on the site of what is now the Royal Opera House. He moved his company of players there in 1732 and gradually phased out performances at Lincoln's Inn Fields: the last performance of the *Necromancer* was given there on December 26th 1733. His financial and artistic success had aroused a great deal of jealousy in the business and so it was put about that at the end of the show and after all the other performers had been paid, there was left on stage one 'supernumerary demon'. This particular fiend asked for no money but instead 'flew up to the ceiling, made his way through the tiling and tore away one-fourth of the house'. An allusion to Rich himself? An envious fancy of course – that's if you don't believe in the Devil.

AN ENTRE-ACTE

Theatrical performances have been produced throughout Great Britain for far longer than London has had theatres. If the monopoly of Mystery and Morality plays which had held sway throughout the Middle Ages began to decline with the Renaissance, it disintegrated with the Reformation. John Skelton's *Magnyfycence* of 1515, while outwardly an allegory play concerning Vice and Virtue, actually satirised Cardinal Wolsey. The first English comedy, possibly *Ralph Roister Doister*, was written by Nicholas Udall, the flogging headmaster of Eton, in 1553 and one of the first tragedies, Richard Edwards' *Damon and Pythias*, dates from 1564. We must also thank Robert Dudley, Earl of Leicester, for possibly introducing Shakespeare to drama for on the 18th July, 1575, he staged a water pageant for Queen Elizabeth at Kenilworth Castle. Young Will may well have been among the crowds who saw a dramatisation of the story of *The Lady of the Lake*. In it, set against a background of fireworks, a singing mermaid - played presumably by a boy - rode on a mechanical dolphin. An amazing sight for a Tudor audience and one not forgotten by the playwright, for, some twenty years later in *A Midsummer Night's Dream* we have Oberon proclaiming:

> *My Gentle Puck, come hither, Thou rememberest*
> *Since once I sat upon a promontory,*
> *And heard a mermaid on a dolphin's back*
> *Uttering such dulcet and harmonious breath*
> *That the rude sea grew civil at her song,*
> *And certain stars shot madly from their spheres*
> *To hear the sea maid's music.*

If performances of Elizabethan and Jacobean drama were mostly confined to the palaces and playhouses of London, from the Restoration onwards proper indoor theatres began gradually to be built throughout the country. By 1805 it is estimated that some 230 playhouses were in existence and companies of actors playing regular circuits of nightly or weekly dates were well established.

But not all troupes were always able to perform on stage. The 1737 Theatre-Licensing Act effectively introduced state censorship and demanded that a person acting in or producing a play had to have a letter patent or licence from the Lord Chamberlain. The higher production costs of working in legitimate venues also meant that other venues were more viable for those performers more closely identified with their legal description of 'rogues and vagabonds'. The topical symbolisms of Hogarth's print *Strolling Actresses Dressing in a Barn* may not be obvious today but our sympathy is surely stirred by these players preparing for their brief pursuit of illusion. It is doubtful their stage will be a theatre, so let us visit an alternative location before starting with the ghosts of proper, purpose built theatres.

'Strolling Actresses dressing in a Barn' by William Hogarth:
'The Readiness is all'

THE ROYAL SEVEN STARS HOTEL, TOTNES

Here's an old coaching inn that dates from around 1660. Daniel Defoe definitely visited it in 1720 for he stayed at the 'great inn next to the bridge'. The high roofed central courtyard into which carriages would once have rumbled now contains the hotel's reception and a wide imposing staircase that leads to the equally-imposing first floor ballroom. Having explored it, I was told that it was originally known as the Assembly Rooms and sure enough, posters in the downstairs bar indicate that it was used for shows. Earlier play-bills from the 18th Century are not on view but on Saturday June 8th 1861, Harry Templeton's Original African Minstrels and Ethiopian Burlesque Opera Troupe - 'The only Ethiopian Burlesque Opera Troupe in the World'- gave a unique performance for the citizens of Totnes and Mr Neebe and his 'Talented Dramatic Company' from Exeter's Theatre Royal played a more extensive six-night run of *Our Little Emily*. But it was another poster that really fascinated me. It announced that on Tuesday February 9th 1875 '*Seances Myterieuses*' would be performed. There was no cancellation sticker so presumably the French prestidigitateur Monsieur Duprez did perform the amazing feat of turning two living birds into one. It was after the interval that this necromancer must have come into his own for he was able to summon up 'The Black Wizard of the Wilderness'. Carriages were called for a quarter to ten and I imagine they arrived not a moment too soon.

I asked the hotel receptionist whether theatrical evenings in the Ballroom still formed part of the Totnes night life but was glumly informed that 'these days you know it's all about weddings, weddings, weddings, weddings'. As her delivery made them sound more like wakes I thought I should cheer her up with a snappy show biz question.

'Where', I asked, 'did Monsieur Duprez change when he did his show in the Ballroom? Because I couldn't see any door up there to a dressing room'.

'Who? And changed into what?' she asked. 'The conjuror, Monsieur Duprez and into his costume', I explained.

She frowned and then gave me a slightly conspiratorial look. 'Well,' she said, 'there's certainly no other room up there but may I show you something?' I followed her down a passage, past the restaurant and into another room. There was a slightly old-fashioned air about it despite efforts to bring it up to date. 'This is the library,' she said. 'Part of the old building. We use it for meetings and receptions and last year there was a small wedding party booked in. They took the usual photos of the bride and groom and then one over there by the fireplace of the whole group. When they got the photos back from the print shop they showed me the group one because there was some-one in it, a stranger who no one knew.'

'Some wedding crasher?' I asked. 'Maybe, yes, perhaps,' she replied, 'but then why would you dress up like Edwin Drood?'

ACT 2
On Tour

Tours are still alive and kicking today even if some productions deserve to be dead and buried. Much planning goes into putting a show on the road. Logic should decree that shows be toured in sensible easy stages, travelling to venues neither too near nor too far apart and so avoiding an overlap of audience catchment areas. Such bookings also evenly spread the transport costs of the production and help to ensure that at each new date the cast somehow manage to arrive in time for curtain up.

Sadly, theatrical theory and practice are often incompatible bed mates. Say a show starts a weekly tour in Plymouth and the producer has a private alphabetic fetish for the letter P; then it would be sensible for him to combine business with pleasure by booking the next week no nearer nor further than Portsmouth. But, the unavailability of that date and the financial undesirability of a 'dark' week may force the poor old deviant to pack his play off all the way to Perth in a frenzy of passion. We ourselves will not go that far, but in homage to such producers we will start this tour with an appropriate P, and please prepare to be led all over the place on 'a merry road, a mazy road and such as we did tread the night we went to Birmingham by way of Beachy Head'.

Scene 1: The Adelina Patti Theatre

To find our first location, we must take the road from Swansea to Abercraf in Brecknockshire where the Brecon Road leads on upwards to Pen Y Cae and Craig y Nos Castle. It is here, within its Neo-Gothic walls that one can discover a perfect miniature jewel of an opera house, the Adelina Patti Theatre. The castle itself was built in 1843, which curiously was the year of Miss Patti's birth. It was the creation of a Captain Rice Davies Powell who unwittingly courted misfortune by having mutual ancestry with a Dutch family from Calcutta and the Cape. The Overbeeks were cursed for reasons unknown to us today, but the malediction was virulent enough to dispose of the Captain's younger son by cholera, to ensure that his wife and younger daughter predeceased him and to arrange for his eldest son to be killed in a hunting accident.

In 1876, the estate was sold for £6000 to one Morgan Morgan. Morgan Morgan had a son, also named Morgan Morgan, who shared the castle with him. They would, it is said, greet each other only by name at the breakfast table. This avoided any delay and disruption of valuable feeding time by the superfluous use of further words. Suitably if silently refreshed, they cut down a fine fir plantation and decimated the red squirrel population before selling the estate in 1878 to 'a certain Miss Patti, boyos'. If they had been a little more knowledgeable about Miss Patti they could have doubled their asking price.

Adelina Patti ranks as one of the 19th century's greatest opera singers, on a par with Jenny Lind. She was in the immortal Verdi's opinion 'a stupendous artist' and a skilled billiard player to boot. She was born in Madrid on September 19th 1843. Her parents, the Sicilian tenor Salvatore Patti and the soprano Caterina Barelli, moved to the Bronx in New York. Patti followed the family profession by becoming a coloratura soprano and made her operatic debut as Lucia in Donizetti's *Lucia de Lammermoor* at the age of sixteen at New York's Academy of Music. She first performed at Covent Garden two years later as Amina in Bellini's *La Sonnambula* and became an overnight sensation. Adopting Great Britain as her home base, she conquered Europe and then the White House where, in 1862, her rendition of 'Home Sweet Home' made even the grandeur of 1600 Pennsylvania Avenue seem humble and reduced President and Mrs Lincoln to tears. This song was to remain in her repertoire and would be pulled out whenever she deemed it necessary to moisten *les mouchoirs*.

George Bernard Shaw observed that, 'on Saturday afternoon the Albert Hall was filled by the attraction of our still adored Patti, now the most accomplished of sopranos. It always amuses me to see that vast audience from the squares and villas listening with moist eyes whilst the opulent lady from the celebrated Welsh castle fervently sings, "Oh give me my lowly thatched cottage again." The concert was a huge success; there were bouquets, raptures, effusions, kissings of children, graceful sharings of the applause with obbligato players - in short, the usual exhibition of the British bourgeoisie in the part of Bottom and the prima donna in the part of Titania'.

Adelina Patti: rich of voice and fortune

Having been born to subjects of the Kingdom of the Two Sicilies, the fair Titania was quite at home entertaining European royalty. Princes, Princesses, Grand Dukes and grander Duchesses were enthralled by the score and Patti sang command performances for Queen Victoria, King Victor Emmanuel of Italy and the Emperor Louis Napoleon, in between touring the world's opera houses and halls for opera engagements or concerts. Her fame was naturally accompanied by fortune.

Patti had an astute business sense. During the long peak of her career she was able to demand 5,000 dollars in cash in advance of a performance and had a parrot rehearsed to squawk 'Cash! Cash!' on cue at any impresario who hesitated to cough up. When asking 100,000 dollars for a twenty-date Unites States concert tour and being told that that was more than the President's salary, Patti merely retorted that the producer should ask the President to sing. For many of the great female personalities of the 19th century, money earned was money spent, but unlike others, after the experience of a costly first divorce, she managed to retain the rest of her fortune through shrewd investments and cast iron contracts. It was when she was living with the French tenor Ernesto Nicolini, who would become her second husband, that she bought Castle Craig-y-Nos from the Morgan Morgans. She lavished improvements to the estate and commissioned the Swansea architects, Bucknall and Jennings, to design a theatre inside the castle for private performances.

The proscenium house can seat an audience of up to 150 and has the capacity for a 24-piece orchestra. It has a mechanical floor that enables the raked auditorium to become a level ballroom, a fly tower, and retains original scenery, effects and a spectacular drop cloth portraying Patti as the Queen of Babylon in Rossini's Semiramide, riding a two- horse chariot.

The first night was on July 12th 1891 with a programme that, naturally, featured Patti. She sang arias from *La Traviata* and *Faust,* leaving the Swansea Opera Company to fill in the gaps and an opening address was given by none other than our tragic hero from the Adelphi, William Terriss. It would appear to have been a successful evening for the assembled company polished off some 450 bottles of champagne at the post-show buffet. Patti outlived Monsieur Nicolini and gained a title at the age of 56 through her third marriage to the 29-year-old Swedish Baron Rolf Cederstrom. She died in the Castle on September 27th 1919 and was later buried in Pere Lachaise Cemetery, Paris, so as to be close to both Nicolini and the composer she adored above all others, Gioachino Rossini.

The grieving widower Baron Cederstrom promptly sold the estate. It became a TB sanatorium for adults and children in the 1920s, then a hospital for the elderly in the 1950s, before being sold in the 1990s and converted into an hotel. It was during its period as a sanatorium that it began to acquire a haunted reputation. Tuberculosis took many a young life, but, as well as reports of children's ghosts being seen and heard in what were the top floor wards, there are claims that Patti, Nicolini and even Rossini haunt the theatre. The last named may seem slightly fanciful but it must be remembered that Rossini retired from composing to devote his life to eating. Was it then the diva or the maestro who threw a heavy saucepan from a table onto the kitchen floor as a film crew were debating why Patti had had a singular failure in the role of Carmen in 1885 and had also withdrawn from an earlier Covent Garden production in 1878?

It would seem that it was definitely Patti who materialised in 1928 before Anne Davies, a young patient at the then sanatorium. Anne loved singing and had become a member of the choir that gave recitals for parents and staff. At one concert, the girl designated to sing solo was taken ill and Anne took her place. Standing in the wings, waiting to go on and feeling very nervous, she became aware of somebody standing beside her. She turned to see a woman in a Victorian dress with her hair in a bun and a bustle at her back. The woman said, 'You will be alright' and kept telling her this, offering words of encouragement until Anne stepped forward and sang 'as she had never sung before'. She went back to thank the woman but she had disappeared.

Patti's final bow before the champagne pops

This story was told by Anne to Haydn Harris, another patient at the sanatorium and then passed on to Ann Shaw, the author of *The Children of Craig-y-Nos*, herself a patient between 1950 and 1954. It is an uncomplicated account but Haydn added that 'Anne used to belong to the same Writers Circle that I did in Swansea. She was eighty-three. We urged her to write it down as a short story, to make it a bit more dramatic. But she refused. She would say "That is how it happened. That is my story. It is true."' Her tale has the refreshing honesty of a real encounter.

If Patti is still about the Castle she has little time to relax 'off stage' as it were. The last time I looked, spectral manifestations were in high demand. Guests could enjoy not one, but five different ghost hunts on winter weekends. Their choices were 'Ladies Fright Night', 'Share the Experience', 'The All-Night Investigation', 'The Teen's Terror Night' and the seasonal 'Nightmare Before Christmas'. Bed and Breakfast was available for those bold enough to brave a night at the castle and the Haunted Bar would naturally await them; a room guaranteed to be awash with spirits – if only of the liquid kind.

Scene 2: The Grand Theatre, Swansea

It is possible that Patti also haunts the nearby Grand Theatre Swansea. After all the great diva graciously performed the grand opening ceremony on the 26th July 1897. Patti duly arrived by train from her castle to be met by the Lord Mayor, Sir Robert Morris, at the station and was escorted by him in an open horse-drawn carriage to the theatre amidst the cheers of the massed populous. Once she was safely inside, the orchestra struck up the overture *Raymonde* by Ambrose Thomas, the Choral Society sang 'Hail Bright Abode' by Wagner and she was invited to lay the memorial stone with a polished mahogany mallet. *The Era* of 31st July 1897 reported that ,'The stone declared by Madam 'Well and truly laid,' christened with the orthodox bottle of wine, she said, 'I name this building the Grand Theatre,' and the ceremony was completed'. Brisk and to the point one might think, but then she had not been asked or paid to sing.

The ghost seen at the Grand is described as a woman in a dazzling white dress associated with a strong smell of violets. It may be Patti, but in the past the spectre has also been identified as 'Jennie', a young actress. She is said to have played the theatre in 1912 before making a bad career move by attempting to try her luck in America and get there via the Titanic. However, I can find no trace of her in the ship's records. The passenger list for that ill-starred liner reveals only one identifiable actress on board. Her name was Dorothy Gibson, a silent movie star, who survived the sinking and soon afterwards made the film *Saved from the Titanic* wearing the actual salt-stained clothes she had escaped in. Whether her performance was as authentic is unknown for the footage is now sadly lost.

Now be it Patti or the elusive Jennie, journalist Antony Harris and photographer Ian Kennedy, who staked out the theatre overnight for the South Wales Evening Post in 1984, had a rather troubled vigil.

At 1.20 am, Antony reported that they heard noises in the bar - bottles clinking together - and then an hour later, the temperature suddenly dropped sharply. For half an hour they felt something was up: "I could feel the gooseflesh rising and I shivered involuntarily. Then IT happened. A woman began to cry. Softly at first and then with increasing desperation." They couldn't believe their ears. "The noise had come from the stage and it was the start of the longest three hours of my life to date. We could hear shuffling footsteps all around us... then from deep beneath us a harp played. Just one swift run of the fingers along its many strings. It was too weird to be true. Then ever so softly, music played. From whence it came we know not, but it was enough to make my flesh creep...my hair stood on end and I felt each tiny blade of stubble pushing its way through my chin." At 5.00 am they hid in one of the theatre's four boxes, "huddled together like children". There they stayed until the staff opened up the building. "We thought we had been set up and looked forward to morning when the 'ghosts' would reveal themselves and share the joke with us. They never did." A month later one of the resident electricians did apparently confess to having hidden himself in order to give them a fright, but he only owned up to Antony as being responsible for clinking the bottles. The rest is down to conjecture.

Finally, there is one more ghostly candidate in the person of an unnamed Irish wardrobe mistress who is said to have drowned while attempting to return home. But whether this was at sea or crossing the River Tawe is unspecified and so, discounting this bare-boned possibility, I believe we should come down in favour of Patti or Jennie for, if nothing else, their names when warbled with a Welsh lilt roughly rhyme with Swansea. See you now?

Scene 3: The Theatre Royal, Bristol

This leg of our tour is a doddle for it is less than sixty miles between Swansea and Bristol, now once again a county in its own right having fully regained a title historically held since 1373. The city proper has for centuries had a vibrancy and importance due to its maritime trade especially with Africa, the Caribbean and the Americas. Its port vied with those other maritime centres of London, Liverpool and Southampton and by the middle of the 18th century the merchants of Bristol had grown exceedingly rich from the profits of sugar, molasses, rum and slavery.

The Theatre Royal in King Street, designed by Thomas Patey, opened on May 30th 1766 with a performance of Sir Richard Steele's *The Conscious Lovers*, the prime 'sentimental comedy' of the age, a comedy only in that it had a happy ending, but written by this soldier, member of Parliament and journalistic founder of the Tatler as an antidote to the bawdiness of the Restoration drama. In truth, society carried on its wicked ways with gusto, but sentimentality and the high moral ground were regarded as acceptable, if watched from a theatre box.

A prologue written by David Garrick started the evening. He knew his audiences then but his words have a timeless truth about our business of acting and should be a mantra for the producers of today.

> *...That all the world's a stage, you can't deny,*
> *And what's on stage?- a shop - I'll tell you why*
> *You are the customers, the tradesmen we,*
> *And well for us, you pay, before you see.*
> *We give no trust, a ready money trade,*
> *Should you stop payment, we are bankrupts made...*

The new theatre had approximately the same dimensions as Wren's 1672 Theatre Royal Drury Lane, for Mr Patey had obtained plans of the designs from a Mr Saunders, a stage carpenter at that very theatre. The Lane was completely rebuilt in 1794 and so the Theatre Royal, now run by the Bristol Old Vic Company, can claim to be the oldest surviving Georgian theatre in Great Britain and the oldest theatre with a continuous working history. It has of course had many various exterior and internal alterations but the auditoorium is still remarkably intact even if the backstage area, essentially original, together with its Victorian stage machinery and effects, was ripped to pieces in the 1970s in order to be replaced by a new stage and fly tower, offices and technical facilities. Luckily though, the diktats of modern architecture have failed to remove the Theatre Royal's older spiritual inhabitants.

For many years it has been claimed that this great 18th century theatre is fittingly haunted by the first lady of the Georgian stage. With humble apologies to Anne, Dorothy, Elaine, Lavinia, Kitty, Peg, Perdita, and of course the late, great Mrs Bracegirdle, may I firstly give you, ladies and gentlemen, the one, the only, the Mrs Sarah Siddons.

As previously mentioned, Sarah was born on July 5th 1755 in The Shoulder of Mutton Inn in Brecon. Her parents were fittingly theatrical, her father being the actor Roger Kemble and her mother Sarah Ward, whose own father had acted with Thomas Betterton and Barton Booth. Mr Ward did not approve of his daughter marrying an actor but consoled himself by the thought that Kemble was 'none'. Sarah performed from childhood with her family, together

with her brothers John Philip and Charles Kemble, touring around the provinces and in particular the West Country. At eighteen she married the actor William Siddons, and was later talent-spotted by Tom King in *The Fair Penitent*.

On King's recommendation, David Garrick engaged her 'upon very low terms' for his Drury Lane company. She had neither an artistic nor personal success. Garrick was nearing the end of his management and Siddons believed that the reason behind his 'exaltation of poor me . . . was the mortification of Mrs Yates and Miss Younge, whose consequence and troublesome airs were, it must be confessed, enough to try his patience'. She became 'an object of spite and malevolence'.

Garrick cast her as Venus in the revival of *The Jubilee*. 'This gained me the appellation of Garrick's Venus; and the ladies who so kindly bestowed it on me, rushed before me in the last

Sarah Siddons as Lady Macbeth

scene, so that if Mr Garrick had not brought us forward with him with his own hands, my little Cupid and myself, whose appointed situations were in the very front of the stage, might have as well been in the island of Paphos at that moment'. Backstage problems were compounded by onstage terror and critical disdain.

Garrick revived his *Richard III* in 1776 and Sarah was cast as his Lady Anne. He had directed her to always stand with her back to the audience when speaking to him 'and her forgetfulness of this direction was punished by Garrick with a glance of displeasure that unnerved her powers'. The London Magazine duly noted that 'most of the other characters, particularly the female ones, were wretchedly played. Mrs Hopkins was an ungracious Queen, Mrs Johnston a frightful Duchess, and Mrs Siddons a lamentable Lady Anne'.

The season over, Sarah took an engagement in Birmingham and it was there that an official letter from the Prompter of Drury Lane arrived to tell her that her services were no longer required. It was not until 1782 that she would be invited back, but the time away was time well spent. 'Tragedies were becoming more and more fashionable. This was favourable to my cast of powers; and whilst I laboured hard, I began to earn a distinct and flattering reputation'.

The Tragic Muse To Be continued to hone her craft in Birmingham, Liverpool and York, before undertaking three seasons at Bath and Bristol, often rehearsing daily in one city while playing the other that night. Her first recorded appearance at Bristol was in Hall Hartson's play *The Countess of Salisbury* in 1778. Coincidentally it should be noted that the real Countess fittingly haunts the Tower of London for it was there that she was beheaded in 1541. Margaret Pole was the 67-year-old daughter of the Duke of Clarence, that 'false, fleeting, perjured' Clarence whom, if one believes Shakespeare, was drowned dramatically in a butt of Malmsey. Her death was witnessed and it was not a clean-cut execution, in fact it was a butchery; the old Countess, refusing to lay her head meekly on the block, tottered off in a vain attempt to escape. She lapped Tower Green with the executioner swinging his axe in hot pursuit until eventually, after some eleven jagged strokes, he managed to hew her head from her neck.

Mrs Siddons was to play over a hundred roles in these two venues, citing in her farewell curtain speech three reasons for quitting the theatre and then, on cue, bringing her three children on stage. Nonsense of course, for she had been approached by Sheridan to return to the Lane, and theatrical children have seldom got in the way of theatrical ambition. Certainly, many other actors leave the stage but their three main reasons are lack of health, wealth or talent.

The number of Mrs Siddons' performances at Bath and Bristol would at first appear to be matched by the claims of sightings of her ghost over the centuries. The stock description is of a lady in a grey silk gown coupled with the smell of lavender. Somewhat differently, the late Chili Bouchier experienced the sound of a sobbing phantom in a quick-change room, who also seems to have 'borrowed' a piece of her stage jewellery. Perhaps the sobs came from the realisation that it was paste.

Samantha Bond however told me that while at the Bristol Old Vic Theatre School and in dress rehearsal for her final student production at the theatre, she had been running down a backstage staircase to get from one wing to the other when she bumped into a lady in a silken dress. She instinctively turned to apologise to discover that there was no one there. 'Was it the ghost of Sarah Siddons? I really hope so!'

After a Royal Gala performance of *Wild Oats* by John O'Keefe on 19th November 1982, four of the cast, Carolyn Moody, Ian Price, Ian Lindsay and Roger Bisley were standing on stage in the now empty theatre. Their loyal post mortem on the exact meaning of Prince Charles' after show comments was interrupted by their mutual sighting of a figure moving across the back of the gallery and disappearing before their eyes. They could only presume that Mrs Siddons had also wanted to glimpse H.R.H. The suggestion that Sarah has observed other performances is backed up by John Symonds, the theatre's manager in the 1980s. He told me his story of watching a dire visiting company's performance and seeing that 'things were going wrong'. John stood at the back of the Side Upper Circle wondering sadly whether 'things would improve'. They did not. As the show stumbled never onwards, he heard a voice behind him saying 'Tut, tut, tut'. The words were repeated a moment later but when he turned around to agree with the criticism there was no one there. Mrs Siddons had obviously seen quite enough.

Cleaning staff have also attracted her interest. One particular cleaner would always and loudly 'sing for Sarah'. This ritual stemmed from one morning when, while working in the middle stalls close to the prompt side door to the pit, she tried to move her bucket from the top of the shallow flight of stairs. It was seemingly immovable. 'OK, Sarah', she sighed, 'I'll come back for it later'. Turning back to her work she saw the bucket suddenly tip over, spilling water all over the floor as the pit passage door moved on its own.

The clairvoyant Stephen Alexander was given permission by John Symonds to visit the theatre and try to communicate with the ghosts. Using the writing method of communication he received the following message:

'My name is Sarah Siddons. I am here to look after things because I love this theatre it was very good for me and I will make sure that everything will work out well bye for now Sarah'

This note may seem to smack of the twentieth century but I have proof of at least the genuineness of the session in a copy of the actual writing on a piece of appropriately headed paper. 'Sarah' is certainly the name by which the Bristol ghost is known but a most intriguing complication has arisen. It is now a case of two Sarahs both alike in dignity because recently, the school of thought has veered somewhat away from Sarah Siddons and towards Sarah M'Cready as being the spectre seen.

Sarah M'Cready was a formidable woman. She was faced with an equally formidable task when she took over the management of the Theatre Royal from 1834 until her death in 1853. Upholding that time-honoured theatrical tradition, she had become the leading lady, mistress and eventual wife of the old actor manager William M'Cready who was some thirty five years her senior.

When he died, he left her all his rights in his theatre ventures. She battled successfully against great odds to somehow keep the theatre going as a valid business concern catering to the changing tastes of the Bristol audiences. She tried to stem the constant deterioration of the building, 'a dingy old place, every year getting more and more gloomy' and booked an eclectic mix of turns to entice a full house, from crowd pleasers such as Signor Hervio Nano, the man-fly, to non-pleasers such as George Owen, tragedian, of whom the Bristol Mirror wrote, 'We witnessed his personation of Macbeth. Macbeth did "murder sleep", and Mr G. Owen did murder Macbeth, and that too most effectually'. In between such dross, occasional class acts such as Jenny Lind and Charles Macready would result in 'House Full' boards. Sarah was described towards the end of her tenure as 'a very eccentric and sybillitic old lady' but against all odds she kept the theatre open and never once missed paying her actors' wages. Her commitment to the Theatre Royal was obvious. On her death it was recorded that she was 'scrupulously just in all her transactions' and as the Bristol Mirror noted, 'a caterer for the amusement of the public'. It would seem churlish therefore to deny that Mrs M'Cready has every right and reason to return to check on how her theatre is faring. Indeed, according to no less a witness than Andrzej Blonski, the architect responsible for the redevelopment of the theatre in the years 2010 and 2011, she has done exactly that.

Mr Blonski told the BBC journalist Robin Markwell in July 2010 that he met Sarah as he climbed the stairs backstage one lunchtime. She was, he said, wearing a long white crinoline dress, had black hair and a pretty face. Unfortunately he had no time to ask her opinion of work in progress for when he tried to speak to her, she upped and vanished. Mr Markwell reported that 'Mr Blonski told the BBC that he has never believed in ghosts and - prior to their meeting - was not aware of her legacy at the Bristol Old Vic'.

'The thing that really got me', he said , 'was that she smiled - she was a friend and then she vanished. But then I was really very, very happy - at the moment I'm quite emotional about it because I think that if there is a ghost, it's someone who cares about this building'. The architect had apparently felt before this encounter that there was something supernatural on these same stairs and had at least, like so many other witnesses in other theatres, smelled the scent of lavender.

However Mr Maxwell also reported that 'the project manager from the team . . had a more shocking experience. Mr Blonski says that he was physically pushed. He ran away and now will not use the "haunted" staircase'. Now, knowing from experience that a leading lady never graciously gives up her position, I can only wonder whether the project manager met the other Sarah.

Mrs Siddons'
'message'

Scene 4: The Theatre Royal, Bath

O ur next date is a mere 16 miles or so away so there are no excuses for missing the half hour call other than death. Oft used no doubt at the Theatre Royal Bath because it is so singularly haunted. I am however not at all envious of the multitude of people who have had a ghostly encounter at this location, for here, I can claim to have been a bit of a ghostly experience myself.

In the spring of 1976, Sir Michael Codron was producing Alan Ayckbourn's play *Confusions,* and decided, prior to its London opening at the Apollo, to give it a nifty pre-West End tour. We were to start off at Bath and duly arrived there on a Sunday for an after lunch Get In.

Confusions is an evening of five loosely-connected one act plays and simple to stage manage with the possible exception of *Gosforth's Fete.* That play's setting is the interior of a large canvas tent which is required to collapse at the end of the piece. Easy enough in real life for anyone nimble footed and armed with a sharp knife, but our designer Alan Tagg also had to solve the problem of how it could be quickly removed from the stage floor so that the next and final play could begin. His solution was that it would be flown out immediately it had hit the deck. Simple to do in a modern theatre, but this was Bath circa 1976. Bonnie Tyler was unfortunately lost in France and those local heroes, the Wurzels, were cider drinkin' and combine harvesting away . . . whatever that entailed.

The frontage of the Theatre Royal looked older than the Roman Baths that day and its interior proved to be bucolically shambolic. The auditorium still maintained an air of faded red plush elegance but backstage was in a far more delicate condition. We tiptoed our way between large holes where floor boards had collapsed to arrive for our meeting centre stage.

There waiting was the resident stage manager, an enormous figure of a man with a delightful Bath burr. Our carpenter opened up the plans to explain what was what, but it was not long before he was countered with what was wasn't. The revolve would go down fine if the "good" joists were underneath it, but when it came to flying. . . We looked up and saw a grid that resembled the rigging of HMS Victory the morning after Trafalgar. 'It be all 'emp. It's goin' to take some boys up there'. We looked at his four-man crew. If his tonnage resembled Oliver Hardy's, they together weighed less than Stan Laurel. 'Ave to get more of 'em in tonight' he said staring at them, or rather through them, for they had a delicate transparency which I put down to a surplus of Bath's spring waters.

Our production manager was not one to spoil the ship for a ha'pence of tar. 'Double 'em up, if needs be', he declared. Deal done, hands spat on and shaken, the dock doors were prised open and the Get In began.

The enervating Bath air was alarmingly soporific and work dragged on until it was time for dinner. I went to try to freshen up in my room at the Garrick's Head, the pub next to the stage door, but the landlord's huge Alsatian had taken possession of my suitcase where I had earlier left it at the top of the stairs. He was sprawled on it, alternately snoring and snarling. It seemed sensible to let said sleeping dog lie, so I joined the others downstairs in the public bar for a Cheddar cheese platter. This was the genuine article and produced a prodigious thirst. Luckily our break was extended by an hour to allow our lighting designer to find enough live circuits to finish rigging his onstage and front of house lamps. Eventually we tottered back to try to deal with what jobs remained outstanding.

By midnight all the legs and borders were in position and we turned our attention to the hanging of the cyc - a shortened theatrical term for a back-cloth or cyclorama. The resident stage manager shouted up to the flys and seven small heads popped up and peered down at us. Our thoughts turned to panto as he bellowed 'Drop in the back wall bar'. The dwarves obeyed his command literally. When the dust settled enough to see, he called them to take this gnarled wooden bar up to working height so we could tie on the cyc. Job done, he checked our collective ties while we removed the collective Georgian splinters from our hands. Satisfied the ties would hold, he bawled 'Yous can take it out then' and the cyc rose jerkily in the air in fits and starts until some five minutes later it was more or less in position. One task was still left to do. Our carpenter tossed a selection of billy blocks into a bag, hauled some coils of rope onto each shoulder and began his ascent to the grid. We held our breath. Would the stairs take his weight? They did.

By two o'clock on Monday morning all the lines had been attached and the tent was lying on the stage and ready to be flown. 'Take it up now' ordered our production manager to the fly floor and, looking appropriately lopsided and rickety as per design, it slowly rose to reach its initial show position. Time for the final test but well past bed time for the dwarves. For on the command to 'drop it in and take it straight out', the whole tent indeed gently deflated to the deck as required for the show but only its centre next managed to rise a few feet in the air leaving its sides slumped sadly on the floor.

'What's happened?' shouted the production manager. 'Sorry' came the carpenter's reply. 'The long and the short . . .' His technical explanation was cut short and his sentence finished by the production manager . . . 'Of it is that it just doesn't bloody work.' 'No. Listen. You got it wrong. It'll work. It's only because the boys on the long and the short aren't strong enough'. 'But I am!' growled the resident. 'So', shouted the carpenter, 'You get up here and give them a hand on the long and I'll join the lads on the short'. 'Right!' cried the resident and rumbled off towards the stairs to the flys.

It took another hour for total synchronisation to kick in but as the city's clocks struck three, we watched in awe as the tent soared up and away into the grid. 'One more go?' ventured the production manager but the resident vetoed this forlorn hope. 'I must be off now. Time for moy round'. 'Round'? As the pubs were still closed, only golf sprung to mind. 'What round??' we chorused. 'Moy milk round' came the reply, and, as if from nowhere, a Benny Hill type hat popped up on his head. 'Oi'll be back at noine', he said, 'and all me boys at ten to toidy up'.

We drifted off to meet again when his last pint of pasteurised had been delivered. The Garrick's Head beckoned. Not a candle flickered as my key turned in the lock. But I had forgotten Cerberus. As the front door creaked open the growling began. I knew it was ridiculous to be frightened of a pet, even if this pet was the size of the Hound of the Baskervilles. But I doubted whether the nearby Hospital for Rheumatic Diseases could combat rabies and besides I had some very urgent paper work to do at the theatre.

Half an hour later, with the last dressing room name card in place, I crawled into the dressing room I had commandeered to be the company office. A high window overlooked the old Georgian carriage entry to the theatre. I sank between the springs of a battered armchair by the gas fire and dozed off as the skyline opposite as the rooftops began to take shape in the coming dawn.

I was dreaming a woman was screaming at me and woke to find one actually was. There in front of me was a lady in a pinafore armed with a feather duster but shaking with fear. She was pointing at me with a trembling hand. 'You're not real' she screamed, 'You're dead!'

This was a serious accusation. I sat bolt upright and, to make sure, pinched my nose. 'Sorry, lady. Not today'. 'No? You sure?' 'Yes. Quite sure.' 'Oh I really thought you was him. You look just like him and you're in his chair, just like we found him'. 'Found who?' I asked. 'The front of the pantomime horse. He sat in that chair with the gas on and then he never got up'. I leaped to my feet and smelt the air. No gas today, just a faint whiff of drains and damp and not a sniff of death. She said she'd give me a good dusting as compensation for waking me up, but breakfast at the Garrick Head seemed more appealing, even if it was probably by now inside the dog.

The pub, originally part of the Georgian theatre, has these days been reincorporated into the original building. There is still an excellent bar on the ground floor but no longer a chance of a bed for a night, or for an hour for that matter. However, on a positive note, many nervous breakdowns have been avoided since the refurbishment, for the dog was not the only thing to loiter at the top of the stairs.

I had heard that the Garrick's Head was haunted before we arrived for *Confusions,* but, because it was so close to work, laziness had overcome fear. Two others members of the stage management team were also game to give it a go, so we all duly booked in. I had been warned that the haunted bedroom was reputedly at the back of the building. All rooms were available and so, for the sake of a peaceful night, I pulled rank and booked one of the front rooms facing the street. The DSM took the other but the ASM, who was sniffy at my 'superstitious rubbish' bagged the largest of the two back doubles. At breakfast the next morning, she looked as rough as our scrambled eggs.

'Something' had woken her throughout the night. 'Something' that made her believe that she was not alone. She had at first put it down to auto suggestion, no doubt stemming from our talk of ghosts. But finally, when the blankets were actually pulled off the bed by 'something other than my nerves', she had switched on the light to try to banish the malignant presence and had lain awake for the rest of the night, cringing at the slightest creak. The landlady accepted her demand to change rooms with weary familiarity. It was, we gathered, a pretty regular request.

I returned to the Theatre Royal a few years ago and marvelled at the changes that had happened since the days of my first visit. The building now had an air of confidence and success. It had become an intentional crowd pleaser, completely different from the days of cavalier decay and peeling paint and though the auditorium was much the same, in other places it has been altered so much as to be quite divorced from its origins. Or so it would seem at first glance, for beneath the present of any old theatre always lurks the past.

The remaining Georgian architecture and Victorian additions to the theatre bear silent witness to the past but there also hangs backstage the famous

Butterfly cloth. This piece of scenery is connected with the Butterfly of Bath, a fleeting phenomenon but indeed at times a living legend which has been witnessed by hundreds of people for over seventy years, though the first set of wings - if there are indeed more than one - may well have fluttered into the original structure of the building in 1805.

The story begins in 1948 when the theatre was run by the Maddox family. Reg Maddox's panto for that year was *Little Red Riding Hood* and he decided to have a Butterfly Ballet in the forest glades in between bedroom japes with the Big Bad Wolf. The chorus girls were accordingly fitted out as

multi-coloured butterflies and to reinforce the illusion and to guarantee that no one would think them mouldy old moths, a huge cut out butterfly was designed to fly in behind them.

During the ballet's re-hearsal, a dead butterfly drifted down from the grid. It fell onto the stage and then, to everyone's shock, Reg Maddox himself, while

The Butterfly Cloth... has this summoned a host of tiny fluttering imitators?

lighting the cloth, dropped dead from a heart attack. Understandably the scene was deemed to be unlucky and promptly dropped from the show, but, at rehearsals just before the opening night, the cast and crew were greeted on stage by a live butterfly. Taking this as a sign of good luck, both ballet and cloth were swiftly reinstated and the season did huge business. Ever since then the appearance of a butterfly is regarded as a token of success. This applies especially to annual pantos, and, despite December not being the best viewing month for aspiring lepidopterists, sightings have frequently occurred.

Perhaps the most famous recorded incident happened during the opening night of *Aladdin* in 1979 starring the comedian and presenter Leslie Crowther. He was aware of the belief but throughout rehearsals not so much as a maggot crawled into view. Nervous at this absence of larvae, Leslie made his very first entrance as Washee and received a customary round of applause from the audience. The front of house follow spot was trained on him as he stood still, waiting for the round to fade; and then a tortoiseshell butterfly descended down the beam of light towards him and came to rest on his costume's lapel. Leslie was utterly convinced that Reg Maddox had returned, reincarnated. He scooped it gently up and released it carefully into the wings, telling the audience that he would explain all at the end of the show. He duly did and the butterfly indeed brought luck. The panto sold out and Crowther returned to television to compere *The Price Is Right*.

The butterfly has appeared many times and gave a Royal performance in 1982 when Princess Margaret attended the gala reopening of the theatre with *A Midsummer Night's Dream*. There is also the strange story that when the crew were clearing out an old store room during the redevelopment in 1981, they came across an old, locked box covered in dust. On prising the lid open, six tortoiseshell butterflies fluttered out and away towards the stage. Recovering from their surprise, the crew next found a photograph of Reg Maddox nestling amongst the yellowing documents and dated 1932. The box did not appear to have been opened since that year.

Today the cloth still hangs upstage in the grid, a gaudy vision. I was glad that when I last viewed it there were no defunct butterflies lying around for I was told that when the Compass Theatre Company played Bath in 1989 with *The Royal Hunt of the Sun*, its founder, Sir Anthony Quayle, was too ill to attend the opening and shortly before he died during that very week, a dead butterfly was found in the wings. However, I draw the line at the story of a fellow company manager, who, on finding another winged corpse and discovering that one of his cast was late for the half, hurried to the actor's digs only to find him really late for he had hung himself. Nonsense of course; it's actors who drive us company managers to suicide.

If the question remains as to whether any of the butterflies are truly supernatural there is no doubt that Bath has other spectres that are not remotely living. In March 2008, the actor Louise Ford was appearing at the Theatre Royal in Shared Experience's production of *War and Peace*. This was a seven hour, two-part production and fairly exhausting for even the youngest and fittest of the company. Having time to spare between battles and balls, Louise took the opportunity to have a quick nap in her dressing room. One evening she was woken up by something suddenly hitting her body. Turning the light on, she found that a metal coat hanger was lying on top of her and looking up she saw that some other empty hangers were swaying wildly on the costume rail. The dressing room door was securely locked from the inside, the

the window closed, and so she was absolutely certain that no one in the company could have been playing a trick on her.

Some ghosts are particular as to whom they appear to. In this category I would place the phantom 'flunkey' who materialises in the front of house bars, corridors and foyer. This gentleman will only manifest himself to actors. He wears, according to thespian witnesses, buckled shoes, stockings, knee breeches, and a velvet coat topped by a red wig and a tricorn hat. Bearing that in mind, I would suggest that he's no flunkey but one of your old actor laddies after a bit of company.

Like Bristol, the Theatre Royal too has a Grey Lady. Although Mrs Siddons played Bath on many occasions and Mrs M'Cready ran the theatre for a time in conjunction with Bristol, neither Grande Dame is credited with being this particular ghost. A popular theory is that she is an unnamed actress who committed suicide by hanging herself in a room in the Garrick's Head on discovering that her husband had murdered her lover. She wears, as one would expect, a grey gown which some witnesses have identified as being of the 18th century and sports a headdress that is sometimes described as being feathered, but her general appearance seems to be of a faded, misty nature. Her most distinctive feature is the smell of jasmine. Her favourite spot to materialise is in the top left hand box of the auditorium though she has been seen in the dress circle corridor. She was seen by Liza Goddard and Christopher Timothy in September 1991 when *Moment of Weakness* by Donald Churchill was playing the theatre. This was confirmed by Miss Goddard in an interview with the Shields Gazette in June 2014, but her most famous and public appearance was in 1975.

On August 23rd of that year, Dame Anna Neagle was appearing in William Douglas Home's play *The Dame of Sark*. Dame Anna had been a box office name for over forty years. Starting as one of Mr Cochrane's Young Ladies, her break came via the film musical *Goodnight Vienna* with Jack Buchanan and by the early 1950s other films such as *Spring in Park Lane* and *Odette* had made her a huge star. She could still pull them in thirty years later in the right vehicle and that night an audience of over 850 were in to watch a real-life Dame playing a dame and getting the better of the Nazis yet again.

The first act was psychically undemanding but, during the interval, one of two Canadian girls who were sitting in the stalls glanced up and saw the profile of a woman in the upper circle box who seemed to be strangely transparent. She alerted her friend and they both kept on staring at her to try to determine what was wrong. As the house lights faded for the start of the second act, the woman began to dematerialise before their eyes. As they watched this happen, the curtain rose and the stage lighting came up. Dame Anna was standing with four other members of the cast in their opening places on stage. She was astonished to see a column of whirling smoke appearing next to her. She backed away from it as it solidified and cast and audience all saw it take the shape of a grey coloured woman in a period costume. It was at this point that one of the Canadian girls screamed and fainted. As members of the audience began to climb over their seats in their panic to get away, the rest of the cast beat a hasty exit from the set, the Grey Lady drifted away towards the wings and Dame Anna was left all alone on stage as the curtain was hurriedly brought in. The indomitable Dame completed the week's run without further spectral disruptions but was never to play Bath again.

*Juliana Popjoy aka
'Lady Betty Besom'*

I have an alternative theory as to the identity of the Grey Lady, for there is someone whose fate was equally as tragic as that of the woman who committed suicide. The present Theatre Royal is an amalgamation of the 1805 building and constructions of an older date including of course the Garrick's Head which was Beau Nash's original house. Adjoining the theatre in Saw Close is yet another Georgian building, now a branch of the Italian pizza chain, Strada. This location was until quite recently a very upmarket French restaurant called Popjoy's and took its name from the house's original owner.

Juliana Popjoy was the last accredited mistress of Richard 'Beau' Nash, the man who transformed Bath from a sleepy backwater into the epicentre of 18th century fashion and society. As Master of Ceremonies the Beau had the

the Assembly House built and, once installed as arbiter of extravagant good taste, forbade all private parties and began his domination of Bath's social life. Lord Chesterfield wrote that he 'wore his gold laced clothes on the occasion, and looked so fine that, standing by chance in the middle of the dancers, he was taken by many at a distance for a gilt garland'. He banned swords and swearing, but not games of chance and it was his addiction for gambling that eventually brought Nash low.

Juliana was born just outside Warminster in Wiltshire in 1717. She was a fashionable dressmaker when she met the Beau and was nicknamed 'Lady Betty Besom' because she would ride about in public sporting a whip that resembled a twig broom stick, and a similarly shaped wig. Towards the end of his social reign the Beau's card debts forced him to move into Juliana's house. Nash had a steady turnaround of mistresses. He may have parted from her, for one account states that he lived with a Mrs Hill for the last two decades of his life. An unpleasant experience if true for 'Poor Nash had no Small Degree of Punishment in living with this termagent woman, Solomon could not describe a worse'. However other reports state that Juliana returned to Saw Close to nurse the declining Beau until his death in 1762 at the age of eighty-seven. Without doubt his death affected her deeply. She quit Bath, moving to 'a large hollow tree' near Warminster, sleeping on 'a lock of straw resolving never more to lie in a bed'. She spent the last fifteen years of her life there as a decaying, rustic hermit. Finally, in 1777, knowing that her time was about to come, she made her way back to Bath and her old house, where, one morning, her rag-bound corpse was found huddled on its front steps. I believe that her association with both buildings means that Juliana could indeed be the theatre's Grey Lady and she may certainly haunt Strada.

I breakfasted there one morning and the manager told me that a ghost of a lady in an old dress had been seen by the staff in the upstairs dining room. He had no knowledge whatsoever of the house's history but then neither did a diner in the Popjoy's days of 1975.

One evening, a gentleman from Berkshire made a reservation via his hotel but arrived a little too early for his table. To pass the time, having looked at the menu and ordered his meal, he accepted the waiter's suggestion to take an aperitif upstairs in what was then a room for pre and post dinner drinks. But a minute later, the staff heard screams and witnessed the gentleman come tearing down the stairs, out of the restaurant and away into the night.

The manager, being most anxious to find out what had happened, rang the man's hotel and the desk informed him that their guest had just checked out, vowing never to return to Bath. He had told them that when he had taken his drink upstairs the room had appeared empty but, as he was about to sit down on the sofa, he became aware that there was a woman now standing on the far side of the room, wearing what he described as an evening dress with jewellery. He smiled politely at her but she glared angrily back as if he was intruding on her privacy. Deciding to ignore her, he sat and turned to concentrate on his drink, but then suddenly realised that she had somehow crossed over the room and was now sitting beside him. He leapt to his feet in alarm for the figure next began to transform itself into an old and filthy hag covered in rags. It was at that moment that a return to Slough became an attractive proposition. Grey Lady? Juliana Popjoy? Ladies and gentlemen, I rest my case.

Scene 5: The Everyman Theatre, Cheltenham

Having now sampled the spirits, if not the waters, of Bath it would seem sensible by way of comparison to move directly on to Cheltenham, another spa town swimming in spooks. Historically, the town is famously linked with the haunting of a house named Garden Reach in Pittville Circus Road, possibly one of the most authenticated cases in the records of the Society for Psychical Research. This house was already rumoured to be haunted when, in 1882, it was rented by a certain Captain Despard to accommodate himself, his invalid wife and their six children. Rose, one of the Captain's daughters, was the first of the household to see the ghost, that of a tall lady, 'dressed in black of a soft woollen material'. But, in a short space of time, seventeen separate people, family, friends and servants, had positively witnessed her and at times had even taken her to be a living person. The ghost appeared most often between the years 1884 and 1886 but has occasionally been seen since then and into the twentieth century.

No doubt encouraged by this fine example, other unworldly apparitions have also made their appearances in Cheltenham and no more so than at the Everyman Theatre. The Everyman only came into being in 1960, but, as befitting a building in a town that was the birthplace of the great magician Maskelyne, its creation was a sleight of hand recreation involving a mere name change and a reconstruction of the front facade and foyers to bring its image into line with modern times.

The New Theatre and Opera House had originally opened on Thursday October 1st, 1891. It was a double thrill for Cheltenham. There had indeed been theatres in the town stretching back to 1782 when John Boles Watson's theatre opened in York Passage, but in this instance the architect was none other than the great Frank Matcham and the opening attraction the incomparable Mrs Lillie Langtry. The Jersey Lily arrived with her company from the Princess Theatre, London to perform the four act play *Lady Clancarty*. She had been booked for this 'special and important engagement at enormous expense.' Lillie may have lost some of that early bloom that had first attracted that ardent horticulturist Edward Prince of Wales, but their affair had made her an instant society celebrity and, on taking up acting at Oscar Wilde's suggestion, she cemented her fame with a passable stage presence. Neither the audience nor the management could have felt short changed by the grand opening for the now vertical artiste received repeated rounds of applause from her first prologue onwards and even the architect was called on stage at the end of the second act to receive an accolade.

The Opera House, as it came to be called, would play host to a wide spectrum of shows during its lifetime. The D'Oyly Carte Company were frequent visitors and following them came a succession of West End plays, operas and musical productions. Panto became an annual fixture and as the century progressed the theatre echoed the changes in popular entertainment. A cinema between 1929 and 1934, it then played host to repertory seasons, variety shows, touring companies, pier entertainments such as *Twinkle* and that dimly remembered staple of the 1940s and 50s, revue. But that veneer of sophistication as found on Shaftesbury Avenue was not quite so glossy in Gloucestershire. Here, audiences were treated to *French Follies, Bon Soir Mesdames, Hotter Than Paris* et beaucoup plus encore. Less nudity was on view in productions such as *Separate Tables* and *All My Sons* and, possibly because of this, dwindling attendances doomed the Opera House and forced its closure in 1959. It was only then of course that the good citizens of Cheltenham realised what they had lost. Funds were raised, the building saved and the Everyman came into existence with its fortnightly repertory company.

The Everyman is but one of our many theatres that have witnessed the same highs and lows of our profession and the same profusion of good or bad productions. It has played host to both a galaxy of stars and the unknown, the unnoticed and the unloved who have lived their nights in expectation or despair, on or off its stage. It is another fine example of a building positively helping the visible and audible retention of the events and memories that have occurred within its walls.

Roger Hendry started working at the Everyman in 1969 and is even now after more than fifty years the Theatre Service Engineer. He thus saw the 1983 closure which involved preserving Matcham's auditorium whilst gutting the entire backstage from the iron backwards.

Before this though, in the 1970s, during a first night's performance of *A Streetcar Named Desire,* Roger was working the counterweighted house tabs. Behind his position on stage left was a creaky old wooden staircase that led up to the dressing rooms and the makeshift crew room. Carol Evans, then stage manager, was on the book. The prompt corner was a bastard prompt - not because of any doubts to its legitimacy but because it was an exception to the rule and positioned on stage right rather than left. At the top of the show, Carol via her headset gave the cue to Roger for 'tabs out'. Roger released the brake, pulled down on the rope but nothing happened. The tabs simply refused to go up. The rope seemed to be stuck in its original position. Not knowing what to do, he put the brake on again. It was at this moment that he heard a creaking coming from the staircase behind him and Carol shouted to him over the cans, 'Say hello to John'. Roger, somewhat confused, said 'Hello John' and with that the brake suddenly released itself and 'the tabs went up on their own'. John has been identified either as a fly man who tumbled to his death down the stairs from the fly gallery, or the victim of another accident at the theatre, a labourer named James John French who, whilst cleaning the wall of the Upper Circle, 'was seen to suddenly fall. Pitching on the front rail of the Dress Circle below, he then turned a somersault and dropped on his stomach on the back of the seats in the Pit-stalls.' Either way, neither suspect was 'the Human Counterweight', a fat and jovial postman, who, with a rope tied around his middle girth, would leap regularly from the fly floor into mid-air and thus fly out heavy pieces of scenery. He must have enjoyed this work for he seems to rest in peace to this very day. Others were more restless.

On March 21st 1983, after the theatre had closed its doors for the total redevelopment of the backstage areas and shortly before the builders were scheduled to move in, Roger and four other members of the staff arrived at what was now the theatre's only point of access, the stage door. They had been detailed off to remove the safe from the catering office of the Café Bar, three floors upstairs in the front of house. The only way to get it down to street level was via an awkward spiral staircase. It was a particularly large and heavy safe and so, to ease their task, they secured it by ropes and began to lower it, hand over hand, step by step, down the stairs. At that moment, an elderly man suddenly appeared from below them on the far side of the safe. He had 'busy sideburns', was wearing an overcoat and a bowler hat and had the air of 'an undertaker'.

The stranger's arrival meant that the crew were obliged to stop lowering the ropes and take the full strain of the weight. 'What's the show tonight?' The man asked. 'There's no show tonight,' Roger replied, 'the theatre's closing'. This seemed not to register for the man kept repeating his question. Roger, beginning to lose patience, spelled it slowly out for him. 'There - are - no-more - shows' he said and added with some exasperation, 'how did you get in here, anyway?' The man stared at him and simply replied, 'I got in'.

He then raised his hat and bowed his bald head in a courtly gesture. Roger, suddenly convinced that he recognised their visitor, was about to ask his name when the man turned suddenly around and started to descend the stairs. As he disappeared from sight and to everybody's horror, one of the support ropes snapped in half. The crew's balance and grip were lost and the safe began tumbling down in the direction of the departing stranger. Everyone was convinced he would at least be trapped by the safe, probably maimed or even possibly killed, but, to their astonishment, there was no sign of him at the bottom of the stairs. He had completely disappeared. They searched the immediate area but, failing to find him, could only presume he had miraculously escaped injury and had somehow left the building.

The next day on March 22nd, the staff returned backstage for some last clearing up jobs. Carol Evans was now with them. She had been stage manager for a considerable time and like everyone else was feeling rather melancholy that the old stage with all its personal memories would soon be demolished. Over the years, at the end of each evening's show, she had got into the habit of putting a lit standard lamp on stage so that the cleaners could see their way into the auditorium in the morning. She now asked if she could do this for a final time. It was a gesture that no one would see but all agreed that it was a fitting end to an era. She set her ghost light for the last time while the others went to sign out at the stage door. However, once she had re-joined them, she asked if she could be granted one more final request.

Years before, during a rep season, an old portrait had been bought locally to be used as a dressing on one of the sets. It was a useful decoration, employed regularly on other plays, and in time it became a symbol of good luck for it seemed that whenever it was absent, shows were inclined to fail. Eventually one artistic director, refusing to believe this superstition, banned it from appearing in yet another production but the crew ensured that fortune would continue to smile by simply hanging it permanently on the back wall of the theatre.

Carol now asked everybody if she could take the portrait home with her as a final memento and Roger and the lads agreed. As they waited impatiently to get to the pub, she raced back to the stage and returned safely clutching her prize. But, as they all began to troop out of the stage door they heard a thunderous crash. Running out into the street they found that the central portion of the theatre's back wall had collapsed on itself leaving a huge hole in the structure. As they stood there in utter amazement watching the dust settle, Roger looked closely at the portrait Carol was clutching. The subject, he now realised, was none other than the bald man, the very 'undertaker' he had spoken to on the day before at the top of the stairs.

The building work began and, during the reconstruction of the fly tower, scaffolding was erected within the walls and on the stage to the height of some twenty meters and the roof was removed and tarpaulined over. One night the security guard phoned Roger at home and told him that there seemed to be intruders in the building and that he had called the police. Roger arrived and went on stage to join the officers already there. The work lights were on and pointing upwards and they all could see what appeared to be shadows running around the top of the scaffolding by the tarpaulin, accompanied by the sound of running feet. The police, believing the intruders to be children, shouted at them to come down but the shadows and noise continued. Exasperated, the officer in charge sent some police dogs and their handlers up the walk way to scare them down. However, when the dogs were three quarters of the way up, they started to howl as if in agony and fled back to the stage. More police arrived and the officers eventually reached the top to find that they were alone. No logical explanation could account for what several people had seen and heard and the incident is still classified as 'unsolved' or perhaps unresolved.

Musical memories seem also to have stayed in the fabric of the theatre. Snatches of opera have been heard in the auditorium at night when legitimate tenors are tucked up with their sopranos. In 2006, psychic researchers were conducting an investigation when a transistor radio which was being used as a prop on stage switched itself on to play *Land of Hope and Glory*, before switching itself off. This may have been at the bidding of a lady in grey whom the then General Manager, John Ridley, witnessed sitting in the stage right box in the 1960s, or a request by the tall bearded man wearing a 1940s suit and tie whom builder Walter Charnock saw in July 2011 for some full thirty seconds before that apparition vanished.

Roger Hendry and the crew experienced another unusual happening in 1987. They were on stage working on the counterweight bars which had been flown in to head height on the deck. Roger's back was to the auditorium and the others were facing it. Feeling a strange sensation, he turned around and saw a woman standing half way back in the Dress Circle. He was struck by the fact that she looked like a porcelain doll. Turning to the others he asked 'who's that woman?' 'What woman?' they all replied. Roger stared out front again to find that there was no one there now. He insisted that he had seen someone but the others were emphatic that nobody had been there. He began to get annoyed. 'I had seen something. I told them that I didn't believe in all that chain-rattling nonsense but . . . At that moment all the bars and the safety chains for the lamps started to rattle. The stage left pros arch moved onto the stage by three foot, and, as everybody fled the stage, both boxes cracked and dropped and the shield on the top of the pros arch swung out. An earthquake had struck as I spoke.' One could classify *that* as an uncanny coincidence, but my last Everyman story is a seemingly impossible occurrence that would mystify Holmes himself if the great man was still alive and not condemned to flicker before us in endless television repeats.

In 1959, a Mr Ernest Dyson was working at the theatre as a night watchman. One night, two police constables, similarly employed on the graveyard shift, dropped by the stage door for a chat and a cup of tea. While brewing up they heard footsteps coming from the direction of the fly gallery. Ernest and the two officers went to investigate but though they searched the whole backstage area they found nothing and were certain that nobody was there. They returned to their tea but then the noises started again. By now thoroughly unnerved, the constables made their excuses and bolted, leaving Ernest to face the sounds alone. Deciding that discretion was the better part of valour, he locked himself into a dressing room until the morning. At dawn he ventured out and walked on stage. An astonishing sight met his eyes. Facing him were two upright, eighteen foot high, scenery flats. Their wooden frames were no more than four inches thick, no brace nor line was in place to support them and yet one was balanced on top of the other. The flats stood still there for a moment before they swayed and came crashing down to the deck. As the saying goes, top that!

Scene 6: The Lyceum Theatre, Crewe

A train is the correct means of transport to our next date for when we alight at our destination we are not only en route to our next psychic encounter, but paying tribute to what was the most famous meeting place for touring theatre companies in the whole of Great Britain.

Crewe Station may not be the most glamorous of locations. You don't have to take my word for it, but I assure you that tens of thousands of spectral actors could testify to this plain truth. That's if they weren't so busy avoiding a veritable Fred Karno's Army of other ghosts. They're dodging officious ticket collectors, short changed landladies, dangerous debt enforcers and a host of irate husbands, wives and lovers as they scarper from platform to platform to catch the first available connection to the relative safety of their next weekly booking.

If the days of theatrical train calls are long gone and the touring companies of such actor manager knights as Forbes Robertson and Frank Benson now all but forgotten shadows, Crewe still has twelve platforms and is rated one of the busiest railway junctions in the country, linking, as it does, all points of the compass. The original purpose of The Grand Junction Railway of 1837 was to reach the four largest English cities of that time, Liverpool, Manchester, Birmingham and London. Other destinations then became attainable and by the 1890s up to a thousand trains were passing through the junction every twenty-four hours. Despite cuts, there are still some twenty-three trains to count each daylight hour if you are that way inclined. If you are not, may I instead guide you through the ticket barrier, not towards The Ghost Train but to what is billed as 'The Only Edwardian Theatre in Cheshire'.

First, we must enter Crewe proper, and walk down the Nantwich Road and right into Vernon Way. It's a lively place and comparatively new. After all, in 1831 before the railways came there were only 70 inhabitants. Nowadays there are over 67,000, though Crewe's most famous son is still the late Jimmy MacDonald, the voice of Mickey Mouse for thirty years. Note too the churches, seventeen in all, which may account for the 2008 closure of 'Lunacy', a shop selling Pagan and Wiccan products, forced out of business by Bible-throwing protestors. Crewe derives indeed from a Welsh word, 'cryw,' which means a creel which is of course a large wicker fish basket and here we are at last in Heath Street, outside the Lyceum.

A theatre has been on this site since 1881 when a professional actor from Manchester, a Mr Henry Taylor, encouraged by the large audiences who had turned up to see the town hall productions he had staged for the Crewe Amateur Musicals Society, decided to open a full- time venue. The site chosen in Heath Street was an old Roman Catholic Chapel which had been built for the Irish railway workers and to this day the chapel's original well is still visible below the current stage. The first makeshift alterations gave way to a complete rebuild in 1887 when a 1500 seater, The New Lyceum, opened. Charlie Chaplin played there in *Sherlock Holmes* as did Stan Laurel and Wee Georgie Wood in *Sleeping Beauty*. Wood was sometimes billed as the world's smallest comedian but, at four foot, nine inches, he was three inches taller than Little Tich. But sadly, the theatre's success was short lived. For during the pantomime of 1910, Dick Whittington or his Cat may have left a cigarette burning in their dressing room and the New Lyceum became the Late.

Undeterred, the then owner Mr Dudley Bennett decided to rebuild it again and from the ashes of disaster rose the New Theatre to open in 1911, 'sumptuously fitted with Wilton carpets and tip up seats'. As Edward V11 died in 1910 purists may question its present claim to be Edwardian but the rotund sweep of the auditorium's dress circle puts one definitely in mind of that monarch's stomach and there is a saucy rotundity to the plaster goddesses on the front of the circle boxes that Bertie would have approved of. The Lyceum remains to this day a busy venue and a vital asset to the town. It has hosted some rather unique acts such as Syncopating Stanley, who played the piano for one hundred and thirty-four hours in 1958 and Saxon Brown, the world's strongest man who pulled a bus with his teeth.

Another value-for-money headliner was the magician Chung Ling Soo, actually the American William Ellsworth Robinson and the bitter rival of Ching Ling Soo, an authentic Chinese magician. Chung's Crewe date passed successfully, even if the audience were confused as to who was playing the bill, for his teeth caught the bullet when it was fired from a gun at the climax of his act. Tragically they failed to do so at the Wood Green Empire in 1918. The bullet missed his ivories and hit him fatally in the chest and for first time an audience heard him speak in English: 'Oh my God, something's happened. Lower the curtain'. It was almost curtains too when the circus came to Crewe for one Tommy Ellis, a trainee lion tamer, for he was mauled in front of the Lyceum audience by a lion called Satan. I cannot discover if anyone has actually died on stage but taking into account the sheer number and variety of shows from burlesque to opera, music hall to revues, musicals, rep seasons, pantos and tours it is small wonder that Crewe's theatre can claim the odd ghost, indeed five, at the last count.

The first two are both formless: a poltergeist, known as Charlie to the staff, who hides props and equipment left on stage, and what I would call the 'Smoking Man'. This spirit no doubt really disturbs new duty fire officers, for he is, for most people, just a strong stench of smoke, smelt both backstage and in the lighting box at the back of the auditorium. We will have to take as an identification the report of a psychic who described the presence of a man in a long cloak or evening cape, holding a lit cigarette in a cigarette holder and exuding an air of menace. It would be interesting to know whether the smoke smells of Balkan Sobranie, or the more pungent tobacco of a Belomorkanal papirosa.

More visible are the ghosts of a small girl and of a dancer clothed in white. The child has been seen both backstage and in the rehearsal room. She wears an old fashioned dress and is inclined to appear when other rival children are on site. The dancer has often been seen over the years. In October 2010, a member of the theatre staff spotted her going through her paces in the dress circle. She is described as wearing period clothes. Local opinion is that she is the spectre of a ballerina who committed suicide in a dressing room and when she fades from view she leaves behind, as curiously do so many ghosts, the scent of lavender. Lastly there is the monk, described as a cowled figure whose face is always hidden beneath his hood. He has been seen hovering about the stalls and backstage. Some credit the original Catholic chapel as the reason for his presence in the theatre but I believe that that structure is too recent and there is the possibility that his appearance may to do with nearby Combermere Abbey.

The present stately home has its own celebrated ghost, the second Lord Combermere who was photographed sitting in a chair on the hour of his funeral in 1891, but the Lyceum connection is with the Cistercian monastery which was sited there from 1133 until its dissolution in 1538. In the last two centuries of its existence it acquired a very unsavoury reputation. Disputes and feuds were the order of the day; monks were accused of forgery and theft and one abbot was even killed by a labourer with a bow and arrow. In 1520, a monk was murdered by a servant of Abbot Christopher Walley who was then accused of covering up the murder and sheltering the murderer. The Abbey at that time held some 22,000 acres in Cheshire and so it is not, perhaps, inconceivable that the Lyceum's monk haunts the spot where he fell.

Lastly, as evidence that sightings of ghosts are taken seriously at the Lyceum, I can report of an attempt made in 1969 to exorcise the spirits from the theatre. If it succeeded, its success was temporary, for, during a performance in the middle of the 1970s, the cast on stage spotted not only the dancer in one of the boxes but also her companion, a gentleman who appeared to be flagrantly disregarding the theatre's no smoking rule. . .

The platform at Crewe railway station is, of course, not as empty as it looks

Scene 7: The Opera House, Jersey

M ost tours go off the rails at times and ours is no exception. For there are boats and planes instead to get us to our next engagement. The island of Jersey has a splendid history and its inhabitants are of an independent creative nature and not only in the world of finance. *Les Crapauds* as they are known, which translates into English as 'Toads', have their own fine Opera House and of course mount enthusiastic productions of *The Wind in the Willows*.

The present Opera House, built to replace the previous theatre destroyed by fire in 1899, was designed by Adolphus Curry and was opened on July 9th 1900 by the island's most celebrated daughter, Lillie Langtry. She came from the Theatre Royal Haymarket with her production of *The Degenerates* by one Sydney Grundy, a prolific if sadly now forgotten playwright and librettist whose work includes *Popsy Wopsy, Frocks and Frills* and *Slaves of the Ring*. At the end of the show 'The Jersey Lily' stepped forward to the footlights to address the audience. 'I thank you most heartily for the welcome you have given me', she said. 'I am not surprised at it, for Jersey people are very clannish. We do cling. I promised after your old theatre was burnt down to open your new one, and I have performed my promise though it is in the midst of my holidays. As a matter of fact, I should have been jealous had anyone else opened it, for it seemed to me my right to do so'. She concluded her address with a quote in Jersey patois, Jerrias, in which she was fluent. Russell Labey, the director playwright and Deputy of St Helier in the Assembly of the States of Jersey, holds that this curtain speech finally cemented her reputation as a legitimate actress because of her recorded grievance at not getting the holiday allocation she wanted.

Emilie Charlotte Le Breton was born to a famously philandering Dean of Jersey, the Reverend William Corbet Le Breton and his wife, Emelie, on October 13th 1853. Her marriage to Edward Langtry at the age of twenty enabled her to escape from the island to London where international fame awaited. John Everett Millais, another Crapaud, painted her, as did Burne Jones. Her beauty and wit attracted hosts of admirers before she began her three years' stint as the Prince of Wales' mistress. As royal passions drooped, financial problems arose. Mr Langtry had taken to drink and was veering towards inevitable bankruptcy - he would eventually die in the Asylum for the Insane at Chester in 1897 - and so she reinvented herself and became an

THE OPERA HOUSE, JERSEY 149

instantly successful actress. She hired a stage coach to teach her the craft and boarded a stagecoach to tour America. 'She is so pretty she takes away a man's breath', declared Theodore Roosevelt. Seasons followed in London. She played Rosalind, Kate Hardcastle and Cleopatra and, no matter what the critics wrote, Lillie was big box office. 'My agent tells me I am drawing the largest salary ever paid in the halls of England. Wonderful, isn't it? For a quiet rural gardener like myself', she wrote. The time, though, eventually came to hang up her secateurs and she retired to spend the last decade of her life in Monaco before passing away in the early hours of February 12th 1929. She made her final return to Jersey on February 22nd, to be buried in St Saviour's churchyard next to the rectory where she had been born. But it is claimed that she remains above the ground at the Opera House where the resident ghost is referred to and addressed as Lillie.

My friend Russell cut 'his theatrical molars' as he puts it, as a boy actor with the Jersey Green Room Club at the Opera House. This organisation has been providing the islanders with theatrical fol-de-rols since 1909. It especially flourished during the Nazi occupation, keeping morale up with shows that included daring subversive references. *The Paladins*, a locally written romantic operetta, contained the stirring anthem 'Faithful and Free'. A cast member recalled years later that 'the whole audience joined in with us, to the chagrin of the German officers in the auditorium; it's a wonder we were all not shot.' Another production that gave great offence to the Germans was *The Merchant of Venice* for each night the audience saved all their applause for Shylock.

After the Liberation, the club continued its annual pantomimes and Easter musicals but by the time Russell joined in the late 1980s membership had dwindled. He told me, 'Members of the Green Room Club are well used to hearing the sound of empty seats tipping up and not always during perform-ances, no, I'm talking about when the house is empty during get ins or fit ups. At the age of twenty I directed *Mame*. Late on Good Friday one devoted actor and I were alone in the whole of the building, painting the stage in readiness for the opening night on Easter Saturday. Our travails were accompanied by the sound of tipping seats, mostly from the upper circle where the ghost was said to reside. "Good evening, Lillie" we said, as tradition dictates and the tipping stopped. These seats had survived the German occupation along with my family, thank God. They were sturdy but beautifully counterbalanced, and so were the seats. It was impossible for them to be anything other than closed

MRS LANGTRY   *PHOTO LAFAYETTE*

Lillie Langtry: saviour of a falling flyman?

if vacant and yet the infamous tipping has been heard by many. There have been sightings too in the auditorium of a lady in Edwardian dress which is perhaps why she was christened 'Lillie' but no one knows by whom.'

Alan Wareham, who was stage manager at the Opera House remembered in 1991 when 'five or six of us were rehearsing a Care Bear Show on stage one morning in summer. We were talking generally about the production when someone turned round because they thought they saw someone in the auditorium. We immediately thought it was an intruder as the theatre had trouble with kids. We went and looked around but couldn't find anybody. We returned to the stage and carried on with what we were doing and then the choreographer just stopped and told us all to look around. Up in the gallery we saw a woman walking slowly in a straight line from one exit door to another. She had short black hair and was wearing a white blouse and a red tunic. We thought at first it was one of our usherettes but then realised our usherettes wore blue tunics. We shouted up at her to stop but she didn't. She opened one of the doors and went through it. So we split up into two teams to block the two exits of that staircase from the gallery. We all met up without meeting her halfway up the staircase on the (auditorium) level where there were two boxes. We heard the door shut in the box furthest away. There was no way it could have been the wind as it was a spring door. All of us pounced into that box but nobody was there. As we looked across at the opposite box its door seemed to shut and that confirmed my belief in ghosts'.

Peter Pearce, a local jeweller, is not a man prone to exaggeration or fantasy. Indeed in the 1970s he was a prominent member of the St Helier Honorary Police. Peter also acted as flyman for many productions. One evening, while working on the top level fly floor, he lost his balance and started to fall to a certain death when an unseen hand reached out and pushed him onto the lower level directly below. Both floors were of equal projection so there was no ledge below to have somehow stopped his fall. The only explanation is the benevolence of 'Lillie'.

The States of Jersey, the Island's government, acquired the Opera House and closed it in August 1998 for a two-year, £7million refit, including the installation of new seats. The newly-restored theatre opened for business on July 9th 2000, exactly 100 years to the day that Lillie Langtry had stepped on stage to open the new Opera House. 'From that day on' confides Russell, 'the ghost has never again been seen or heard'.

Scene 8: The Wolverhampton Grand Theatre

O ur tour now takes us back to the mainland close to England's meridian where a great city venue has managed to survive redevelopment through the determination of its citizens to keep the flag of culture flying, even if that *drapeau* has more holes in it these days than a Swiss cheese. The Middlelands can take it. Take Wolverhampton for example. Labelled by the Lonely Planet guide in 2009 as the fifth worst city on the planet, the Wulfrunians took it on the collective chin, carried on regardless and then stuck a collective finger up at their rival citizens of Westminster by voting overwhelmingly for Brexit. Narrow-minded anachronisms are anathema to them. After all, this is the city where the first set of automatic traffic lights in England was installed and, though they brought assorted automobiles and animals to a standstill in 1927, the city has embraced the adventure of modernity ever since. The splendid Grand is linked to a continuous tradition of Wulfrunian theatre appreciation ever since the 1750s when plays were performed in the town hall. In 1844, the Theatre Royal opened on the corner of Garrick Street, named after neighbouring Lichfield's second most famous son. This has now become the Central Library, for in 1894 the new Grand opened, splendidly designed by Charles J. Phipps and able then to seat 2,151 patrons. It has attracted audiences ever since with a mix of touring companies, variety and weekly rep in the 1930s to 50s. From Irving onwards, stars have played the Grand. Marlene Dietrich even sang there and sometimes in tune and, in November 1918, Lloyd George used its stage to declaim his rousing 'Building a Land fit for Heroes' speech.

The Grand is yet another theatre not haunted by the ghost of Charlie Chaplin, though he worked there in 1902 as company call boy and later on tour in *Sherlock Holmes* playing Billie, Doctor Watson's page boy. But by way of compensation it does have two apparitions in the front of house, for an unknown lady has been seen in the box on the right hand side of the auditorium and then there is also a certain Mr Percy Purdey. Mr Purdey was the theatre manager in the 1920s and a thirsty one at that, for he still haunts the circle bar. He can be heard pouring himself drinks and occasionally causes both glasses and light bulbs to smash - no doubt after a few stiff ones. Backstage is also in on the act for it has a lingering and, at times, helpful presence. Alexandra McQuillen-Wright, the director and choreographer, was looking after the tour of *Midnight Tango* when it reached the Grand in 2012. 'I had dressing room number 5 with Teddy Kempner next door in 4 and Tony Renshaw on the other side in 6. All of these dressing rooms have wall mounted TVs which have show relay as well as live TV. One day before the show I asked Teddy what channel I needed in order to get something other than the show relay. I think he must have told me, but my remote didn't seem to be working. I went in next door to Tony to see if his TV was okay, which it was. I told him my predicament but said I'd deal with it later. By this time it was show time and I gave up and went to watch the first half. When I came back the TV was on and tuned to BBC1. I immediately thought "Oh lovely Teddy, he's helped me out and fixed the TV for me." So I went in to him to say thanks. He looked at me and said he'd never been in my room. So I went to Tony because it was now obvious that it was him who had fixed it. Again, I received a rather blank uncomprehending look and an assurance that he hadn't been in my room. I thought it a bit strange but was happy to look at a bit of telly in the interval. During Act Two I stayed backstage and caught up with Tricia Deighton and told her about my experience. She said "How funny, I've felt that someone has been following me." I mentioned it also to Caroline Hannam our wardrobe mistress and to Vincent Simone who said that only that day he thought that someone was in his dressing room toilet. There was the sound of running water but when he checked there was no one there'. At the end of the show Alexandra mentioned what had happened as she gave her dressing room key back to the stage door. She was told very clearly and matter of factly 'Oh yes, dressing room 5? That often happens, it's the ghost'. Alexandra recalls being, if not stirred, more than a little shaken at the time.

* * * * *

Our phantom bookers, as you may well have realised, have followed no logical route on this tour. We now must move to another, completely contrasting theatre, tiny in comparison with the Grand. Indeed, its only connection is that the city in which it is located shares its beginning letter with Wolverhampton.

Scene 9: The Theatre Royal, Winchester

Theatres Royal come in all sizes. The Theatre Act of 1843 had helped loose the stringent past regulations regarding patronage and nomenclature and by the middle of that century venues with monarchical longings began to spring up with a fecundity to rival their monarch's. After all, the insertion of the prefix Royal to the theatre in Humber Street, Hull could only but add a whiff of something and I'm not talking kippers.

Winchester has indeed a really ancient royal connection for it was the Saxon capital of King Alfred and intermittently witnessed the presence of kings and queens throughout its medieval history. More recently, Charles II was of a mind to completely relocate there from London and in 1683 commissioned Christopher Wren to design and build a palace to rival Versailles on the site of the old castle. Work commenced but the King died when only the outer shell of the central building had been finished. There was indeed a Palace of Winchester but it belonged to the eponymous bishops and its remains are on the South Bank of London in Southwark, located next to those other vanished freehold sources of clerical income, brothels, bars and bear gardens. There is a theatricality too about King Arthur's Round Table which hangs in the Great Hall of Winchester Castle for it is a magnificent medieval fake dating from the 13th century. Next door to it is another impressive building used by a theatrically inclined institution, Winchester Crown Court. Lawyers in Winchester today are indeed legion, though none have yet publically surpassed the infamy of Lord Chief Justice George Jeffreys, whose Bloody Assizes started their circuit in Winchester's Great Hall.

The Theatre Royal Winchester is a very humble building by comparison, positioned on the corner of Jewry and Tower Streets. It stands on the site of the old Market Hotel which opened in 1850 next door to the cattle market and the Corn Exchange. In 1912, two brothers, John and James Simpkins, bought the hotel with the aim of converting it into a theatre. They were also early pioneers of the silver screen and were running cine variety shows in the incongruous setting of the 15th century banqueting hall of St John's House on the Broadway.

Their new theatre opened on August 24th 1914 just in time for the start of the Great War. The huge wave of patriotism caused several of the staff, including one of the follow spot operators or, as they were known in those days, 'lime boys', to duly sign up and march away to join Kitchener's New Armies and onwards to the Somme. To help boost morale at home the two Simpkins mounted a show entitled *Soldiers of the King*. One of the actresses, glancing into the wings, saw the bloody apparition of a Tommy and promptly fainted. When she came to she described the soldier in detail. James Simpkins had had a portrait photograph taken of each of his staff who had volunteered and the actress identified the 'lime boy' as being the ghost. It was then discovered that the boy's mother had received a War office telegram the day before notifying her of her son's death.

During these early years as a variety-cum-newsreel house, the Royal played host to a stream of names including Chesney Allen, Gracie Fields and Florrie Forde who knocked them out nightly with her rendition of 'Down at the Old Bull and Bush'. Time came, however, when audiences for a live show began to never get back on their feet and the brothers Simpkins decided to concentrate again on the silver screen.

They eventually sold up the Royal to County Cinemas who in turn sold it on to the Odeon Theatres Ltd but, despite this change of ownership, one of the brothers would never leave the building. In 1914, when the painters and plasterers moved in to finish the interior of the new auditorium, they decorated the top of the proscenium arch with a scroll. When finished it had two engraved initials which simply read 'JS'. These obviously represented both of the Simpkins but it caused an almighty sibling spat. John was furious with this curtailment and pedantically demanded that it should be altered to 'J & JS'. James promised to attend to the matter but owing either to a lack of long ladders or to a short memory the missing initial was still missing when John dropped dead.

The Theatre Royal itself bounced back to life in 1979 with a first professional production of *Who Killed Agatha Christie?* closely followed by *Wot! No Pyjamas?* The former starred Richard Todd, who complained about conditions backstage and the latter, Fiona Richmond, who didn't, but who may have made John Simpkins rise again. In any event the upright, stern figure of his ghost has been seen regularly by staff. He comes out of the wall on the left-hand side of the auditorium to cross the circle and peer angrily at the scroll from the middle of the right-hand boxes before disappearing through the right-hand wall. He has also been seen when audiences have been entering the circle, standing by Box 4. Perhaps he is looking at the dancer, another, but unknown spirit who has been seen occasionally going through her paces on stage. But John Simpkins does not only appear at show time.

In the 1970s a couple were employed as cleaners and the husband would daily say an unconcerned good morning to a 'gentleman' he would meet in the corridors until his wife heard him and managed to convince him that they, and they alone, were the only living people in the building.

The theatre is now a thriving concern and perhaps this has also attracted other visitors from the far side. Footsteps, voices and music are regularly heard and an attempted séance on stage in 2005 by a group of mediums from the UK Society of Paranormal Investigation was interrupted when one of them was thrown off their chair. The presence of John Simpkins' wife Annabel was detected at another investigation on October 31st 2006, so perhaps it would be fitting to conclude that Michael Bentine - the fourth Goon and the creator of *The Bumblies, Potty Time* and *It's a Square World*, was performing his one man show, when he also observed 'a Victorian lady'. Why believe a myopic comedian? But then why not believe a past President of the Association for the Scientific Study of Anomalous Phenomena?

Touring companies, adept at taking the rough with the smooth, seldom moan if the next date is on their itinerary, for next is a city which combines all conceivable manner of contrasts and tastes.

Scene 10: The Theatre Royal, Brighton

Brighton conjures up different images for different people. Many memories are still drenched in nostalgia, influenced by *One Man, Two Guvnors*, the West Pier and Max Miller. But the first's a fiction, the second's mostly underwater and the third's dead. If it's your hometown now, Peter James' gritty crime novels may paint a more accurate picture of everyday urban neuralgia. Brighton has always been London by the Sea, bracing but corrosive, partly because the sea air batters people's faces and rots the buildings. All the paint in all the world can't cure the peeling stuccos but there's no denying the damp jauntiness that comes with that breeze. It is well epitomised by Rex Whistler's 1944 allegory, originally painted on the wallpaper of his billet at 39 Preston Park entitled 'H.R.H. The Prince Regent Awakening the Spirit of Brighton.'

It is a misconception that theatres only followed in the wake of 'Prinny's first arrival in 1783. Mr Johnson, who ran theatres in Salisbury, Chichester and Portsmouth, opened for annual business in a barn on the Old Steine in 1764 and the first proper theatre was erected in North Street in 1774. The Theatre Royal in New Street was built to plans approved by the Prince and fittingly opened on 6th June 1807 with Charles Kemble playing the Prince in *Hamlet*. With fashionable society flocking to what would for a few years become a briny rival to Bath, the then idols of the London stage - Mrs Siddons and Mrs Jordan, Braham, Grimaldi and Kean - all played the theatre and this star trend has continued throughout its chequered history. With the ascent of William IV, Brighton and the theatre began to lose its noble clientele. Next, royalty deserted altogether, for young Queen Victoria, disliking the lack of privacy and deploring the Royal Pavilion's racy past, sold the palace to the town in 1850.

Brighton was no longer fashionable, middle-class audiences were, as now, hard to please and the theatre changed hands several times. But in 1866 it was bought by Henry John Nye Chart who engaged the great theatre architect Charles James Phipps to redesign and enlarge the building. It was Henry's widow, Mrs Ellen Elizabeth Nye Chart who, from 1876, really turned around the theatre's fortunes. She knew her audience and had the knack of picking both the right touring show to entertain and the right star to admire, be it Shakespeare, Gilbert and Sullivan, Henry Irving or Lillie Langtry.

She started the tradition of an annual pantomime and invented what became known as the Thursday 'flying matinee'. This involved neither wires nor harnesses. Mrs Nye Chart would simply book a London production for the afternoon, and train down the cast and scenery in the morning. Curtain up would be at 2.00 pm, curtain down by 4.45pm and by 5.35pm the show would be back on the train to Victoria so that by 8.00 pm, the cast could be standing by for the start of their evening West End performance. Unrepeatable these days. It would all end in tears somewhere outside Clapham Junction.

Ellen Nye Chart: still keeping a spectral eye on her beloved theatre?

Mrs Nye Chart's reign lasted until her sudden death in 1892. She had turned her theatre into a respectable, respected institution and given it a national reputation. She was furthermore admired for her generosity for, every year, she would invite the staff and inmates of the Brighton Workhouse to a free matinee panto performance. A poignant foyer testimonial reads 'Many of us will, on the reoccurrence of your invitation, be in the world of shadows, but when we meet at the last great transformation scene, the things which you have done for the poor and friendless will be written in letters of gold above your head'. That very final walk down is still to come but I am glad to say that Nye Chart has been known to leave the world of shadows and return to inspect her theatre. She is described, of course, as the Lady in Grey and has been seen by several actors and staff including the late Danny La Rue. She has been known to appear in the back of the Grand Circle examining the auditorium and tipping the seats up and down. She has also been caught sitting in the Royal box, most recently during a performance of *The Twits*. The lad who saw her was so insistent in his belief that his father, to disprove his story, phoned the box office. He was disappointed, for they confirmed that the box had been unsold, locked and therefore empty for that show. A small girl child has been seen backstage who runs away giggling when challenged and there is a report of an old lady appearing from a ground floor dressing room in the corridor by the stage door during a performance of *My Fair Lady*.

The old stage crew also used to talk of seeing 'Myrtle of the Circle' though this again could be Mrs Nye Chart.

Another ghost, seen around the foyer and by the Colonnades is that of Bill Tupper who worked at the theatre from 1920. He was the front of house commissionaire for the last twenty years of his employment. Bill had a stentorian voice which he used to great effect when summoning taxis or making sure latecomers didn't hold the curtain. He may be silent now but his presence is still around.

There is a further gentleman who haunts backstage. Jonathan Coy recalls that 'I was standing in the stage right wing waiting to make my first entrance as Dick Dudgeon in *The Devil's Disciple*. Perhaps it was the character's satanic tendencies that gave offence, but I heard a deep male voice from above and behind me. I turned to look, and was thus late for my entrance! And this was the days when they still had a call-boy running around backstage so it was certainly not the distant rumblings of a tannoy'.

If you should catch the faint sound of a piano coming from the covered pit, it could be emanating through the ghostly fingers of Miss Hero de Rance who would play for incoming houses in the 1960s. Hero was a great character, an accomplished composer of songs such as *You're Mine* and incidental music for plays, one of which, B*ats in the Belfry* at the Ambassadors in 1936, featured a young Vivien Leigh. Hero had been born in 1900 but soldiered on to a great age fortified by the occasional cocktail. She was playing pre-show at the Savoy Theatre in the 1970s and was furious one night when there was no applause at the end of her repertoire. The management was summoned for an explanation but could only suggest that next time she should try playing with the lid open.

My own experience in Brighton was with her successor Hazel Dorling. Wearing a smart evening frock, she would appear at my elbow on the half before the first night of each show to ask, in a manner reminiscent of Olivier as Dr Christian Szell in *Marathon Man*, 'Is it Comedy? Is it Drama?' I would set her right each time but the music of course would always sound the same.

Lastly it is claimed that Sarah Bernhardt also haunts the offstage areas, in particular the passage from the prompt corner to New Road, and that her aggressive phantom has pushed people forcefully out of the way. The reason for this may well be because of an injury.

Sarah played the Theatre Royal four times, and on her first visit in June 1895 performed Victorien Sardou's *La Tosca*. Her right knee had already been damaged in 1887 by a fall on board ship while returning from America, and it is said that she injured it again in Brighton by throwing herself too violently into the part at that very moment when Tosca jumps off the ramparts of the Castel Sant'Angelo. It was a role and fall that often featured in her repertoire and it is documented that she missed the mattress completely at the Teatro Lirico in Rio de Janiero in 1905. Her knee became so damaged that the artist Georges Clairin reported to her doctor that 'she cannot walk as far as the post box'. In 1914, and by now an acknowledged National Treasure, Sarah was ordered to Bordeaux by Clemenceau in order to avoid German capture. There, encouraging her surgeon with a bravura humming of the opening bars of *La Marseillaise*, she had her leg amputated above the knee to avoid the lesser evil of death by gangrene. In 2009 the severed limb was found in a Bordeaux University storeroom pickled in formaldehyde. There was great excitement coupled with firm statements from the University that it had not been lost but merely 'mislaid'. And then the awful truth dawned. This leg was the wrong leg. It was a left leg and Sarah's missing leg was indubitably the opposite. So, be tolerant. Perhaps that is what she is looking for as she barges so rudely past one backstage.

Does Sarah Bernhadt still elbow her way to the stage?

Now let's ditch our buckets and spades and man up a bit. for we have been wafted by the soft winds of England for far too long and our tour needs a bracing pick me up. It's time to gird our dirks, air our knees, don our sporrans and, like Brigadoon, make a singular appearance north of the Border.

Scene 11: The Royal Lyceum Theatre, Edinburgh

If all reports are taken at face value, a complete list of the Northern Kingdom's ghosts would fill many a volume. The Scots have always had a connection, even an affiliation, with the afterlife which may account for why, over the years, so many have descended into England.

In past centuries, some of those who stayed behind also fervently embraced the dark side. Few stories are as devilish as that of the Wizard Major Weir, and the covens of Scotland clearly led the way in the Satanic League table of Sorcery. Over 1,500 Scottish witches were executed between 1563 and 1735. They easily trounced their English counterparts' score and, if that number were detected, who can with any accuracy calculate how many more remained to cast their foul spells in the shadows of the gloaming?

But this is not to imply that Scottish theatre ghosts are by any stretch of the imagination secret, black and midnight hags. After all, the vast majority of stage hauntings have only been recorded in the past century for, though plays have been performed in Scotland since the Middle Ages, theatre buildings themselves are relatively newer in comparison with their English counterparts. John Knox and the Scottish Reformation can take a major share of the blame for this. Presbyterianism frowned strictly on such louche entertainment and dictated taste and public conduct until the beginning of the Age of Enlightenment. Even then actors were denounced as 'the excrement and refuse of all mankind' and in 1739 a performance of *Macbeth* was banned by the Presbytery. It was not until 1747 that Scotland's first purpose-built venue was opened in Edinburgh. This was the Canongate Concert Hall which in 1767 became, after obtaining its Royal Charter, the Theatre Royal. Following Edinburgh's lead, Scotland began wholeheartedly to embrace the dramatic art; theatres followed in Glasgow, Aberdeen and Dumfries and then throughout the country, and though many of these early 19th century buildings would burn down, the blame lay firmly with falling candles and faulty gas lighting rather than with human arson or divine indignation.

The Royal Lyceum was built in 1883 for the actor managers John Howard and Frederick Wyndham who would later found their eponymous theatrical empire. It was named after the Lyceum in London and fittingly the stars of the very first performance on September 12th were none other than Henry Irving and Ellen Terry in *Much Ado About Nothing*.

The Lyceum has thrived ever since, witness to a host of plays and operas but it would seem that the building may retain some visual memories of its first leading lady. Before becoming Director of the National Theatre, Richard Eyre was the Lyceum's Associate Director between 1967 and 1972. The scheduling was intense. 'During most of that time', he told me in 2015, 'we used to do shows for three and a half weeks. We would open on a Tuesday and then start rehearsing the next one on a Wednesday and rehearse for three and a half weeks. I was doing the Scottish Play and in those days we always worked Sunday nights. This was because the get out would start on Saturday night. You'd begin the get in overnight Sunday, work all day and then you'd be lighting on Sunday night for a tech dress rehearsal, if you were lucky, on Monday night, but, generally on Tuesday afternoon. Then you'd do a performance on Tuesday night and the press would come in on the Wednesday. And so what it meant was that - we were all very young at the time - you habituated to working through the night, which does very, very odd things to you when you get very tired. It must have been a coffee break at around two on the Monday morning and I was alone on the stage. I looked up to the back of the circle - and you could walk round the back of the

Ellen Terry: does this leading lady still put in an appearance?

circle, there was a waist high wooden partition which you could lean on to watch the show which was lovely, and a feature of a lot of those Victorian theatres - and there was a figure crossing at the back of the circle, a figure in white and it was a woman dressed, I would say, in late Victorian clothes - now I may of course be just fabricating that because of my knowledge that the theatre dated from around about 1885 - and this figure just crossed the back of the circle and looked down at me. I didn't feel it to be a threatening figure at all, and then it passed on. Sadly there was nobody to corroborate my sighting. I've explained it to myself as a phantasm growing out of excessive tiredness and a sort of hallucination but on the other hand it seemed at the time to be a real figure and there was absolutely nobody apart from the technical staff working in the theatre'.

If Richard maintains an 'open verdict' regarding his encounter, this must be accepted as a perfectly correct personal assessment and one which I have met regularly throughout my research. Rationality, more often than not, holds sway, be it a questioning sway, over wishful uncertainty.

But another sighting at the Lyceum in 1996 was witnessed by two separate parties at approximately the same point of the evening. It was during a performance of *The Steamie,* that perennially popular play North of the Border by Tony Roper the actor, perhaps best known 'down South' for his portrayal of Jamesie Cotter, Rab C. Nesbitt's appallingly funny crony. By then, the gallery - the third tiered level above the stalls - was no longer on sale to the public, but the follow spot operator was positioned there for the production's musical numbers. As she waited for her cue, she saw a figure in blue walk across the aisle of seats. At the same time as the figure seemingly disappeared in front of her eyes, one of the actors, waiting in the wings for her entrance, looked up and saw standing in the gallery the same figure in blue, which waved at her and then faded away. Ghostly approval? Ellen Terry? Why not? A great actor always has the confidence and generosity to acknowledge other great performances, as long as they know they are still being watched themselves.

Scene 12: The Grand Opera House, Belfast

Having left the Athens of the North we're off next to Linenopolis and, if you fancy, by boat. That is of course after we've got to Dumfries and Galloway and the port of Cairnryan. Once the ferry's docked, our destination is a short taxi ride away, but, if the crossing has been rough, the City centre is in walking distance so give it a go and lose your sea legs before visiting our next date.

The Grand Opera House on Great Victoria Street is an absolute gem of a theatre and it was noticed when it opened that the balustrading and minarets adorning the exterior gave it in the words of the Northern Whig, 'quite a continental appearance'. To add to this image, that evocative French word 'Cirque' was placed on the exterior panel directly above the frieze that spells out 'Grand Opera House'. This was not only for decoration, for the stage and auditorium had been specifically designed to be adapted and become a circus arena, taking bookings in between proscenium-based shows. Furthermore, the founder of a circus which played here, Jean-Pierre Ginnett, was a French cavalryman. Having been captured at Waterloo, he was held as a prisoner of war in Ireland before becoming an equestrian performer and circus owner. The double signage was also essential because, as any box office manager will tell you, patrons always need a little help to know where they are heading to. This became essential from 1907 for then a rival variety house, the Royal Hippodrome, opened immediately next door. This theatre,designed by Bertie Crewe was later to suffer the indignity of becoming a bingo hall and was demolished in 1998, but Frank Matcham's magnificent creation has somehow thankfully survived despite all that has been thrown at it.

The Grand Opera House was opened officially on the 16th December 1895 with the unveiling of a memorial stone by the actor manager Frank Benson, whose touring company had often played at Belfast's Gaiety Theatre. Benson had broken his journey from London to Newcastle to officiate at the ceremony, and the very next day nipped smartly back to Newcastle to lay another stone, this time a foundation one, for the future Grand Theatre, Byker. Benson's company had already been engaged to open it in July 1896 so the engraved symbolic trowel with which he was presented with was further proof that the future booking was set as it were, in concrete.

The first show for that Christmas was the pantomime *Blue Beard*. We don't see many *barbes bleus* these days, perhaps because the story is ultimately based on the macabre antics of the murderous Gilles de Rais. It may not have worried Victorian audiences but they were possibly unaware of its origins. Then followed a steady stream of the great actors of the day such as George Alexander, Martin Harvey and Sarah Bernhardt before the building was renamed the Palace of Varieties to do battle with the new Hippodrome. It reverted to its original name in 1909 and from then on has played host to a great mixture of bookings. Pavlova danced, Gracie Fields sang and Laurel and Hardy 'Sold Out' in 1952 in between a steady diet of opera, plays and pantomimes. The Second World War's restrictions on civilian travel stopped most touring shows but caused one positive result with the formation of the Savoy Players weekly rep company.

In May 1963, the local Grand Opera Society unknowingly made history by mounting their production of *Madam Butterfly*. For in it, cast as Lieutenant Pinkerton, a certain Italian tenor made his professional debut in the UK. As Luciano Pavarotti started to sing, fellow cast member Nan Murray recalled 'you felt this sort of shiver, a feeling, a fantastic feeling when he began to sing. He was such a lovely man, but the voice just blew you away . . . on the First Night people didn't know what they were going to hear and they heard this magnificent voice and at the end the place just erupted'. But with the start of the Ulster 'troubles' the Grand Opera House had to face other less friendly eruptions. By then the theatre, faced with ever-dwindling audiences, had been converted into a cinema and the bombings of the next-door Europa Hotel literally rocked the old building. The man responsible for leading the team that restored it to its present glory was the architect Robert McKinstey. He returned to assess the venue of his childhood memories in 1975. He was struck by 'the extraordinary abandoned look of the inside, as if everyone had suddenly quit the theatre in a great hurry. The house manager's black jacket still hung on the back of his office door, the ashtrays attached to the seats had never been emptied and in the bar there were still half-full glasses and crates of bottled beer. It was like the Marie Celeste'.

A perfect location then for the spirits of the dead and still, despite its restoration, one that they have not yet abandoned for there has been, as far as I know, no spiritual deep cleansing. One firmly identified ghost is J.C. Magee. Mr Magee was a long-serving assistant manager in the early days of the last century. It is said that he suffered a heart attack and died in the box office in 1928. Since then his spirit has been repeatedly seen lurking in the foyer. Various people have not only sensed a presence but seen a shadow moving about and it is generally supposed that, having worked there for so long, he is still most attached to the location.

But if Mr Magee clings limpet like to his surroundings he is not alone. Other presences have also been reported. Various casts in the 1980s, when making their way to the stage from the top floor dressing rooms, reported a ghostly face which would appear to gaze at them through a round window set on the staircase. The dressing rooms were re-developed in the theatre extension of 2006 so this ghost if it still appears sadly has no audience to startle.

Two more ghosts, Harry and George or George and Harry - depending on who is either on last or seen first - are identified as being a pair of old caretakers whose double act appearances date from the 1980s. They do not seem to haunt the stage itself and their sightings are always in the auditorium and dressing rooms. The Gods is home to two more spirits. An unidentified lady has been spotted there and also a phantom film projectionist who worked up there in the 1960s when the theatre was a Rank cinema. Finally, to date, the Circle Box Right is reported to have a ghostly occupant in the shape of a soldier from the First World War. I do believe that there are other presences in the Grand Opera House but they are not openly discussed. In Gaston Leroux's novel, the backstage staff of the nineteenth century Paris Opera are furtive about what lurks beneath the stage. The *Phantom of the Opera* may be a work of fiction but is there the possibility that there are other phantoms of the Grand Opera House, Belfast too frightening to reveal?

Scene 13: The Gate Theatre, Dublin

S ome tours have 'dark' weeks meaning that certain slots in the schedule cannot be filled through lack of suitable venues. We will pretend we are experiencing one now for it would be criminally negligent, to say nothing of bad manners, not to board the train at Lanyon Place Station and take the two-hour journey to Dublin, a city where theatre and ghosts are seemingly entwined.

Dublin's first playhouse, the New, opened in 1637, a mere twenty-one years after Shakespeare's death. Although it was closed down by the Puritans in 1641 during the Civil War, this was not a permanent dramatic glitch, for the Restoration heralded the opening of the first Theatre Royal in Smock Alley in 1662. Since then Dublin has had its share of touring houses but its reputation as an innovative theatre city is primarily because of new and outstanding plays and performances over the last century at the Abbey, the Gaiety, and the Gate. The Abbey may be haunted by memories of Yeats and Synge and the Gaiety by Archbishop John Charles McQuaid but in this instance, it is the Gate which we will visit.

The Gate Theatre, founded by Hilton Edwards and Micheál MacLiammóir in 1928, has been housed since 1930 in a Georgian building, originally part of the Rotunda Hospital at the top of O'Connell Street. Their artistic policy was to produce a mixture of new and old international plays. Many of their productions during their tenure were stunningly innovative, some even commercially successful, but their careers were to be dramatically interrupted by the arrival in 1931 of a certain sixteen old American youngster.

Having announced to the press that their next production would be *Jew Süss* they realised they had an immediate problem. Edwards would play the lead but they were lacking an actor for the second principal part of the Duke. In his autobiography MacLiammóir recalled:

Hilton walked into the scene dock one day and said: 'Somebody strange has arrived from America; come and see what you think of it.' 'What,' I asked, 'is it?' 'Tall, young, fat: says he's been with the Guild Theatre in New York. Don't believe a word of it, but he's interesting. I want to give him an audition . . .'

The young man amazed them; they offered him the job. He seized the role, turned in an extraordinary performance and stole the reviews. It was of course the start of Orson Welles' meteoric career. The three of them were to have an intermittent working relationship and friendship for the rest of their lives.

MacLiammóir may have been influenced by the Celtic Twilight but he definitely experienced a spiritual encounter one night in the mundane location of the paint frame. The actor was also a set designer and the Gate's scenic artist, and often had to work alone till the dawn in the scene dock to meet the deadlines for their forthcoming shows. This, archivist Pat Turner told me 'mostly didn't bother him a scrap but one night he heard steps coming down from the stage - there was a ramp, not steps there, in those days - and he turned to see who it was and there was no one there, but the footsteps kept on coming until they were on a level with him. Then they stopped and he knew something was there watching him. The feeling lasted for seconds or minutes - he couldn't tell - and then the footsteps went back the way they'd come. Needless to say, Micheál got out of the theatre as quickly as he could.'

Empty, creaking theatres can challenge the imagination and are irresistible for some betting men. Actor Aiden Grennell agreed to spend a night alone in the Gate for a wager. In order to keep both himself company and the shadows at bay, he had brought along a selection of flamenco records to play. He was particularly taken with one because of the distinctive voice of the singer. The night passed safely but at home the next day he played the record again and discovered that it was purely instrumental.

In 1971, Niall Buggy was appearing at the Gate in *Its Later Than You Think*, a translation by Lucienne Hill of Jean Anouilh's *Ornifle ou le Courant d'air*. He had been allocated dressing room 6 and one afternoon came in early for a lie down before the show. Pat Turner arrived at the theatre at about seven and went into dressing room number 5. 'About a quarter of an hour later I was startled by Niall rushing in - white as paper. He asked me had I come into number 6 and stood beside the bed looking down at him. I replied that I hadn't even known he was in the theatre and that I wouldn't have done that anyway. If I'd wanted to speak to him I'd have done so. He said he had wakened with this feeling of someone beside him and was filled with a terrible dread which made him too frightened to open his eyes. After a while the feeling passed and when he did pluck up the courage to look there was no one there, but the door was wide open'. Pat was certain of two things. Firstly no one went up or down the corridor after she arrived because number 5 seeming stuffy, she had left the door open and would have heard anyone going past, however quietly. Secondly the door to number 6 was shut when she arrived for 'if it hadn't been I would have called out a "good evening" or popped in to say hello to whoever was in the dressing room . . . I don't think he stayed alone in the dressing room for the rest of the run!'

Dressing room 6 was also the location for a psychical vigil in October 1983. It had been organised by the Northside News for a Hallowe'en feature and three mediums, a reporter, a photographer and Pat duly sat in the dark waiting for something or anything to happen. It was at times contradictory, like so many of these sessions, the photographer complaining of cold though sitting with her back to the radiator and the mediums claiming to experience presences both evil and benign. The session came to a sudden end when the oldest of the mediums became very frightened by what he was experiencing. Pat thought that he and the young girl medium were 'very credible' but 'the third . . . was rather a poseur and didn't ring true with me. In speaking of the benign presence, the oldest described Micheál MacLiammóir which at the time was a little too pat for me. He said the presence was writing on something in French and that the words were '*Toujours L'Amour*'. The reporter had told Pat that she was the niece of a former Gate employee and had visited the theatre as a child. She had met Micheál and he had signed her programme. On the mention of the writing in French 'she made no comment, like a good reporter, but in the next edition of Northside News revealed that what Micheál had written on her programme with his signature, was '*Toujours L'Amour*'. Surely two most apt and final words for the Gate.

Scene 14: The De La Warr Pavilion, Bexhill-on-Sea

Not all haunted theatres on our tour are ancient. Some are beacons of modernity standing alone in the midst of a mishmash of architectural mediocrity. In other words, back to Blighty and in particular to the South Coast. Bexhill-on-Sea conjures up a real life Walmington-on-Sea. When walking very slowly along the front, so as to avoid possible collisions with senior skateboarders, I always keep a lookout for Corporal Jones, Sergeant Wilson and Captain Mainwaring. A futile vigil of course for they - Clive Dunn, John Le

DE LA WARR PAVILION, BEXHILL-ON-SEA. · 1935.

Mesurier and Arthur Lowe - have long gone to God, in stark contrast to the vast majority of the town's real inhabitants who retire here and then forget to die. Bexhill-on-Sea has indeed had an enviable reputation for longevity stretching back for over two centuries.

On June 4th 1819, a very peculiar dinner was held in the Bell Inn to celebrate King George III's eighty-first birthday. It was a loyal gesture but I wonder whether it passed off in the manner intended. For eleven of the twenty-five guests were older than their monarch - the youngest being a mere seventy-five - and there is no record to suggest that they were any less insane. If they were geriatric maniacs and liable to all manner of violent fits and troubled starts, then their volatile meal may have been further disrupted by the fifteen waiters who attempted to serve them, for the combined age of these worthies was 1,076 years. Picture them tottering from the kitchen, soup tureens and roast beef dishes held at dangerous, shaky angles. As they circle jerkily round the bemused guests, they leave a dribbling trail of Brown Windsor soup and an individual Yorkshire pudding in each octogenarian's lap. To add further to the celebration it is recorded that six bell ringers, mere lads in their sixties, were engaged for the evening; ostensibly to chime joyfully. but perhaps to drown out the cacophony of breaking glass and crockery.

Apart from its perpetual pensioners, the town can boast of some famous past residents including Fanny Cradock, Eddie Izzard and David Hare. It also adventurously embraced the future when Herbrand Sackville, the ninth Earl de la Warr, whose ancestors had basically owned Bexhill since the reign of Elizabeth I, instigated an architectural competition in 1934 to design an entertainment hall and complex. Some 230 architects sharpened their pencils and the winning 'Modernist' design by Erich Mendelsohn and Serge Chermayeff resulted in the famous Pavilion. It stands proudly on the front and has somehow survived both wartime bombing and 'logical' redevelopment. The Pavilion is now rightly recognised as a very important piece of architecture and has Grade 1 listed building status. It sums up the very best of that era's style, a perfect time capsule where Hercule Poirot would have felt right at home. Indeed, the second murder in The ABC Murders takes place in Bexhill, and though its fictional location is the beach, a far from imaginary spirit haunts the Pavilion.

Tony Williams was stage manager of its theatre from 1988 to 2009. Over the years he experienced several uncanny happenings that led him to explore the archives of the Bexhill Museum and even to consult a London medium, a certain Dr Brown. He had never met the doctor before, but she was immediately able to tell him that he worked in the theatre and that he had what she described as a guardian angel, identified by the initials IRA, who was prone to sit on the edge of the stage. Tony's research later uncovered the fact that the Pavilion was built over the site of some old coastguard cottages. He managed to track down a coastguard's widow who informed him that it was here that one of her husband's colleagues had murdered his wife. Tony subsequently discovered that the site of the murder was where his office now stood but the question remains whether this seaside uxoricide is the cause or has connection with any of the following inexplicable happenings.

During a rehearsal of a tour of Thunderbirds the ASM Peter Lockwood was forced to leave the stage when the auditorium became suddenly filled with a smoky mist. Smoke again appeared one night in the lighting rack area above Tony's office when he was about to lock up. The fire brigade was called but despite extensive investigations no explanation could be found as to how it had materialised or where it had come from. The Pavilion is a stone's throw from the sea but that could not in any way be the reason why Tony, having locked up the theatre, returned one morning to find the Green Room's ceiling covered in hundreds of pieces of wet tissue. Someone or something is in residence, for on one production a dresser, while waiting to do a quick change just outside Tony's office, saw a figure which so alarmed her that she dropped the costume and fled the theatre.

Doris Stokes, the spiritualist and psychic medium, was made of sterner stuff but she too had her qualms. One afternoon in the 1980s she arrived to give a live presentation. Tony was summoned to show her to her dressing room and led her through the auditorium towards backstage. Miss Stokes suddenly stopped dead in her tracks and asked him 'if there was another access point as she was unable to proceed due to an uncomfortable presence'.

Tony himself has often felt that there is someone behind him when walking through the auditorium and in the backstage corridor and this feeling has been reinforced by the occasional sound of footsteps. He has also seen a shadow sitting on the front edge of the stage which could relate to the mysterious IRA. Bob Marsh, the front of house manager, has also had his share of strange experiences. He, together with fellow staff members Chris Bullock and Natalie Trimby, have heard whispering and whistling in the corridor by the Elizabeth Room. He recalls that during a production of *Cinderella* in 2005, there was a very fast change in the wings where Cinderella herself would be unzipped, got out of her ball gown and then helped back into her normal rags. During one performance, the dresser was late and completely missed his cue but, when he arrived, there were no angry histrionics. The change had simply happened and Cinderella was safely back both on stage and in time for her next scene. Afterwards, neither she nor anyone else could explain who had unzipped her or robed her again.

On another occasion, Bob had arrived one early morning at seven to open up the theatre. He had just switched off the alarms when he heard footsteps above him on the Pavilion's terrace. Thinking there were intruders, he ran upstairs to discover he was alone but then witnessed an opened magazine on a table being slowly closed - by no one. The Modernist De La Warr Pavilion would seem to be a theatre that has retained its past.

Scene 15: The Royal Theatre, Northampton

We've walked the mile on this tour but if you're feeling a bit down at heel don't despair. Our next date is where you can refresh your plates with some nice new ones and twos. . . Mind you, things aren't what they were. Despite having inspired a British film, a Broadway musical and furthermore manufactured over 23 million pairs of decidedly un-kinky boots for our Tommies in the First World War, there are now, according to a recent newspaper report, only fifteen shoe factories left in the Shire. Don't worry unduly. If it's quality rather than quantity you're after, then you can combine culture with comfort, for the Royal Theatre is up there with Lobb's, Tricker's and Church's. It continues its tradition of producing innovative, new and popular shows in not one but three venues, for the Derngate and the Underground are in the same location as the Royal. Now add the allied Core at Corby and you and your trousers will be hard pressed to escape the cause of artistry in Northampton and its close surrounds.

It started simply enough. C.J. Phipps drew up the designs and the Royal duly opened in 1884. Due to the limitations of space, it was one of Phipps' smaller theatres. It was and is only a 583 seater, but this intimacy means that it has weathered both temporary economic problems and the rise of those alternative popular forms of entertainment in the last century that bedevilled and indeed helped destroy so many larger theatres. Home to the Northampton Repertory Players from 1927 to 1992 it spawned a host of famous names including Roger Lloyd Pack, Nigel Hawthorne and Julian Fellowes and even one of the world's greatest film stars, Errol Flynn. Flynn joined the Players in 1933 because, so his unreliable autobiography claims, he managed to convince its then director Robert Young that he could play cricket. His subsequent first performance on the field was so disastrous that the Players lost to Coventry. Young was furious, but relented from sacking him when Flynn agreed to take a pay cut.

A dubious tale perhaps but he did stay for some eighteen months, appearing in over twenty productions, and, as you did then in rep, learnt his craft. He may not have given his Othello to Freda Jackson's Desdemona - his roles being listed as First Senator and Lodovico -   but paradoxically he did play the lead in Frederick Lonsdale's *The Fake* before being talent spotted and signed up for Warner Brothers. Only one reliable memento of Flynn now remains in Northampton. It is his unpaid tailor's bill for £300 still owed to Montague Jeffrey Ltd, for his shade has never returned to settle up or, for that matter, to even strut the stage. Instead the Royal has to make do with that well known shadowy fall back spectre, a Grey Lady, but a Grey Lady in this case convincingly documented.

The late General Administrator, Andrew Thompson, told me that there were stories of entire companies seeing her sitting in the stage left box during dress rehearsals and that there are reports of a presence walking between that area, the circle corridor and the workshops. In 1991, I interviewed Jim Sharman the lighting designer. He told me that, 'in the autumn of 1979 I was alone backstage at about 4.00 am when I heard the sound of footsteps walking around backstage on the old wooden floor of the workshop'. He had also seen the Lady in Grey. 'During a musical, I was at the lx board at the back of the stalls when I saw her standing by the side of the auditorium underneath box A. Over the cans I told the follow spots and prompt corner that there was a woman standing there in what appeared to be old time music hall clothes but they couldn't see her. Other people too have seen her in box A.'

The wardrobe mistress then told me that her father remembered as a child there being slaughter houses at one end of the street and had the memory of a story of a girl murdered there by a lover or father. Certainly there was a gravestone which was used as the doorstep to the entrance to the old workshop and this bore the name 'Fox'. Bryan Douglas worked the Royal for 32 years as master carpenter and then front of house manager. He witnessed a ghost three times in the 1960s before the Derngate was built. The locations may now have changed but not his accounts of what he saw.

'I was sitting one day in the old green room, having a well-earned cup of tea, when I saw a woman wearing a grey cloak walking along the upstairs corridor towards my workshop. I popped up the stairs and followed her to ask what she wanted, only to find she had completely disappeared. At that time, there was no other way out of the carpenter's shop, the exit to the old theatre manager's house in Derngate being blocked by several tons of scenery. I would not have gone upstairs if I had not seen anyone, but where had she gone? It was then I realised I had "seen the ghost". The second occasion was even more incredible. It was dusk, during a pantomime performance, and I had just gone out into Swan Street (which in those days went from Derngate to Victoria Promenade) to put something in the boot of my car. parked next to the old bus station. On returning to the stage-door, I saw a woman wearing a similar grey cloak cross the road as if to enter the stage-door. I expected her to open the door, allowing the interior light to shine out in the darkening twilight. Instead, she just walked straight through the door without opening it. It was only a few yards away, so there could be no mistake, and I followed her - having to open the door properly myself. She was walking along the corridor past the electrician's shop, towards my workshop, and once again she walked straight through the door without opening it! I followed, only to find my workshop empty, and a strange feeling of presence.'

Bryan's third encounter was a different manifestation. It was again during a pantomime and he was watching from the wings, standing in front of 'the entrance to a very small room that Henry Irving used to use as a quick-change room'. It was being used for that purpose once again.

'I felt a hand on my shoulder, and thinking that someone had just done a quick change, and wanted to come out, I moved out of the way, only to find there was nobody there. Yet I had distinctly felt a hand on my shoulder!' Whose hand was it, I wonder? No bets taken but my wishful money in this case has to be on Sir Henry.

Theatre is broadly truthful fiction so we should end our visit to Northampton with a story that possibly demonstrates the morbid power of what some interpret as a supernatural story.

In the autumn of 1999, while a production of *The Turn of the Screw* was being mounted, inexplicable incidents happened during rehearsal. As reported In the Chronicle and Echo, the stage manager Joss Matzen said, 'Every morning I go to the rehearsal room and set up all props, the table, the chairs, books and cups, then leave the room locked. When I return half an hour or so later with the actors, everything has moved. I am the only one with the keys, so I don't know how this happens.' Did the power of suggestion in Henry James' story take control of the witnesses or did this fiction unlock the boundaries of reality?

Scene 16: The Kenton Theatre, Henley on Thames

Despite Henley on Thames being one of the main locations for *Midsomer Murders*, the last recorded homicide to date was in 2006 and that was the first for some sixty years. It presents itself to this day as a safe and affluent town, its image the very essence of respectable middle class England and one that even becomes regal by association during its Royal Regatta. But, once past the picturesque centre, I do wonder what really lies behind the immaculately kept hedges and driveways of its outlying houses and mansions. After all, here's a town that recently allowed itself to be represented in Parliament by Boris Johnson. Detached or even semi-detached, passion can still be a dangerous pastime, and even more so in the eighteenth century when its consequence proved fatal.

The Kenton in New Street opened as the 'New Theatre' on 7th November 1805 with *The School of Reform, or How to Rule a Husband*. It was the day after news of Nelson's final victory reached England and the first night takings were sent to the Patriotic Fund 'for the benefit of widows and orphans and for the relief of the wounded of those brave heroes who . . . gained the unparalleled victory off Trafalgar'.

Henley society was already well accustomed to theatre-going, primarily because of the enthusiasm of a local aristocrat, Richard Barry, 7th Earl of Barrymore, Viscount Buttevant and Baron Barry of Ireland. Inheriting his titles at the age of four, 'Hellgate', as he was nicknamed, was a pre-Regency rake, boxer, jockey, cricketer and passionate amateur actor. His immense fortune allowed him to build his own playhouse in nearby Wargrave in 1789 but his 'Theatre Royal', designated as such by his crony the Prince of Wales, did not survive his early accidental death in 1793. The town's appetite for drama was next fully fed by Mr Jonas and Mr Penley's touring company. This troupe would regularly arrive to play at what was grandly called the New Theatre. This in fact was an enclosed courtyard at the back of the Broad Gate Inn in Market Place but such was their success that Messrs Jonas and Penley eventually decided to build their own permanent theatre on New Street.

It seemed a good idea at the time, but within a few years the smart Henley set began to drift away to be replaced by ale throwing rowdies. In 1813 Jonas and Penley threw in their make-up towels, closed up the theatre and moved on to the Theatre Royal, Windsor.

Henley's elegant Georgian playhouse changed into a non-conformist chapel, a school house and finally suffered the indignity of becoming a mere hall for hire. For over a century it entered the dramatic doldrums until the 1930s when professional and amateur performances started again on a regular basis. Renamed the New Playhouse, it at last became the Kenton in 1951 and remains so to this day. It is of course haunted but strangely the hauntings go no further back than 1969.

To find an explanation for this date it is now necessary to go back in time to April 6th 1752. On that day in Oxford, Mary Blandy, as the Newgate Calendar reported, 'left her apartment to be conducted to the scaffold, habited in a black bombazine dress, her arms being bound with black ribbons. On ascending the gallows, she begged that she might not be hanged high, "for the sake of decency"; and on her being desired to go a little higher, expressed her fear that she should fall. The rope having been put around her neck, she pulled her handkerchief over her face and was turned off on holding out a book of devotions which she had been reading'.

Mary Blandy

Mary Blandy, a thirty-two year old wealthy heiress, had been hung for poisoning her father Francis, a prosperous lawyer and the Town Clerk of Henley. Six years earlier she had met an unscrupulous Marine officer, William Cranstoun and they had become lovers. Cranstoun asked for her hand in marriage despite the inconvenience of having a wife and child in Scotland. He managed to fool both his wife and the Blandys for some years until Mary's father became suspicious enough to forbid him from seeing his daughter and barring him from Blandy House. Cranstoun retreated to Scotland but secretly kept in contact with Mary. Writing to her, he enclosed packets of arsenic trioxide labelled 'powders to clean Scottish pebbles'. She would testify at her trial that he persuaded her to mix them into Mr Blandy's food and drink because he assured her the powders would change her father's opposition to their union.

Mary was either a total innocent or a willing accomplice. She seems to have openly followed his instructions for her servants would later give damning evidence against her that they had witnessed the administering of the poison. Her father fell ill but managed to survive the first two attempts to change his mind or take his life. But on the third attempt, she added an even larger dose to his gruel and this proved fatal. In agony, the dying man realised that Mary had poisoned him and tried to save his daughter by stating that he believed her 'pebbles' story. But her deed quickly became common knowledge throughout Henley. Threatened by a mob, she fled from Blandy House to a friend's inn, the nearby Little Angel, where she was duly arrested. Though Cranstoun managed to flee abroad and escape justice, she, despite her vehement denial, was found guilty of the capital crime of murder.

Unsurprisingly Mary's spirit does not seem to rest in peace. There have been reports of over the years of her ghost being seen not only at the Little Angel Inn but standing beside an old mulberry tree in the garden of her old home in Hart Street. After all, guilty or not, what better location for a ghost to haunt than the actual scene of a crime? But her appearance at the Kenton Theatre is much more curious and seems only to have come about because of a play.

On 19th May 1969 a new company of actors, HM Productions, presented the premiere of *The Hanging Wood* by Joan Morgan, a dramatisation of her own book on Mary Blandy. The author, once a British silent screen star, was also a long-term resident of Henley but this did not prevent her play receiving a scathing review from the Henley Standard. The bad notice however was only part of the production's troubles.

As soon as rehearsals began, an unseen presence started to make itself felt. Sitting in the green room, the cast witnessed a large mirror jump off the wall by itself, lights turning on and off, doors opening and closing by themselves and a selection of glassware being unaccountably shattered. These manifestations seemed to indicate poltergeist activity by an as yet unknown spirit. But next, when rehearsals moved to the stage, the cast noticed the figure of a young woman watching them from the back of the stalls. One of the actors was sent to find out who she was, but the woman simply disappeared. An immediate search was made of the building but it was established that no one had been seen to enter or leave the theatre. During a subsequent rehearsal break the conversation turned to Mary Blandy and Joan Morgan reported that in full view of herself and the actors 'a cup jumped about six inches off a table and smashed on the floor.' From the date of that production onwards, sightings and sounds have been reported at the Kenton. There have been descriptions of a lady walking about the back of the stalls and being seen to disappear through the wall seemingly into the green room. There is even a report that in 1966 when the trial itself was re-enacted at Henley Town Hall, a similar female figure was spotted watching the performance. Evidence would therefore indicate that the ghost of Mary Blandy, rather than restricting her appearances to her actual past surroundings, is curious enough to move to new locations to check out her impersonators.

MISS BLANDY *at the place of Execution near Oxford, attended by the Revd. Mr. Swinton.*

Scene 17: The Theatre Royal, Margate

We come now to our final date for all tours must come to an end. Indeed, that's the fervent prayer of some companies on the first day of rehearsals. But we are not concerned with living moans and groans, for our ears are finely tuned for whispers of the dead. So, let us use the last of our touring allowance to take a ride on Charon's ferry over the Wantsum Channel to the Isle of Thanet, that most easterly point of Southern England. There facing us is the North Sea and for those blessed with exceptional eyesight, Holland, for we have arrived in Margate. We have already met several past lady producers and theatre owners on our itinerary. All are important for all were united in their drive to succeed and in their determination to uphold and advance the sometime crumbling cause of drama. Let us now make the acquaintance of another such heroine, namely Sarah Thorne.

Theatre came early to Kent for we have evidence of the recently re-discovered 12,000-seater Roman theatre in Faversham. But both the Dark and Middle Ages set back the dramatic arts in Kent until the year 1504 when a theatre, which stands to this day as the Shakespeare pub in Butchery Lane, opened in Canterbury. Some have it that the Theatre Royal Margate is the second oldest theatre in the country. This is disputable but, as it did open in 1787, it can claim to be the second oldest existing playhouse in Kent. This theatre which has had such a chequered history was built by the partnership of Charles Mate, a retired sea captain, and Thomas Robson, a singer from Covent Garden, on the east side of Hawley Square at the junction of Prince's Street, which is now named Addington Street.

Captain Mate, already owner of a theatre in Dover, had opened his first venue in Margate in 1785 by leasing and using the stable of the Fountain Inn in King's Street. Unhappily for him, he came up against the formidable Sarah Baker. Sarah was owner of 'an excellent heart with much of the appearance and manners of a gentlewoman' even if her language did smack of Peckham Fair. She was another early lady producer whose touring company traversed Kent and Sussex. She would go on to build the Tonbridge Wells Theatre in 1802 and be the first employer of Edmund Kean, but at this point of her career, she was determined to succeed in Margate.

Undeterred by the fact that there was no suitable venue available, she had a wooden theatre constructed so as to be in direct competition to Mate and soon saw his venture off. However, the Captain's landlord, Mr Cobb of Cobb's Brewery, being deeply distressed at the loss of rent, organised a local petition and managed to achieve a Royal Charter and the 'Margate Playhouse Bill'. This gave him, as licensee, the theatrical monopoly for the town and this in turn saw Sarah Baker off - not that that lady took it lying down. She ordered her carpenters to dismantle her theatre plank by plank and then shipped it round by sea and re-opened it in Faversham.

After a few good years of business, the Theatre Royal began to endure that common Dickensian complaint, hard times. It would consistently close and then re-open as a succession of short, and, at times, shoddy managements tried to entice audiences to enter through its doors. This uncertain period continued until 1874 when the building was extensively reconstructed.

Sarah Thorne, eldest daughter of the actor manager Richard Samuel Thorne, then took over in 1878 and would remain in firm and successful control until 1899. She described herself in an address to the house as 'the captain of a ship that has just left harbour and was spreading her sail in the breeze'. These

SARAH THORNE, MANAGERESS OF THE THEATRE ROYAL,
MARGATE, BETWEEN 1867 AND 1899.
(By courtesy of Mrs. Henry Oscar)

'The captain', Sarah Thorne

were suitably apt words for her seaside patrons, for if they didn't immediately splice the mainbrace, they soon rallied to support the theatre. Her success as an actor manager was mirrored by the success of her school of acting, the first proper academy in the country so it was claimed, whose alumni included Harley Granville-Barker, George Arliss, Irene Vanbrugh and Seymour Hicks. She was reputed to have declared on her deathbed 'so long as the Theatre Royal is there, I shall be there'. It would appear she has been as good as her word for she seems to have returned when the theatre's wellbeing or future has been in doubt, periods when it has suffered the indignities of being used as a wrestling venue, a warehouse and a bingo hall.

After Sarah's death, her son Edmund McKnight took over the management and it is reported that he would often regale visiting companies with stories of her ghost. Filial pride and belief in the afterlife may have prompted his disclosures but he was not alone in seeing Sarah. In April 1934, a Mr Caspar Middleton obtained the lease in partnership with a formidable and gravelly baritone-voiced actor manager, Miss Pat Nye. She was one of the few actors of her sex to have an active naval career and to receive a military OBE for, as a First Officer in the Wrens, she reputedly kept her girls safe and sound in Scapa Flow from randy Jack Tars.

Perhaps it was the presence of such a rival that prompted Sarah to appear at this time. Within weeks Mr Middleton saw her ghost three times. He explained that 'twice on coming out of the circle buffet sometime after the performance I saw it walk through the doorway from the stairs leading to the boxes and gallery on one side and go slowly round the back of the circle and disappear through a wall on the other side'. Mr Middleton would later discover that there had once been a doorway in this wall with stairs leading down to the stage and to Sarah's small office. On another occasion 'the ghost passed so close that I could have almost reached it with my hand. On another night, I was standing in the circle when I saw it by the door in the stalls leading to the boxes'.

He reported her as wearing what he described as Lady Macbeth's sleep walking costume, loose flowing, blue and intriguingly transparent. One wonders whether Mr Middleton could possibly have known that in 1895 Sarah, when asked as to what was her favourite part in an interview for the Sketch, had replied that she had 'bestowed the most time on Juliet, Desdemona and Lady Macbeth...and I think they are my greatest successes'.

But Mrs Thorne's ghost did not walk only for him that year. One evening some members of the new repertory company were busy rehearsing for their next week's production of *The Naughty Lady*. They were using the circle bar as space on stage was limited because of the current show's set. Rehearsals dragged on and just after midnight one actor, Peggy Ford-Carrington, slipped into the back of the circle to run through her lines by herself. There was only a small gaslight on in the darkened auditorium and the iron was in. 'Suddenly I was startled by a gentle moan or cry which broke the stillness, and glancing up I saw something leaning over the box on the other side, waving its arms about. It was terrifying and I could not stop myself from screaming'. Another actor, Chic Elliott, ran into the circle to find out what was happening, saw what was happening and promptly fainted. Mr Middleton was next on the scene and in the circle box 'saw something swaying and waving over the edge'. Despite his previous experiences, he hoped it was a practical joke and so ran round the circle and into the box but 'no one was there and nothing had been disturbed'. In the meantime, Peggy Ford-Carrington saw the transparent figure of a bluish grey lady rise into the air in front of the box and then disappear into the ceiling.

In the autumn of 1954, John Baxter Somerville, the lessee of the Theatre Royal Brighton and the Lyric, Hammersmith acquired the theatre. He also had an interest in the Malvern Players and decided that his opening show that Christmas would be their production of Terence Rattigan's *The Prince and the Showgirl* starring Bernard Archard, designed by Stanley Mills and directed by James Belchamber. Baxter Somerville also asked Mills to design and supervise the redecoration of the auditorium. There was little time to achieve this, so Mills began working alone overnights but stopped because 'he began to feel uncomfortable, as if someone was watching him'. The others were used to Stanley's 'histrionics' and paid scant attention at the time.

Belchamber told me that 'the dress rehearsal was on Christmas Eve afternoon. We were opening on Boxing Day matinee'. The majority of the cast broke in time to catch the last train back to London but 'we had a hiccup that had to be put right. In the play the Showgirl dances for the Prince when she hears a barrel organ in the street below play a tune from the musical play she is in. The synchronisation of dance and organ had gone wrong. We opened a flat in the scenery on the OP side so that David, the stage director, could get a better view. On stage was Bernard, Dawn (Leslie) and me plus a very powerful torch, a Christmas present from my brother. Dawn did her dance and at the end added a little kick; the timing worked, but with that little kick came a peal of laughter from the auditorium. We all turned to it, I shone my torch, there was no one there'. They searched the theatre which of course was empty with all the doors locked. 'That peal of laughter was definitely female. I would like to think that she wanted her theatre open.' James remembers that later on 'Reggie Birks of our company left us to manage the theatre after our departure and form a permanent rep company. He was seated one time in the circle watching a rehearsal with his young son who said to him "how did that lady get into that box?" He was pointing to a closed off one. Reggie looked but could see nothing'.

Other reports would indicate that Sarah Thorne is not the theatre's solo act but part of a ghostly ensemble. According to general manager Michael Wheatley-Ward, an old stage manager wearing a pork pie hat has been seen several times stage left. He told me in 2006 that 'Personally I have witnessed the following. On the side of the stage there rests the ashes of Pat Whitcombe, related to one of the owners. During a visit from a psychic research group their specialist equipment did not work, until I took them past 'Aunt Pat' and the machine came alive, lights flashing all over the place. Also, during one of the pantomimes, arrows were fired off stage and, to prevent them hitting anyone, a blanket was held up in the wings in front of Pat's photo. It was witnessed that one of the arrows directed itself over the top of the blanket and smashed the glass in her picture! Myself and a colleague have had our watches reset, staff have seen glasses move in the bar, tools and keys vanish and then reappear and the technical stage manager will not go up to the grid on his own as he was spoken to! There is a great deal of activity in the old gallery, mainly children's voices'.

Michael also explained that a television company had caught the outline of someone sitting in a stalls seat which may be linked to a letter he had received from the Reverend John Houston in 2005. It read, 'an Australian visitor and I attended a performance at your theatre earlier this year. On two occasions I noticed him turn around sharply to the empty seats behind us - I think we were in row D. After the show ended, he told me that he twice felt someone tapping him on the shoulder but when he turned, the seats behind were empty. Neither he nor I knew anything of the ghost stories associated with your theatre . . . I'm new to the UK myself . . . he was quite un-nerved by the experience'.

In contrast, Lynda Baron's experience made her initially not so much un-nerved, as angry. In April 2002, she was starring as Mrs Hardcastle in Hettie MacDonald's production of Oliver Goldsmith's *She Stoops to Conquer.* It was not the first time that this classic comedy had been seen in Margate for it had been in fact the very play that had opened the Theatre Royal on June 27th 1787.

During the run, Lynda had heard stories of the ghosts but had taken them 'with a pinch of salt'. The staging of the production meant that for about the last five minutes of the evening she was positioned downstage and facing the audience and so was able surreptitiously to study the house while keeping firmly in character. As she would tell her fellow actors and later relate to me, it was at this moment during one performance that she noticed two people getting to their feet from their seats in the centre of the stalls. She realised that they were going to leave, seemingly oblivious to the fact that they would be disturbing the rest of the audience around them. 'How rude, I thought, and I decided to give them a really steely glare if they were to look up at me'. What was odd, she thought, was that no one in the audience seemed to be aware of the couple as they started to make their way past them. Lynda watched their progress along the row of seats and then, to her utter astonishment, saw them, on reaching the aisle, suddenly and completely disappear.

Venues win all sorts of accolades but the Theatre Royal's five-star rating according to Mr Wheatley-Ward as a multi haunted theatre makes it rather special. I can only hope that the Ghost Hunt events it now regularly hosts will not completely exhaust audiences and ghosts alike, encompassing as it does séances, vigils, EVP experiments, ouija boards, glass divination, automatic writing and table rapping. How better just to keep things simple and not scare spirits, timid or otherwise, away.

A GRAND FINALE

All productions, Ladies and Gentlemen, need a big dramatic ending and so, although our tour is now over, may I present yet one more location which will in turn, aided by a unique performer, lead us to the most famous haunted theatre in the world.

Sadler's Wells Theatre

These days Sadler's Wells is dedicated to the dance and is visited for the most part by lovers of leggings and lycra, unless, like myself in search of something dramatically stimulating, you set off on a number 19 bus bound for Shaftesbury Avenue, doze past *Harry Potter and the Cursed Child* and are woken in Roseberry Avenue by the massed clack of the Dutch National Ballet's clogs. Should you have such a similar experience, I urge you too to jump off at the nearest stop for Sadler's Wells is well worth the visit.

You must not be deceived by the building's very modern appearance. It is of course, but five previous theatres have stood here since 1683, thus making Sadler's Wells almost the oldest continuous theatre site in London. It was in that year that the well which had once bubbled away in the grounds of the Priory of Clerkenwell was rediscovered by workmen digging for gravel on the property of Richard Sadler, a road surveyor.

Local tradition had it that a slug of this mineral water per day had kept the Black Death at bay and so Mr Sadler decided it would be sensible to revive the tradition for both universal health and personal profit. He promptly opened a wooden Musick Hall where paying patrons could imbibe the elixir and thus fend off scurvy, dropsy, virgins' fever and other 17th century ailments. The Hall soon acquired a scandalous reputation before being demolished and replaced by a new stone built theatre in 1765. Thomas King from Drury Lane would become manager and raise the tone of the house by attracting quality shows and audiences.

The semi-rural location of Sadler's Wells meant that in order to escape cut-purses and highwaymen, your cautious 18th century play goers would have to employ flambeau-carrying, armed escorts to see them safely home but the theatre nevertheless thrived. Its lack of a Royal Patent meant though that it was obliged to present an ever changing bill of novelties, acrobatics, patriotic re- enactments and pantomimes with casts that included martial dogs, singing ducks and dancing horses.

From the age of two and a half until his retirement, the great Joseph Grimaldi regularly played Sadler's Wells. This truly extraordinary actor, comedian and clown raised Regency pantomime to new levels of daring and mirth and his popularity guaranteed full houses wherever he performed. Like so many great comics he was depressive, stating that 'I am grim all day but I make you laugh at night'. His mental condition was partly due to the harshness of his childhood. His father, the malignant Giuseppe, was a ferociously cruel performer who put into practice what his contemporary the Marquis de Sade could only write about.

Joseph's comic energy, invention and charisma could captivate the most brutish house. But on October 15th 1807, after he had finished his performance and left the theatre, a tragedy occurred. In the pit that evening, were Sarah Luker, Mary Vyne and the brothers John and Vincent Pearce. Having continuously antagonised those beside them with their drunken and threatening behaviour, fierce quarrels broke out and constables were sent to evict them. As they were being ejected Sarah Luker was heard to shout to the brothers 'Fight! Fight!' This was misheard by many as 'Fire! Fire!' A panic ensued and eighteen people, mostly women and children, were trampled to death. One mother, a Mrs Price, had allowed her eleven years old son to go to the show in the company of her neighbours. That same evening, before the news of the tragedy broke, her daughter told her that she had seen Benjamin in their kitchen but that he had vanished when she had called to him. Mrs Price, certain that she had seen his ghost, hurried to the theatre to duly find his dead body. I cannot find hard evidence that any of these unfortunate victims have since returned to haunt Sadler's Wells and indeed it is now near impossible to pinpoint the accurate location of the site where they died. There were some major alterations in 1834 before 1879 when the building was rebuilt again. The fifth theatre which opened in 1931 was likewise demolished to make way for the present in 1996. However, before this date, stories persisted of the presence of Grimaldi's ghost in the auditorium. The clown would be seen at night in one of the boxes, or rather part of him would be observed, for only his disembodied head, daubed in his garish makeup, would be visible. This led to the belief that on his instructions it had become separated from his body before burial. A false story but one based on a similar macabre truth involving the Signor, Joseph's father.

*Joseph Grimaldi, the great clown, in his prime in Mother Goose in 1807,
painted by Samuel De Wilde*

The appalling Giuseppe had a morbid fear of being buried alive. On his death in 1788 it was discovered that his will commanded that, firstly, he should not be buried for a full forty eight hours while lighted candles and needles were applied to his feet to ensure that he had passed over. As the old devil had previously faked his death to observe his family's reactions, they waited a further seven days before daring to proceed to the next step. This was because the will stipulated as a final assurance of his demise that Mary, his eldest child, should then 'see me put into my coffin and the day that I am buried to sever my head from my body'. The dutiful daughter duly obliged though she merely placed her finger on the knife that the surgeon so briskly applied. So perhaps the Grimaldi seen at Sadler's Wells was the father, not the son? No matter the identity, I am sure Edgar Allen Poe would have enjoyed the detail.Headless or not, it is now Joseph's cue to lead us on a leaping, frantic race.

Grimaldi in his prime would run from Sadler's Wells at the end of one performance and take just eight lung-bursting minutes to arrive at the next nightly venue for another. His route did lead downhill with fewer road diversions than today, but his 'legs of steel' must have been truly remarkable. His journey may well have led him to a thoroughfare at the northern end of what is now High Holborn. If so, he might have whizzed past The Great Mogul, an inn on the left-hand side of the road. A tavern has been on this site since the early 1600s and if Shakespeare didn't actually drink there, he knew a man who did. The inn fell into disrepute before it was pulled down to become the Middlesex Music Hall in 1851. That building in turn was demolished and rebuilt as the New Middlesex Theatre of Varieties to a Frank Matcham design in 1911. This theatre would eventually have an interior make over and be relaunched as the Winter Garden but a change of name was insufficient to protect it from the wrecker's ball in 1965. The New London Theatre was then constructed. It is a fitting monument to the architectural taste of property developers whose pursuit of profit collectively destroyed so many fine theatres in the immediate post-war decades. Now at least its name has been changed for the better in honour of the late Gillian Lynne whose wonderful choreography for *Cats* inspired generations of young dancers. As far as I know, it is not a building favoured by ghosts but we should not despair at their absence. We merely need to follow Grimaldi's flying footsteps for a few more hundred yards down Drury Lane to reach the location of a site truly saturated in spiritual activity and supernatural sightings.

The Theatre Royal Drury Lane

For the climax of our grand finale we have arrived at the most haunted theatre in all Great Britain. Other theatres may dispute this claim and some with possible justification, but it is undeniable that mass opinion credits the Lane with being our country's most famous ghostly venue.

The irony for me is that this popular belief stems from the report of one strange discovery in the 19th century which in turn led to the appearance of the Man in Grey, a singular ghost who has become synonymous with this theatre ever since his first appearance. He has inspired endless newspaper cuttings and articles but his background remains shadowy. The truth is that hard facts and really credible appearances are few and far between. I myself am not one to completely disbelieve the authenticity of his existence, but because his fame has eclipsed the many other ghosts of Drury Lane, I must first delve into his story before introducing and attempting to restore the names and reputation of his fellow spirits.

Let me immediately state two undeniable truths for both elder and younger readers. This Man in Grey is neither the late James Mason, nor is he in any way connected with the writings of EL James. Having dispatched those two canards, it is time to introduce the man who introduced the world to the Man in Grey, one Walter James Macqueen-Pope.

'Popie', as he was known to his colleagues and contemporaries, appears to have been born with greasepaint in his blood for he claimed direct ancestry to Thomas Pope, a shareholder of Cuthbert Burbage's Globe and one of the Chamberlain's Men. He started out as an aspiring playwright but his short play *The Punctual Sex* failed to satisfy the critics, even those who arrived in time for curtain up. Turning to theatre management, he became press representative for the London Palladium before moving to Drury Lane where he remained for twenty-one years. His encyclopedic enthusiasm for the West End theatre world from the Edwardian era to the pre-war '30s was boundless and from 1945 he wrote some twenty tomes chronicling what was rapidly becoming a lost world. His first book was *Theatre Royal, Drury Lane,* which curiously, considering the importance of the theatre, was its first biography. It was also the first time that the public were made aware of the Man in Grey.

Popie set up the story of the ghost's entrance by recounting how in the 1840s workmen in the upper circle came across what appeared to be a a bricked-up void beyond the main wall on the Russell Street side of the building. The foreman's decision to investigate further led to the discovery, once this section of the wall had been breached, of a secret room in which lay a man's skeleton with a dagger in its ribs. At the inquest, no identity could be proved. An open verdict was returned and the remains were buried in the old churchyard off Crown Court, now a rather hidden public garden.

Once discovered and his resting place disturbed, the presumably murdered spirit seems to have begun to make frequent appearances. Popie declared dramatically that 'the present historian wishes to put it on record that he has seen this apparition on numerous occasions', adding the precautionary proof that 'he' himself 'has excellent sight, is not troubled mentally, has not a fantastic mind, and is not a Spiritualistic medium'. His description of the ghost was most detailed. 'He is a man of medium height, dressed in a long grey riding cloak of the early 18th century, wearing a powdered wig of the period and a three-cornered hat. The cloak covers most of him, but he has a sword which can be seen under it, as it swings at his side, and he has high riding boots. Sometimes he carries his hat in his hand'. Popie also insisted that all the recorded accounts of his appearance were between 9am and 6pm and that he only haunted one part of the building, namely the upper circle.

It has been speculated that Popie knew that a well-reported haunting could be very good publicity for selling his book, but the fact remains that the ghost does seem to have been seen ever since the 1930s. Popie named a Mr Stephen Williams, an employee of ENSA, as having encountered the ghost in 1942 on the grand staircase by the upper circle entrance. On another occasion a cleaner entered the upper circle one morning during a rehearsal. Sitting in the fourth row on the aisle seat of the centre gangway was a man in grey, wearing a hat. Thinking one of the cast was watching what was going on down below on stage, she approached him to have a chat, only for him to seemingly disappear in front of her eyes before materialising again by the right-hand side door and passing through it. She reported what had happened and her description matched Popie's previous encounters. This sighting by an anonymous wartime 'Mrs Mop' could be put down to an early morning vera in her rosie but then it is also reported that more than half the cast of The Dancing Years saw the Man in Grey during a photo call one afternoon in 1939. Besides this company, he has also been witnessed by members of other casts including My Fair Lady and A Chorus Line even if depictions range from most vivid to mere hazy. Morgan Davies was appearing in Carousel in 1950. On a Saturday matinee he unknowingly challenged Popie's authoritative assertion that the ghost only haunts the upper circle level. Looking out front during a scene, he noticed that one of the boxes in an otherwise sold out house was unoccupied. Surprised, he looked again and saw that there was now a figure standing in it, a man wearing a long grey cloak, open at the front and revealing sleeves adorned with ruffles. Astonishment hit Morgan when he realised that the person he saw was actually transparent. The ghost stood for some ten minutes watching the stage before vanishing and this particular sighting was confirmed and witnessed by one of the chorus who was also on stage.

The Man in Grey's appearances are also credited with bringing luck to a show and there is a story that managements would always keep an upper circle seat open for him on press nights to guarantee success. The tale continues that it was inadvertently sold on the first night of *Miss Saigon* and, true or not, the possibly disgruntled Man in Grey has not been seen with any certainty since. His true identity will no doubt always remain a mystery, and though I will later on add more details, I worry about the story of the bricked-up room for this seems to pose more questions than answers.

If we take Popie's description as being totally correct, it would date the ghost as being from the late 18th century. However, the present building only dates from 1812. Prints of the theatre immediately after the fire of 1809 show a skeletal shell, but here I refer to the remains of the brickwork rather than to our Man. Could any hidden room before this date really have survived? Or could the Man have been a Regency patron or player? There is one unquestionable fact. Drury Lane has always endured and so it is time to wind back to *anno domini* 1662.

In that year Thomas Killigrew and Sir William Davenant were granted royal patents from King Charles II allowing each to form a company of actors and build a theatre. These patents effectively prevented other theatres and companies from producing 'legitimate drama' and so established an immediate theatrical monopoly. This exclusivity, first in practice and then in theory, would be supported by the full weight of the law until 1843. Killigrew's chosen site for his theatre was a plot of land bordering Bridges Street, now renamed Catherine Street, and Drury Lane, and it was here that the first Theatre Royal opened on May 7th 1663. It was an instantaneous, roaring success in the first flush of the Restoration, a place where ladies could for the first time be viewed on stage, though Samuel Pepys of course would go one better by being taken backstage and 'into the tiring rooms; and to the women's shift, where Nell was dressing herself, and was all unready, and is very pretty, prettier than I thought'.

True to that time-honoured theatrical tradition, the original building burnt down in 1672 and was replaced by a new house whose design was popularly attributed to Christopher Wren. This building witnessed the likes of Thomas Betterton, Colley Cibber, Charles Macklin and the great days of Garrick before, like these actors, it 'decayed' and beyond repair, was in turn demolished. The new 1794 theatre, which saw the ascendency of John Philip Kemble, Sarah Siddons and Grimaldi, was built to the latest theatrical standards but even the presence of a new-fangled iron curtain could not prevent it being destroyed by fire again on the evening of February 24th, 1809.

Alerted to this disaster, Richard Brinsley Sheridan, both author of *The School for Scandal* and owner of the theatre, was nonchalant in adversity. Hurrying over from the House of Commons he was observed watching the inferno from the Piazza coffee house with the aid of a bottle of wine, for as he said, 'may not a man be allowed to take a glass of wine by his own fireside?' The conflagration may have ruined him financially but the theatre rose again from the ashes to open once more in 1812. Its present incarnation has witnessed the greatest triumphs of Edmund Kean, Macready and a galaxy of Victorian actors. It has seen the management of Augustus Harris usher in the era of spectacular pantomimes in which Dan Leno and a host of music hall stars would entrance audiences and in time watched the eventual domination of musicals which commenced in the 1930s with the shows of Ivor Novello and has continued ever since.

There have been some astonishing changes of style and substance in the productions staged here over the last two hundred years but I can assure you that the supernatural elements have and still remain a constant factor. It is now time therefore to return to their other world.

As he led us here, let us begin with Grimaldi. Having made his very first stage appearance at the Lane it was fitting that it was on that self-same stage he made his last. But though the audience yelled and cheered for their hero he was a tragic shadow of his former self. Years of performing countless extraordinary, and at times, death-defying leaps, tumbles and falls had wrecked his body and left this wonderful clown and acrobat so crippled that he was hardly able to walk unaided.

On June 27th 1823, a Benefit was organised for him by the Drury Lane Theatrical Fund and Joey the Clown tottered on in full motley. He collapsed

Mr Grimaldi's Farewell Benefit on Friday June 27th 1823,
by George Cruikshank

into a chair to perform a final sketch from *Harlequin Captive or the Magic Fire* and sing one of his signature songs, 'Hot Codlins':

A little old woman a living she got,
By selling hot codlins, hot! hot! hot!
And this little old woman who codlins sold,
Though her codlins were hot, thought she felt herself cold,
So to keep herself warm, she thought it no sin,
To fetch for herself a quartern of —

The house roared out 'GIN!' Grimaldi replied 'Oh, for shame!' and chorused

Ri tol iddy, iddy,iddy
Ri tol tol iddy iddy, Ri tol ay!

Dreams are made of such. The audience bravo'd endlessly, calling for encores but his strength was done. At the end of the evening he managed to enter out of costume for a final bow and, once the applause had finally stopped, for a farewell speech. He had, he said, 'jumped my last jump, filched my last custard, and ate my last sausage'. He was just forty-eight years old.

Grimaldi's ghost is one of those that have been variously felt, heard and possibly, seen. His is a friendly ghost, unlike Charles Macklin's, whose baleful presence has been felt chilling the air of the old corridor by the orchestra pit. But then Macklin had an infamous, murderous temper. In the theatre's scene room on May 10th 1735, his ferocious argument with Thomas Hallam over a purloined wig, caused him to drive his cane into and through his fellow actor's eye. Macklin applied first aid by pissing into the wound but the unfortunate Hallam passed away the next day. Tried by jury for murder, Macklin conducted his own successful defence, got away with manslaughter and concluded his career with a partial last performance of Shylock at the age of ninety-nine in 1789.

Let's now leave him to fulminate under stage and return to examine Joey's more amicable touch. It would appear that the comedian is most considerate to the ladies for there are three witness accounts of his unseen activities.

The late Patsy Rowlands who appeared as Mrs Pearce in the 2000 revival of *My Fair Lady* at the Lane claimed that she often heard his footsteps close behind her on stage as she played her part, encouraging her so she thought, and perhaps at the same time sniffing out the whereabouts of Eliza Doolittle's parents' favourite tipple. In 1947, Betty Jane Watson came to London to play Laurey with Howard Keel and the American cast of *Oklahoma!* - the show which overnight revolutionised the concepts and construction of musicals and musical staging. For three performances during one of her scenes she felt hands on her shoulder pushing her gently downstage, until, when judged sufficiently in view, she was patted on the back. The same experience happened to Doreen Duke who was playing Tuptim in the 1953 production of *The King and I*. Again, tender help was given to guide her to a better position on stage so that the audience could see her to her best advantage. Perhaps it was during that Act 1 number, 'We Kiss in the Shadows.'

One evening, at about 5.30 pm during the run of *Hello Dolly* in 1967, the orchestra drummer Stan Bourke was being seen by the masseur Paul Johnson in the inner band room. While the treatment was taking place, they heard someone playing Stan's drums. After the previous show, Stan had covered his kit as he always did with a sheet stretched over the two cymbal stands so that it would be clear of the drum skins. The initial drumming went on for about twenty seconds and sounded like someone was hitting the tom-toms in an un rhythmical, haphazard way. Paul Johnson stopped his massage and said 'is that somebody playing your kit? Do you want to go and see who it is?' Stan certainly did. Together, to the sound of the drums, they left the band room and reached the stairs that led up to where the orchestra sat, but, as they entered the pit the noise stopped. 'The drum kit was still covered up, the sheet being in exactly the same position I had left it the evening before, there were no drum sticks or beaters lying and there was no one to be seen either in the pit or on stage. There was no chance of anyone leaving the pit without Paul and myself seeing them as they would have had to pass us to get out, or again, if they had made their exit on the other side of the pit we would have seen them'.

Some light on the mystery as to who or what was playing his drums was possibly thrown in 1972 during the run of the subsequent *Gone with the Wind*. One afternoon Stan had called into the Lane to collect some kit. Task done, he, together with his son Tony Bourke and a friend, made their way out to the stage door. As they walked across the stage from the prompt corner side, they noticed that a four poster bed from the previous evening's Act 2 was still set on stage.

Lying on it was a person with his hands behind his head. 'He was quite real

CHARLES MACKLIN,

Mr Macklin...ever fiery at eighty-seven

and although laying down we could see he was a smallish person, looked very old and white, and wore a white all in one leotard outfit. As we walked past the foot of the bed he raised his head and sort of chuckled at us. At the time we thought it was probably a stage hand or someone working backstage although we did comment on his unusual clothing.'

They gave it no more thought and left the theatre. It was only some years later while watching a BBC Nationwide programme on 'the old stars of Drury Lane' that Stan and Tony saw a familiar looking costume, as worn by one Joseph Grimaldi. But then, to muddy the waters, Stan told me that the face 'looked very like Dan Leno with his stage make up on'.

Dan Leno towered above his other comic contemporaries. Unfortunately, the comedian was of just too early an age to be captured properly for posterity on film. Some vocal recordings do exist and two flickering 'What the Butler Saw' sketches, but these are inadequate testimonies to his talent. Written patter songs and evocative photographs remain but we must rely on the opinion of his contemporaries. Max Beerbohm wrote that he was 'not one of those personalities who dominate us by awe, subjugating us against our will. He was of that other, finer kind: the lovable kind. He had, in a higher degree than any actor I have ever seen, the indefinable quality of being sympathetic. I defy anyone not to have loved Dan Leno at first sight'.

This view was universally shared and he was incredibly popular. When Charlie Chaplin came back to London in 1921 fresh from his cinematic triumph in America, he went on a return journey of his youthful haunts. Many of the landmarks of his early days had gone but an old photographic studio remained in Westminster Bridge Road where he had had once sat for his front of house shot. In its front window he noticed a framed photograph of Dan Leno. 'My name is Chaplin' he told the owner. 'You photographed me fifteen years ago. I want to buy some copies'. 'Oh, we destroyed the negatives long ago' came the reply. 'Have you destroyed Mr Leno's negatives?' 'No, but Mr Leno is a famous comedian'.

Fashions in humour change. Whether he would make us laugh today is as unanswerable as his own query: 'Ah, what is man? Wherefore does he why? Whence did he whence? Whither is he withering?' What is indisputable is his enduring fame. Here stands a comedian whose material was topical and at times almost surreal, one of the first 'stand ups' and one whose characterisation as the put upon little man would influence comedians as equally successful as Chaplin and as generous as Stan Laurel who willingly admitted to have borrowed his rueful smile. Peter Sellers, that chameleon creator of comedy, was also convinced when the mood took him that he was the reincarnation of Dan, unprovable of course, but a telling tribute from one extraordinary performer to another.

Dan Leno in drag...

Leno was a national star from 1886 until his sudden mental collapse and death at the age of forty-four on October 31st 1904. He was born George Galvin in a ramshackle 'two up, two down' in the slums of London's Somers Town. Having managed to get over the 'inconvenience' of his birth, Dan joined the family variety turn on stage at the age of four, billed as 'Little George, the Infant Wonder, Contortionist and Posturer'. At five he had adopted his stepfather's professional name and was performing a clog dancing act with his brother Henry, billed as The Great Little Lenos. He would become the World Champion Clog Dancer before developing his own patter acts for a cavalcade of invented characters such as

the Beefeater, the Railway Guard and the Shopwalker. His music hall and burlesque popularity brought him to the attention of Augustus Harris, the manager of the Lane, who engaged him for *Babes in the Wood* in 1888, pairing
the slender Leno with the portly Herbert Campbell, a pantomime partnership
which would last for sixteen years. During these shows, Leno would sometimes use a dressing room situated on stage right directly by the proscenium
arch. This, though by no means large or palatial, allowed him instant access
to and from the stage before and after his costume quick changes. It is a light
and cheerful room looking out over the road to the front of the Fortune
Theatre. A large framed mirror used
to hang over the dressing table
which was opposite to the casement
window. An unusual feature is a
spiral staircase which leads to and
from the down to a basement level
where lurks an ornate, late Victorian
lavatory.

    After Dan's death, the actor and
comedian Stanley Lupino succeeded
him in his roles at the Lane both as
Widow Twankey in *Aladdin* and
Buttons in *Cinderella*. Lupino experienced the same hard childhood
as Leno. He was born in a hansom
cab outside the family lodgings in
Petticoat Lane though it is doubtful
that his parents could have afforded
the fare. He made his first appearance at the Lane at the age of three,
being carried on as a prop baby by
his father George during one of

...and out of it

Leno's shows. As a boy, he shared a garret room in digs in Kennington with
his father and his brother Mark. There was no money for coal that midwinter,
so Stanley and his brother were sent out nightly to try to find any off cuts of
timber left over from the construction of the new tram line. As they crouched
down for shelter from the wind in the doorway of the Kennington Theatre, a
hansom cab drew up and out jumped a little man. It was not someone trying

to welch the cabbie but a welcome benefactor. Seeing them, 'he felt in his pocket and said "here sonnies". It was half a crown and before we had recovered from our surprise he had disappeared through the stage door'. If that was his first remembered meeting with Dan Leno it was not to be his last.

One night in 1919 during the run of *Cinderella*, Lupino set off for home but his car quickly skidded on the ice, ran into a hoarding and broke its front axle. He trudged back through the snow to the theatre, and, let in by the fireman, tried to kip down in his dressing room. Having borrowed some bedding, he stoked up the coal fire, bolted the room's iron door and turned the lights out. It should be noted that Lupino was both a very practical man and a teetotaller and so for me his story has not the suspicion of embroidery. He recalled that there was 'no other entrance or exit to or from that room' which then had a corner curtained off for costumes. 'I had not turned off the lights more than a few minutes when I heard these curtains draw back. I sat up in surprise. The glow of the fire made an eerie light and everything was now very quiet . . . peering through the half-light towards the fire I suddenly discerned a pair of man's legs as if he was standing with his back to the fire and looking across and down at me. . . there was no other part of him visible to me. Just those legs! . . . I was about to spring off the bed when the legs began to move away and pass into the shadows of the room. A door opened and clanged back. The iron door that I had bolted! I sprang up. My first action was to switch on the lights. I looked around me. I had heard the curtain draw aside. They were still drawn back. Then to the door. That was shut. I went over and examined it . . . it was still bolted on the inside just as I had left it!' Mr Lupino's rest was not disturbed again that night but there was to be another visit and this time, before a show. It was after the half and 'I was making up and quite unprepared for what happened. As I was looking in the glass, I suddenly saw another face above mine. It was looking at me with a smile, and was also in make-up. There was a line across the forehead where a wig had been removed. There was no mistaking that face . . . there was no doubt in my mind as I gazed at the reflection that I was looking into the face of Dan Leno. Naturally I thought someone was having a big joke at my expense. I winked. The face winked back. Then I swung round. The room was empty . . . the door was shut.'

Still unconvinced that he had seen a ghost and having ruled out a practical joke, Lupino tried to see if it was in any way a trick of the light on the mirror but all his experiments failed. It was only after this that he found out that the room 'had been a favourite one of Dan Leno and the last one he had dresses in for the stage . . .' Two evenings, later his wife Connie Emerald and another lady were in the dressing room with him during the show. 'The pantomime was in full swing. As the call boy popped in his head and said "near you, Mr Lupino", the laughter of the audience could be heard. I rose and went out and as I did so I heard my friend's wife give a short gasp of surprise'. Lupino took no notice and left but Connie asked what the matter was. The lady explained that 'that man gave me such a turn' and on Connie asking, 'What man?' she replied, 'the little fellow behind the curtain. He came from behind the curtains and followed Stanley out'. Lupino returned to find brandy and soda being administered and remembered thinking whether Mr Leno was 'giving me a hand in the playing of his old part?'

The tale of 'the haunted mirror' was handed down to and by successive occupants of the dressing room and was still being recounted when in 1981 I came to work the Lane with *The Pirates of Penzance*. It had become an accepted 'fact' that Dan's face could occasionally materialise in the glass and this belief was coupled with the tale that people would sometimes smell the heavy scent of lavender water with which he used to liberally douse himself. Now some believe that Dan did so to disguise another aroma. Others, in his defence, decry that story as a piece of dubious piss but the actual truth may never be known. The only possible evidence pointing to incontinence is the lavatory beneath the dressing room. One could argue whether any management would go to the expense of plumbing in such a thunderbox if it was superfluous to requirement, but that can always be countered with the logical answer that it was contractually essential.

By the time I arrived, the dressing room had long lost its star status and had a battered atmosphere for it had become assigned to stage management. My stage manager, long before she became a children's casting director, was Jo Hawes, fearless of actors living but a tad timid of actors dead and it soon became apparent that she was nervous of the ghost stories. Her concern made me mischievous. I couldn't conjure up a face in the mirror but I knew I could target her sense of smell.

Before one matinee I came in early and dosed the room with a garden spray full of lavender essence. Jo and her nostrils were suitably wound up, but I kept my council, did not confess and both shows and the scent passed smoothly away. But I was to get my comeuppance. That evening, after all the team had left, I lingered behind to type up the nightly show report. Job done, report ready to post, I had got to the stage door when I realised I had forgotten to put a stamp on the envelope. Chas, the resident fireman, was there manning the door and waiting impatiently to let me out for, until I had gone, he could not start his first round of his nightly inspections. I made my apologies and went back on stage towards the office. As I walked down the side of the wing I was assailed by the sudden and overpowering smell of lavender. The whole wing literally reeked of the aroma. I knew with certainty that Chas and I were the only two people left backstage. There was only one thing to do. I would forget about the stamp. Returning to the stage door I described what had happened. Chas immediately went to check and returned to confirm that he too could smell the lavender. I left him to his lonely vigil in that dark and creaking building. Nobody envied him that side of his job, but no one foresaw that some nameless shadow would get the better of him, for this charming, cheerful man, with no apparent problems in the world, would later in our run be found one morning, hanging by his neck in the fireman's room.

At the end of one performance he alerted myself and the master carpenter that he could smell something burning in the Long Dock, a huge storage area for scenery upstage of the acting area and spanning the width of the building. Everybody on the backstage staff joined the search. We checked through all the stacks of old flats and rolled cloths but though we could all definitely sniff what collectively we described as 'charred timber', there was nothing visible and, as far as we could tell, no identifiable source. Baffled, we all went home leaving Chas to live with the phenomenon. During that night he was so convinced that there was something smouldering that he twice called out the fire brigade, who again would confirm his fear but could not solve the mystery. My only explanation is that perhaps on that night we all witnessed a faint memory of the fire that had destroyed one of the previous theatres.

Mr Leno, having teased my nostrils with his lavender, returned to the assault a few weeks later. That evening, rather than go out front to watch, I was standing directly outside his old dressing room by the downstage masking flat. This allowed me a perfect view of the alleged non-choreographed goings on during the number 'Climbing Over Rocky Mountains'. Just as the Major-General's daughters downed their elbows, finished their jockeying for best lit position and adopted a brief tableau for the customary applause, my right shoulder was suddenly pushed so violently that I swung round in a circle and just avoided joining them on stage. I leapt back angrily to confront my assailant only to discover that there was nobody there at all. My story was received with scepticism by many, with some unkind members of the company putting it down to too many pours of pirate sherry. However, I was vindicated two shows later when Louise Gold, who was standing exactly where I had been, felt an unseen hand tugging gently on the back of her wig. We were both guilty of blocking Dan's stage entrance after a ghostly quick change for old times' sake in his dressing room, but, being a natural gentleman, Louise got the gentler treatment.

It is possible that Dan was up to his old tricks again on April 30th 1956, the first night of *My Fair Lady*. The show's stage manager and one of the West End's best, the late Robert Stanton, had taken the decision that evening to call the show himself and was standing in position in the prompt corner down stage left. As he was standing by to give a lighting cue to the board operator, a hand slid into his trouser pocket and began jiggling around with its contents. Bob was furious someone was playing around with him on this of all nights. Being a visual cue, he could not look round to see who the joker was, though he suspected his DSM, Harry Bowers. The hand wriggled relentlessly, and fighting to keep his concentration, he whispered fiercely, 'stop mucking around'. The hand stopped, he gave the cue and, turned around to see Harry looking at him very curiously from several feet away upstage.

I am very fortunate to have worked with George Hoare, who was general manager of Drury Lane from 1958 to 1982. George was the debonair epitome of what is now almost an extinct breed. He was already an endangered species when I first met him but he faced the future fearlessly each evening in the foyer, standing on the steps by the side of the box office, immaculate in his dinner jacket and smoking a slim cheroot as he saw the house in. Once the curtain was up, he would proceed at a leisurely pace to the Grand Saloon, take a seat at his customary table and dispense liquid hospitality and verbal entertainment. George didn't trouble himself too much with the burden of paperwork for he had some very able assistant managers and had anyway come to believe that that sort of nonsense should be dealt with only during the hours of daylight. He told me that in his early days he had indeed been in the habit of working late in the office but this stopped for good one evening when a metal ruler had risen unaided from its place on his desk, hovered in mid-air and then proceeded to swipe him over the knuckles. He attributed this activity to a previous legendary manager, Arthur Collins, whose dictum was that all work should be done in office hours and that overtime was the work of the Devil. George had an ambivalent attitude towards the other ghosts of the theatre. Regarding the Man in Grey, a Darlington psychic had written to him to inform him that the spirit had identified himself as one Arnold Woodruffe and appeared to be extremely friendly. 'I was advised to ask him "What ails thee, friend Arnold?" if ever we met, but we never have'. George regarded the ghosts as part and parcel of the building, accepting their presence but never in awe of them. He was of the opinion that they would never appear to order and this belief was reinforced by his knowledge of the negative results experienced by various reporters and investigators whom he had allowed to hold vigil overnight. Nevertheless he was witness to a remarkable appearance.

During the run of *The Four Musketeers*, Lew Grade had some American businessmen in to see the show. He wished them to be properly 'entertained'

George Hoare in 1959, during the original run of My Fair Lady

and so it was arranged that they would occupy the Royal box, have interval drinks in the Royal retiring room and that George himself would escort them round at the end of the show to meet Harry Secombe. George duly came to meet them in the retiring room at curtain down and, as they waited for the house to clear, one of the Americans asked him who was 'the clown' they'd seen on stage who didn't seem to fit in any of the scenes.

George had no immediate explanation for this, and, slightly puzzled, then led the guests across the front of the dress circle to go backstage. To reach the pass door they had to walk through the Prince of Wales box's retiring room. As they entered it, the Americans all chorused 'That's the fella we saw!' In front of them, on one of the walls, hung a framed photo of Dan Leno.

Chris Edwards who was house manager with George had his own spiritual experience on the eve of All Souls in 1979 during the revival of *Hello Dolly* with Carol Channing. He told me, 'the show was halfway through the first act and I was in my office when I noticed a figure pass my door coming from the Grand Saloon. He appeared to be wearing a black dress suit or dark short coat and as this area was closed to the public and I did not recognise him as a member of staff I was up and in pursuit of this stranger. As I exited my office I turned left and in a few strides I was at the head of the corridor that runs to the offices adjacent to backstage and the back of the Prince of Wales side upper boxes. Halfway down the corridor was a glazed swing door that indicated the passage of some person, however I could not see anyone through the glass nor had heard anyone run along the corridor. I ran to the end of the corridor coming out behind the boxes and found no one'. Chris retraced his route and asked George, whose office faced his across the corridor, if he had seen the man. 'He was aware of a figure and my giving chase but had no idea as to who it was'. Chris then asked Bill, the catering supervisor, whether he had seen the man. 'Bill confirmed that a man in a dark suit had passed him, coming from the Grand Saloon and heading my way. Finally, I went out into the Grand Saloon where some of the staff were taking a break and asked who had come through the door'. Their answer was disconcerting for they had seen nobody. Perplexed, Chris returned to his office and was still trying to work out what had happened when the same figure 'went across my doorway again heading towards the Grand Saloon. I was up and in hot pursuit to be met by Bill coming out of his office. We entered the Saloon where the same members of the staff were still gathered only to be curtly informed that no-body had come out of the door since the last time I had asked. Bill and I began to protest but then seeing the look of confusion and pity on the staff faces decided to retreat and wonder.'

This incident is only one of several that have occurred in the front of house offices. During Bob Fosse's *Dancin'* in 1981, I recall an instance when Bill Roberts, one of the assistant managers, had to take time off work to recover from the shock of seeing a figure appear literally through and from a solid wall. There was also another sighting in the auditorium during that run. *Dancin'* had an American stage manager, for Tom Arnold had brought the road company from the States to the Lane. Mark Krause, as was the normal American practice, was both technically in charge of the show and responsible for maintaining the required artistic standards. There was of course a dance captain, but Mark's administrative work load was always heavy, especially on tour. By way of compensation, he had commandeered the Lane's number 1 dressing room to use as his office. One evening he decided to stay behind there after the show to have time and peace to catch up with some of the endless paperwork. After an hour or so pen pushing, he needed to rest his eyes and take a break. He made his way into the house for he always enjoyed sitting in empty auditoriums, facing the stage with his feet up on the back of a seat and enjoying the silence.

Only the secondary lights were on, but as he sat there, he saw out of the corner of his eye a movement. He looked to his right and realised that there was a female figure standing in the Prince of Wales box, looking towards the back of the auditorium. He watched fascinated for a minute and then she seemed to nod her head and gradually fade away. Mark, who was unaware at the time of any of the theatre's hauntings, was quite unfazed and took it in his stride. He rested a minute or two longer and then headed back to the paperwork.

Mark Fox is with LW Theatres, the current owners of the Lane, but his involvement with the theatre goes back to beyond their tenure. In 1994, he was working as an assistant manager during the run of *Miss Saigon*. This show needed an enormous staff both backstage and front of house. Some 120 people were employed by Stoll Moss and in those days a completely manual payroll was used to calculate their wages. Theatre wages were and are paid weekly and so, having received all the time sheets by each Monday, the managers then had to deliver their pay sheets to the Stoll Moss head office in Soho Square before 10 am every Tuesday to guarantee that all would receive their pay on the coming Friday. It was a formidable task and had to be done how ever long the hours.

'On one Tuesday morning at about 2 am, on what was your proverbial dark and stormy night, I was sitting at my desk trying to finish the figures.' recalls Mark. 'The managers' office had a skylight above the desks and so, directly over my head, I could see the lightning and hear the thunder and the continual drumming of rain. As I tried to concentrate on my calculations there were three separate occasions when I thought I heard someone call out my name. The first time I went out of the office to check who it was but there was nobody there. The second time I didn't bother as I thought it was someone messing about and they'd make themselves known. But when it happened the third time, I was so behind with the payroll that I didn't want to be bothered by whoever was obviously playing a trick and wasting my time, so I went over to the office door, which was a solid wooden one, and dropped the latch to lock it. Ten minutes later there was the most almighty thump against the door as if someone had thrown something enormously heavy against it and I heard a voice shout out something to the effect of "for goodness sake, get out here". The size of Drury Lane's payroll meant there was no choice but to work into the early hours so I imagined it could only be the fireman whom I thought had been asleep in his office by the stage door. I opened the door, and ran out into the middle of the Grand Saloon. There was still nobody there, it was still pitch dark, but I heard what I can only describe as a waterfall around me. I looked out of the Saloon's windows but there was only the rain outside pouring on the canopy. Next, I went out of the bar and into the Rotunda and here the noise was worse. I then opened the doors that led into the Royal Circle. As I walked into the auditorium I saw that the stage was being hit by a deluge of water, mixed with paint from the ceiling and the walls. It was bucketing down from the roof. I ran back to the office, phoned the fireman and together we went on stage and moved the props and costumes which were always left there overnight to safety. When the stage management came in later that day there was work to do to restore some of the props and it took all day to dry out the pit but if we hadn't discovered the flood we would have lost a performance. I will add that I did actually finish the wages but, still covered in streaks of white paint, had to walk through more rain to deliver the paperwork.'

The ghosts of the Lane roam throughout the building. Different departments have had their own experiences. Olivia Ward was a member of the wardrobe staff in the summer of 2014. 'I was up in the laundry room on the very top floor of the theatre one Wednesday morning at about 8.30 am before the matinee. There was always an uncomfortable presence in the room when doing a laundry call and I had been told by a colleague always to say "Good Morning" and to prop the door open to feel more comfortable'. As Olivia did this and said the words, 'I heard clear as day a little girl's voice say "Good

Morning" in my ear. I spoke to other colleagues and others have experienced the same as me in there, pegs chucking themselves at you, hanger stands falling over of their own accord . . .'

Again, Tony Britton, when starring with Anna Neagle in the production of *No, No, Nanette* in 1973, had his own experiences with the unseen. After each show the dressers would collect all the laundry needing to be washed by the wardrobe. It was a nightly routine and, 'they can be heard arriving - loud footsteps - but one evening the footsteps were heard approaching and went on past the door without coming in. I opened the door. There was no-body in the corridor. At the curtain call at the show's end my coat tails - I was in full evening dress - were tugged several times although there was no one behind me. My dresser and I were talking as I changed and the coat hanger put on the back of the door started swinging as usual. But the swinging continued far longer than usual and had to be stopped by us. Dan Leno, they say, had very big boots and had been making his presence felt - not for the first time'. Tony was so convinced of an unseen presence that he contacted the BBC who put mics in all the appropriate places and recorded any sounds for 24 hours. He had the disc to his dying day.

Brothers Michael and Simon Howe have both played the Lane. In 1974 Michael was playing a scene in *Billy* with Elaine Paige, when he smelt the lavender on stage as did Simon in 1981 during a performance of *The Best Little Whorehouse in Texas*. Simon did one better one Saturday night in 1986 during *42nd Street*. He was about to make an entrance from prompt side when he glanced from the wings at the previously unoccupied Royal box and saw a woman in grey standing there. He turned to tell the stage manager but when they looked again the lady had vanished. She seems to have appeared again in the next decade, for Graham Bickley vividly remembers the panic of the Filipino ensemble during a rehearsal in 1993 of *Miss Saigon* when they realised that a 'Lady in Grey', as they put it, was standing and staring at them from the right-hand side of the upper balcony.

Does this unknown spirit also roam the stalls or is she a familiar ghost? During rehearsals for *Miss Saigon*, one of the show's creative team asked for a theatre manager to come to see him at his production desk in the stalls. Chris Edwards duly arrived and was told off for allowing members of the public to wander about in what was meant to be a closed and off-limit auditorium. He asked what they looked like and was told it was a very odd looking woman wearing a straw bowler hat and a long skirt. Chris then asked whether he had smelt anything and on being told lavender could only reply that he was 'terribly sorry but I cannot help you. I am unable to bar ghosts from the theatre'.

The belief in an unseen spirit presence unites many of those who have worked the theatre. Mark Davis, one of my younger Pirates, was so partial to a regular after show shower on the prompt side top dressing room floor that he would often be the last of the cast to leave the theatre. But one night he was so disturbed by the feeling of a baleful 'something else' beside him in the shower room that he joined the ranks of the more seasoned Brut splashers for the rest of the run.

Special routines are sometimes adopted to appease the spirits. Simon Howe, on his way out of the theatre would follow an old tradition and always cross the stage diagonally from upstage left to down stage right by the proscenium arch. He would then turn and walk straight back behind the iron curtain to the prompt corner before re crossing again diagonally to reach the upstage right exit towards the haven of the stage door.

The diversity of reported sightings must take the Lane to the top of the league of our haunted theatres. It has naturally been investigated many times, but the results range as widely as the ghosts. Perhaps it would be best to leave the Lane by quoting extracts from the remarkable report of a visit on the morning of Saturday 23rd April 1983 written up on the 28th of that month by Wendy Francis, the psychic. Miss Francis had written to George Hoare to try to arrange a visit to the theatre. George, now in his role of historian of Drury Lane, duly invited her and a friend to meet him in his backstage archive office and, at about 11.45 am, after looking at some of his artefacts, he took them down to the stage to begin the tour.

Wendy 'knew very little about the reputed hauntings of this theatre or its early history' but she had previously seen *A Chorus Line* there in 1977.

'I remember quite clearly not being able to concentrate very much on what was going on on stage, I was more involved in the incredible atmosphere and things that were there that somehow seemed as if they shouldn't have been'. She had looked up at one of the auditorium right boxes and seen 'sitting alone a very distinguished elderly man . . . fairly tall, slimish, grey hair swept back, short neat sideburns, and wearing a monocle. What struck me most was his hands beautifully poised. I guessed he was dressed in evening dress around the 1930s. One thing I was sure of, he was no part of a live audience.' It was this experience, related years later to a friend who worked in the theatre that led her to make her visit. When she met George she described 'the man I had seen in the box. Mr Hoare after some searching found a photograph which fitted, right down to the last detail, even his hands in the photograph were poised the same way as when I saw him in the box'. Wendy wrote that 'this man G.G. had been general manager, so I understood, for just one year in the 1930s'. My own research confirmed later that George Grossmith Jnr. - the equally talented son of George Grossmith the actor and co-author of *The Diary of a Nobody* - was indeed briefly the owner and managing director of the Lane in 1931 and according to contemporary reports would often sit in the Prince of Wales box.

George then led Wendy and her friend onto the stage itself. 'We stood talking stage right looking up at the Prince of Wales box . . . I suddenly became very aware of a presence a few feet to my left. I walked towards it and fleetingly saw a lady dressed in grey, what appeared to be a grey habit; her head was bent forward and she walked quickly, very quickly, her hands clasping a large crucifix hanging about her neck on a thong. I walked back to the others and then learnt that many years ago a convent had once stood nearby if not on these very grounds before the theatre was built'. Wendy felt that she was full of sadness and shame and believed that she had died by her own hand. She sensed that after bearing a child the young woman had been 'forced into a convent therein to suffer unbearable penance'. They ascended to the upper circle where 'I was surprised and pleased at the outcome' for it was here that she encountered the celebrated Arnold, the one spirit she had previously heard about.

But before his arrival she saw appear from stage left 'an elderly woman wearing a scarf around her head, a very scruffy green jumper, [a] calf length dark brown skirt, old kind of lace up shoes and what seemed to be men's socks...' A pair of glasses, which Wendy thought were borrowed, were balanced on the end of her nose. 'Although of a fairly frail appearance this woman carried a definite air of authority about her; she stood hands on hips almost as if questioning our presence.' A subsequent search through George's photographs seemed to identify her as a Mrs Jordan, a one-time housekeeper of Drury Lane.

And now it was time for Arnold to appear. '... I noticed Arnold making his way towards us... I made up my mind to say nothing to the others, I wanted to see if they too felt or saw anything. As Arnold walked on and was just a few feet from us my friend said a little nervously "he's here, isn't he?" I said "yes, take no noticed he is just curious." Arnold came and stood behind us. He had made us all very aware of his presence by this time. He seemed curious yet humorous, a strange little man...he appeared not very tall, about 5'6" to 5'7". Dressed rather untidily in a kind of button down smock, shirt, breeches, brown boots almost calf length, his hair I thought a wig, shoulder length, grey, resembling untidy ringlets, a thin moustache and wearing little metal rimmed spectacles. He carried a kind of tricorn hat. I feel Arnold's appearance rather deceiving, for although fairly untidy in dress, for example carrying a hat but wearing no jacket, I felt in his day he carried some weight, a very clever knowledgeable man, especially with money, very insighted although somewhat eccentric. I would put him around 1820s onward. I feel a connection with him and Kean'.

Arnold accompanied them to their next port of call, the Royal box. As he sat down beside them Wendy saw 'a very dramatic figure' appear on stage. This man paraded back and forth before appearing in a box opposite for the purpose of 'seemingly studying us'. Wendy later described his costume in detail and George's archive pictures came up trumps again, proving their watcher to be none other than Edmund Kean. They left the Royal box, followed by Arnold who at this point 'stood behind me and the others and began to playfully tug at my hair'. The tour continued to the Board Room where, 'although I saw nothing in there once again years of atmosphere filled the place. It felt full of people, full of loyalty and love, though also very cold'.

A footman was encountered in the Grand Saloon from 'somewhere around the time of George III, a short very stout man this footman, immaculate in dress and appearance, never leaving that particular area, there he has always served and still waits to do so'. The last encounter on the tour was with 'a man with a cane. He seems to walk up and down the corridor past the general manager's office. He is tall and stately, elegant and flamboyant. Victorian in appearance; long cloak, frilled shirt, dress suit, tall shiny top hat, elegant moustache I would say in mid 40s, very good looking, full of ego and self-importance he strides up and down a slight limp in left leg, tapping the cane as he walks. The head of the cane is carved into a bear's head. The name Victor seems somewhere to connect'.

The thoroughness of these descriptions leaves me convinced of Wendy's ability to 'receive' the past. When the tour was over she left the building, like so many of its past inhabitants, 'with great reluctance. I can honestly say that never during my course of work have I been inside a building so full of every type of emotion, love, loyalty and inspiration'. Indeed, may I add, when taken in another context, is this not what theatre is all about? This would seem a most appropriate moment to say *au revoir* to the spirits of Drury Lane, indeed a most appropriate location to end this journey around some of the theatres that are all, for want of a better word, haunted.

But where there's an end, there's always a beginning. On my very first visit to Drury Lane I saw a production so enchanting that its memory still bewitches me to this very day. It was the play that first persuaded me that other worlds do exist, timeless, fragmentary worlds, worlds of enchantment and imagination for, on that evening in 1957, I watched John Gielgud in *The Tempest* directed by Peter Brook. Gielgud's Prospero was a true magician, a stern sorcerer unequalled and entrancing. Tonight I hear his voice again, and the words are surely echoed by countless other voices in any buildings which proudly bear that simple name of Theatre.

Our revels now are ended. These our actors as I foretold you, were all spirits, and are melted into air, into thin air...or are they?

The Theatre Royal, Drury Lane circa 1881

Acknowledgements

I am so very grateful to all the very many friends and colleagues who have shared their stories with me and helped make this book possible.

May I also thank the following whose names do not appear in either act or interval but whose 'backstage' encouragement and work, assistance and kind permissions, have been vital in making my project, unlike most ghosts, appear in solid form at last.

Dr Mark Bryant
Harry Bucknall
Emma Carter
Anna Charles
Brit Felmberg
Liz French
Moira Goff
Carmen Holdsworth-Delgado
Sye Hyman
Amy Mechowski
Richard O'Brien
Simon Seddon
Richard Walton

Nick Bromley, November 2020

Illustrations and credits

Page

Every effort has been made to trace the copyright owners and seek permission to reproduce images in this book. Please contact the publisher if you think you have detected an error or omission.

As this book goes to print, many of our theatres remain dark because of Covid 19. But we're a resilient profession, innovative and hopeful in adversity. Shows shall return and so, until they do, ghost lights are kept burning on empty stages to keep dreams alive and shadows of despair at bay.

Our final image, therefore, must be our own ghost light, a salute to both the Theatre's future and its past.